Advanced Praise for *The Savvy Musician 2.0*

"Whether you're a music performer, educator, composer, administrator, or all of the above, this insightful resource is the ultimate guide to rocking the digital age. Learn what it takes to amp up your career game, earn a living, sharpen entrepreneurial chops, and make a profound difference!"
—**Brian Shepard**, CEO, Music Teachers National Association

"*The Savvy Musician 2.0* provides what no other book has managed to pull off: a comprehensive exploration of tools needed to build and sustain a career thoroughly integrated with entrepreneurial thinking. Cutler writes with wit, clarity, and deep knowledge, while never losing sight of the reason why all this matters: the art itself. If I could use the word 'magisterial,' I would!
—**Jeffrey Nytch, DMA**, Composer; Author of *The Entrepreneurial Muse*

"In a world where musicians and music teachers must innovate to stay relevant, this book shares a treasure trove of strategic tips I fully endorse (and am inspired by)!"
—**Annie Ray**, High school teacher; winner, GRAMMY Music Educator Award

"A game-changer for any musician ready to break out of the traditional mold! Combining his deep knowledge of entrepreneurship with a passion for music, Cutler's powerful guide teaches how to think like a savvy professional and thrive in today's evolving marketplace."
—**Aaron Dworkin**, Founder, The Sphinx Organization

"Musicians just want to make a living, please, from the art we love. Cutler prioritizes RELEVANCE as he critiques an educational system that tends to create rule followers. This book provides a reassuringly detailed, provocative map for the good hard work required to seize agency and thrive."
—**Mary Ellen Poole**, Dean, College of Fine Arts, Carnegie Mellon University

If the "business" side of music has felt foreign or uncomfortable, *The Savvy Musician 2.0* is for you. Practical insights, field-tested advice, and thought-provoking stories of real musicians empower readers to re-examine hidden assumptions and take action—not just professionally, but in life outside music as well!
—**Noa Kageyama**, Creator, The Bulletproof Musician; Faculty, The Juilliard School

"It isn't enough to play or sing well. David Cutler's 'how-to' guide on becoming an entrepreneurial musician goes into such depth, consider him your personal business coach."
—**Beth Morrison**, Co-founding Director of PROTOTYPE Festival (presenting contemporary, multi-disciplinary opera-theatre and music-theatre works)

"*The Savvy Musician 2.0* fills out my shelf of groundbreaking books by David Cutler. It is not only a must-read, but a must-library for all musicians interested in greater achievement and impact."
—**Tayloe Harding**, President, National Association of Schools of Music

"Addressing the ins and outs, ups and downs, and pros and cons of the music business while offering numerous roadmaps to success, **this is the book you need!!!!** In fact, this is the book I needed to unlock several new ways of thinking."
—**Wycliffe Gordon**, Trombonist, Lincoln Center Jazz Orchestra

"The world deserves thriving artists and artists deserve to thrive. *Savvy 2.0* is not just a book—it's your personal mentor offering a roadmap for sustaining purpose-driven careers."
—**Joyce Griggs**, Saxophonist; Provost, Manhattan School of Music

"Dr. David Cutler is a highly respected, world-class thought leader in music entrepreneurship education. *The Savvy Musician 2.0* is a masterpiece of professional development for musicians at any career stage. David's energy, joy, and relevant expertise leap off the pages. Comprehensive and powerful, it invites readers to think, dream, work hard, have fun, and make things happen with distinctiveness."
—**Michael Millar**, Professional Development Coach

"Every musician is in business for themselves. More than just a resource, *The Savvy Musician 2.0* offers a planning guide for making it on your own terms."
—**Tonya Butler**, Chair, Music Business/Management, Berklee College of Music

"This is a MUST READ! Lifting the facade of romanticism around being a musician, Cutler breaks things down into pieces that can be ingested and understood by working musicians and students alike."
—**Jeff Coffin**, Saxophonist with Bela Fleck and The Dave Matthews Band

"Finally!! Encouragement, inspiration, and realistic advice for today's musician with 0% fluff! David Cutler seems to have a well-prepared crystal ball, challenging and informing us as we progress in this fantastic, scary, fulfilling profession. We ALL need this book – right now!"
—**John Wittmann**, Associate Vice President, Yamaha Artist Relations Group

The Savvy Musician 2.0

Amplifying Impact, Income, and Inspiration

DAVID CUTLER

OXFORD
UNIVERSITY PRESS

Oxford University Press is a department of the University of Oxford.
It furthers the University's objective of excellence in research, scholarship,
and education by publishing worldwide. Oxford is a registered trade mark of
Oxford University Press in the UK and in certain other countries.

Published in the United States of America by Oxford University Press
198 Madison Avenue, New York, NY 10016, United States of America.

© Oxford University Press 2025

All rights reserved. No part of this publication may be reproduced, stored in a retrieval system, transmitted, used for text and data mining, or used for training artificial intelligence, in any form or by any means, without the prior permission in writing of Oxford University Press, or as expressly permitted by law, by license or under terms agreed with the appropriate reprographics rights organization. Inquiries concerning reproduction outside the scope of the above should be sent to the Rights Department, Oxford University Press, at the address above.

You must not circulate this work in any other form
and you must impose this same condition on any acquirer.

Library of Congress Cataloging-in-Publication Data
Names: Cutler, David, 1971– author.
Title: The savvy musician 2.0 : amplifying impact, income, and inspiration / David Cutler.
Description: New York, NY : Oxford University Press, 2025. |
Includes bibliographical references and index.
Identifiers: LCCN 2025004941 (print) | LCCN 2025004942 (ebook) |
ISBN 9780197796368 (paperback) | ISBN 9780197795958 (hardback) |
ISBN 9780197795989 | ISBN 9780197795972 (epub)
Subjects: LCSH: Music trade—Vocational guidance.
Classification: LCC ML3795 .C884 2025 (print) | LCC ML3795 (ebook) |
DDC 780.23—dc23/eng/20250206
LC record available at https://lccn.loc.gov/2025004941
LC ebook record available at https://lccn.loc.gov/2025004942

DOI: 10.1093/9780197795965.001.0001

The manufacturer's authorized representative in the EU for product safety is
Oxford University Press España S.A., Parque Empresarial San Fernando de Henares,
Avenida de Castilla, 2 – 28830 Madrid (www.oup.es/en).

Other books by David Cutler

The Savvy Musician
Building a Career, Earning a Living, & Making a Difference

The Savvy Music Teacher
Blueprint for Maximizing Income & Impact

The GAME of Innovation
Conquer Challenges. Level Up Your Team. Play to Win.

SuperNova
A Suzuki Tune Explosion

More information:
www.savvymusician.com

This book is dedicated to the memory of my good friend Lance LaDuke, one of the savviest musicians I've ever known.

Contents

Acknowledgments   *xvii*

INTRODUCTION: A SAVVY QUESTION   1
   Savvy Genetics
   About *The Savvy Musician 2.0*
   Getting the Most Out of This Book

PART I. ENTREPRENEURIAL JOURNEY

1. THE PATH TO REMARKABLE SUCCESS   9
   Thinking Like an Entrepreneur   10
     Why Be Entrepreneurial?
     What About Excellence?
     A Success Formula
   Professional Frameworks   16
     The Three Job Types
     The Three Position Descriptions
     The Three Career Models
     Setting Your Course
   A Savvy Musician's "How To" Primer   18
     How to Win the Rat Race
     How to Get "Lucky"
     How to Deal with Rejection
     How to Become the Best in the World

2. FINDING YOUR VOICE   25
   Creating Demand in any Environment   25
     Marketplace 1
     Marketplace 2
     Marketplace 3
   What Makes You Interesting?   28
     1 - Get Narrow (and Then Go Big)
     2 - Go Broad (and Then Shrink)
     3 - Blend Talents
     4 - Lean into Personality
     5 - Adopt a Mission
     6 - Subtract a Vision

3. MIND YOUR OWN BUSINESS 35

Entrepreneurial Insights 35
Projects That Matter 36
- What's Your Problem?
- What's Your Solution?
- What's Your Difference?
- What's Your Scope?
- What's Your Model?

Powerhouse Proposals 45
- BIG Idea
- WOWables
- A Little Something Extra

4. SHARPEN YOUR VISION 49

- Empathize for Insights
- Assess Your Positioning
- Distinguish from Competition
- Design the Business Model
- Build a Prototype
- Gather Feedback

5. MARKETING IS EVERYTHING 65

Eight Marketing Myths 65
Arts Marketing A-List 68
- Art
- Audience
- Angle
- Allies
- Arsenal
- After
- Building a Comprehensive Plan

Marketing Considerations 79
- The Goal
- The Lists
- The Timeline
- The Words
- The Look
- The Investment

6. PROMOTIONAL STORYTELLING 85

Storytelling Tools 85
- Name, Slogan, Logo
- Elevator Pitch
- Bio
- Publicity Photo
- Electronic Press Kits

CONTENTS   xi

    Working with Media 92
        The Media Circus
        In the Name of Publicity
        On Becoming Newsworthy
        Pressing Release

7. POUNDING THE VIRTUAL PAVEMENT   99

    Your Professional Website 99
        Step 1: Set the Scope/Domain
        Step 2: Sketch the Map
        Step 3: Compile the Content
        Step 4: Design the Site
        Step 5: Test and Revise
        Step 6: Attract Attention
        Nine Reasons Most Websites Fail
    Your Digital Footprint 107
        Platforms
        Perspectives
        Protocols
        Permission

8. MUSIC BUSINESS IS PEOPLE BUSINESS   113

    Savvy Rules of Engagement 113
    One Handshake at a Time 115
        Building Your Network
        The Schmooze Factor
        Igniting Support
        Professional Communication
        Cold Calling
        Persistence versus Peskiness
        Staying Current
        You're Not Talking to the Right People!

9. WINNING THE MONEY GAME   123

    Money In 123
        Five Ways to Generate Cash
        Filling Your Portfolio
        Setting a Price
        Projecting Revenues
        Tweaking the Formula
        Generating More
        Protecting Yourself
    Money Out 132
        COGS
        Overhead
        Taxes

xii   CONTENTS

        The Bottom Line
        Spending Habits
        Health Care
        There's No Place Like Home (or Is There?)
        A Word of Caution About Debt
    Money Forward   140
        Planning for the Future
        What to Do with Savings
        Investing in Your Career

10. FUNDING YOUR DREAMS   145

    Philanthropic Framework   145
        What Will Be Funded?
        How Much Do You Need?
        When Is It Scheduled?
        Which Campaign Type?
        Who Will Give?
        12 Fundraising Missteps
    Donor Campaigns   148
        Annual Giving
        Crowdfunding
        Special Events
        Sponsorships
        In-Kind Donations
    Grants   154
        Navigating the Maze
        Compiling Submissions
        Selection Process
        Raising Money in Difficult Times

11. A LIFE IN MUSIC   161

    Time Management   161
        Write It Down
        Urgent versus Important
        Work Forward
        Schedule Your Schedule
    Project Management   164
        Projecting and Reflecting
        Choosing the Right Puzzle
        Mapping the Process
    Team Management   169
        Ailments and Remedies
        Team Makeup
        Career Partners
    Life Management   174

12. LEAVING A LEGACY   175

PART II. ART THAT MATTERS

13. OUTSTANDING PERFORMANCE, PLUS...   181

Programmatic Considerations   181
- Setlist
- Duration
- Venue
- Attire
- Speaking
- Persona
- Scenery
- Interdisciplinarity
- Participation
- Surprises
- Pre-/Post-/Midconcert

A Classic Conundrum   189
- "Classical" Has an Image Problem
- "Popular" Has a Musical Problem
- Who's to Blame?
- Is There a Middle Ground?
- Can Classical Be Popular?
- Rethinking the Canon
- Creative Performance Practice
- Is All This Appropriate?

14. THE NEW RECORDING PARADIGM   197

Then and Now   197
- Label Backing
- Recording Costs
- Financial Objectives
- Musical Choice
- Product Psychology

Generating the Product   202
- Why to Record
- What to Record
- How Much to Record
- Paying to Record

The Business of Recording   206
- Record Label Dilemma
- How Recording Artists Get Paid
- Increasing Streams
- Copyright Protection

15. GOT VIDEO???   213

Video Production   213
- Envisioning the Concept
- Filming the Shoot

Editing the Content
Promoting the Art
Music Video 2.0 220
Live Streaming
Live Projection
Virtual/Augmented Reality
Projection Mapping
Holography

PART III.   NICE WORK IF YOU CAN GET IT

16. THE ART OF GETTING HIRED   229
Cover Letters
Resumes
Curricula Vitae
Interviews
Auditions
Negotiation
When to Take a Gig

17. TEACHING   239
Teaching Jobs 239
K–12 Classroom
College
Independent Teaching 242
Private Lessons
Online Lessons
Group Lessons
In-person Classes
Online Classes
Summer Camps
Teaching for Hire
Other Opportunities
Teaching Artistry 249
Designing Workshops
Lining Up Work

18. PERFORMANCE   253
Opportunities to Play 253
Large Ensembles
Military "Bands"
Theatrical Productions
Conducting
Small Groups
Soloists
Sacred Music

Gig Getting Guide   260
    12 Steps to Booking Concerts
    Some Thoughts on Touring
    Landing a Contract
    Competing Priorities
    The Deal with Management
    A Musical Union

19. COMPOSITION   267
    Commissions
    Production Music
    Acquiring Performances
    Selling Notation
    Traditional versus Self-Publishing
    Performance Royalties
    Copyright Protection
    Logistical Considerations

20. INDUSTRY   277
    Arts Administration
    Artist Support
    Audio Recording
    Music Retail
    Instrument Repair
    Software Development
    Music Therapy
    Music Librarian
    Nonmusic Employment
    Coda

Further Savvy Reading   287
Featured Artist Index   293
Subject Index   295
Author Bio   301

Acknowledgments

The ideas presented in this book have been profoundly influenced by friends, teachers, students, colleagues, and musical heroes. Thank you for touching my life. I hope this publication gives back some of the generous gifts you have bestowed upon me.

One of the great pleasures of working on *The Savvy Musician 2.0* was interviewing some 150+ entrepreneurial performers, composers, teachers, and administrators. These individuals were incredibly generous when sharing stories, experiences, and ideas. Beyond incorporating their incredible contributions in this book, I made quite a few friends along the way.

I am grateful to the many individuals who generously shared time and feedback during the preparation phase of this text: Matthew Arau, Martin Atkins, Alain Barker, Joanne Bernstein, Jennifer Cable, Becky Chappell, Michelle Chen, Brian Chin, Fabiana Claure, Andy Heiss, Andrew Hitz, Mary Javian, Alice Jones, Ted Masur, Jeff Nytch, John Parks, Melody Payne, Stan Renard, Kevin Sanders, Vedrana Subotic, Jill Timmons, Audra Vaz, Ellen Woodoff, Xuan, Susan Zhang. The outcome is unquestionably stronger as a result of their insights.

Two people who deserve special acknowledgment are my wife, Erika Cutler, and mother, Tina Cantrell. They each spent countless hours proofreading and acting as a soundboard for my crazy ideas on entrepreneurship and innovation. Thank you for your perpetual support. My kids, Ashton and Alaina—both budding musicians committed to making a difference—have also been constant sources of inspiration.

This book is dedicated to the memory of my dear friend, euphonium player Lance Laduke. You may not know that *euphonium* is derived from the Latin term *euphonos*, which I believe translates loosely to mean "unemployable." I used to poke fun at Lance by describing him as a euphoniumist with way more work than he could handle, defying any inkling of logic. Together, Lance and I toured, performed comedy songs, ran workshops, co-keynoted, wrote a book, spent hours imagining the pedagogy of innovation, and laughed way too much. I miss you every day.

Finally, I'd like to express gratitude to you for reading this. Wishing you a life in music that is deeply fulfilling and meaningful. And get paid for your art!

Introduction
A Savvy Question

If you're like me, the decision to seek a career in music was never under much contention. With your talents and passion, any other option feels "criminal," robbing yourself and the world of incredible gifts. Perhaps you aspire to become a performer, educator, creator, engineer, administrator, business owner, manager, or some other type of music professional.

Despite many strengths, however, you are concerned. Thriving in the "real world" feels illusive. It's not due to laziness. Your work ethic is on overdrive. It's not necessary to be rich either. But there is equipment to buy and loans to pay, not to mention the rising cost of doing business. Someday you might want to raise a family. Or save for retirement. Or balance the books. Or eat lunch. Those things cost money!

What terrifies you most are the statistics. Competition for posted jobs is staggering. Some school districts cut music funding, while others are skeptical about its value. Many record labels have collapsed. Orchestras struggle—with several declaring bankruptcy. Much of the population could care less about the quality music you've spent your life perfecting. How is survival possible? Are you good enough? Was the pursuit of music an unmitigated miscalculation?

Now that I have you hyperventilating, take a breath. Yes, musical professions bring their fair share of challenges. But is this not the case with any line of work? Truth be told, now is an exciting time for our industry. Success is possible—there is a way! However, that won't happen automatically. Realizing ambitions requires flexible visioning, proactivity, and the wisdom to accept that success today requires significantly different strategies from even a few years ago.

Isn't it time YOU got savvy?

SAVVY GENETICS

Adjective: The ability to dream big, turn obstacles into opportunities, innovate solutions, plan strategically, and get things done.

When it comes to envisioning the future, people fall into two categories. The first type has one or two (or maybe zero) ideas about what is possible. If Plan A fails, all is lost. On the other side are those who view the world as an infinite, abundant playground. *The way things have always been* is but one of a hundred possibilities. Their challenge becomes determining which option(s) to pursue. Interestingly, almost nobody lives in the middle ground with—say—four or seven ideas. It seems folks either have the savvy gene or they don't.

This perspective is misleading. Though some musicians are naturally wired innovators, *savvy* is not merely a function of genetics. Rather, it describes a muscle that can be toned and strengthened. Becoming a heavyweight champ requires tools and tricks, courage and creativity, guidance and grit. Fortunately, anyone can develop this aptitude.

Music history classes celebrate savvy musicians. Think about it. Everyone we examine existed within a context yet had the foresight to challenge the status quo, break rules, and think differently. Many of the *masters* flourished despite (because of?) enormous obstacles. Yes, they were creative geniuses. But might there also be greatness within you? The answer is almost certainly "yes." A more important question: How much do you want it? If your quest for success is matched with an ironclad work ethic, this book will help you thrive.

> ### ATTENTION: We Need Leaders!!!
>
> The world has a shortage of creative artists committed to experimentation and evolution. Untold opportunities await discovery from artist-citizens who ramp up relevance, instill spirituality, and foster fresh business models. We need visionaries. We need innovation. We need YOU!!

ABOUT *THE SAVVY MUSICIAN 2.0*

The Savvy Musician 2.0 guides musicians to build careers, lead organizations, found ventures, strengthen viability, and make a difference. Industry challenges are highlighted but not dwelled upon. Instead, these pages burst with flexible, actionable success strategies that address a comprehensive collection of issues for professionals of all stripes.

Readers expecting an answer key spelling out exactly what to do will be disappointed. In today's world, where rules and realities are in constant flux, there are no unimpeachable formulas guaranteed to deliver. Instead, you will find provocative questions and powerhouse tools. Your challenge is to build something uniquely extraordinary, elevating personal aptitudes and relevant priorities. If an idea here feels unfamiliar or uncomfortable, I encourage you to consider its merits rather than immediately shutting down.

When my first book *The Savvy Musician* was released, it was a bit of a unicorn. At that time, only a handful of publications addressed practical career concerns for this audience. The term *music entrepreneur* was largely unfamiliar. University programs focused almost exclusively on artistic excellence, doing precious little to harvest professional success. Practitioners were often conditioned to feel guilty if admitting, even secretly, that they cared about financial stability. *It should be enough to chase the art you love!*

Fortunately, there has been progress. Significantly more resources today champion career strategies and entrepreneurial thinking. The current generation is motivated to build sustainable frameworks. Artists pursuing innovative approaches are more often revered than shunned.

When returning to this project, my plan was to craft an updated second edition. Yet, as I dug in, it became clear just how much the world had changed. Topping that list are extraordinary technological evolutions (for better and worse) including artificial intelligence, streaming services, social media omnipotence, deep fakes, virtual reality, cloud-based everything, and a population glued to smartphones. Scientific advances, an international pandemic, political polarization, and evolving views on diversity have reshaped society. For musicians, each rule-bending paradigm shift simultaneously threatens tradition and catalyzes fresh possibility.

It also occurred to me just how much I had grown. Serving as distinguished professor of music entrepreneurship at the University of South Carolina, and through workshops/keynotes around the globe, I have had the pleasure of engaging with literally thousands of burgeoning "creative geniuses." These forums allowed me to experiment, share ideas, collect feedback, and propel businesses. Extensive reading and participation in organizations/events focused on issues as disparate as food insecurity, AI, health care innovation, whole-child education, globalization, Socratic discourse, and social justice further shaped my thinking.

Another development: I began running immersive problem-solving experiences. Often-diverse teams would progress through carefully architected processes to solve important problems related to the arts, business, education, government, and beyond. It took a while to figure out exactly what these experiences were. (Was it a retreat? A boot camp? A "non-ference"?) After arriving at the term *innovation GAME*, clarity emerged and a new methodology was born. Many gamified techniques my collaborators and I developed were shared in an illustrated book, *The GAME of Innovation: Conquer Challenges. Level Up Your Team. Play to Win.*

As I began reworking *The Savvy Musician*, it became evident this publication should evolve into a sequel rather than a revision—hence the title *The Savvy Musician 2.0*. While core pillars like purpose-driven visioning, opportunity creation, guerilla marketing, people skills, financial literacy, and innovative problem solving remain, a mountain of fresh strategies are introduced. Less than 10% of the original remains. Fourteen chapters morphed into 20. All *vignettes* were replaced, making room for a new set of lessons and artists. (Incidentally, readers with access to both books may reference twice as many case studies.)

That's what savvy musicians do. We start with inherited circumstances/traditions and then tweak, reimagine, and amplify to create distinctive solutions that meet the moment.

> **Savvy Vignettes**
>
> More than 150 real-world stories about individuals and organizations are cited in gray boxes throughout this book. They represent a broad cross-section of instruments, genres (classical, jazz, popular, world, and beyond), organizational structures, geographic regions, and experiences. While I anticipate you'll find direct similarities between some examples and your own background, the specifics are largely irrelevant. All lessons are transferable. *Savvy musicians become masters of the metaphor.*
>
> I have intentionally steered clear of famous superstars. If Taylor Swift, Wynton Marsalis, or the Vienna Philharmonic produce something spectacular, it's easy to dismiss the effort: "Of course they can. They have all the resources in the world!" But if somebody you've never heard of from rural Montana achieved a great thing, perhaps you can too.
>
> Interviewing these artists has been truly inspirational. I encourage you to research them further, as all have interesting discoveries, contributions, and ideas beyond that which is included here. People who view the world as a place overflowing with potential seem to discover untapped opportunity at every turn.

Getting the Most Out of This Book

Part I: Entrepreneurial Journey should initially be read in its entirety. Its twelve chapters examine issues like entrepreneurial mindset, defining success, product development, marketing, financial strategy, project management, and legacy. Regardless of professional aspirations, these lessons will prove invaluable. Don't let the focus on "entrepreneurship" throw you. Such perspectives are paramount to folks in even the most traditional of roles and organizations. No individual or organization is immune from the need for savvy, innovative problem solving.

Part II: Art That Matters takes a deep dive into artistic expressions: live performance, audio recording, video. Beyond practical how-to guidance, it plants seeds for expanding relevance and demand. While not every music profile inherently intersects with all three mediums, keep an open mind. For example, even if video isn't part of your current portfolio, perhaps it could (or should) be.

Part III: Nice Work If You Can Get It is pragmatic, exploring marketplace opportunities and career development. After unveiling tips that help secure employment, chapters address frameworks related to music teaching, performance, composition, and the industry at large. Feel free to jump around, studying that which most closely correlates with your profile.

For those who are willing to do whatever it takes but need some help with the roadmap, reading *The Savvy Musician 2.0* may be one of the smartest moves you make. Whether you're a student, breaking onto the scene, or a seasoned professional, take control of your future. Embrace a holistic approach to your livelihood and art. Balance tradition with innovation. Insist upon relevance. Most importantly, get things done. *Become a savvy musician.*

Thank you for devoting your life energy to the noble cause of music. I hope you find *The Savvy Musician 2.0* to be a useful resource that proves pivotal time and again. And now, without further ado, let's get down to business...

PART I
ENTREPRENEURIAL JOURNEY

Regardless of musical specialty or goals, it is difficult to imagine a career profile today where entrepreneurial insights are anything less than paramount. This is true even for individuals and organizations pursuing the most traditional of paths. The great news is that such perspectives can be learned and augmented. Better yet, many of the same features are necessary for both artistic and professional success: attention to detail, big-picture visioning, creativity, analysis, critical thinking, collaboration, work ethic, patience.

Part I: Entrepreneurial Journey considers:

- What is an entrepreneurial mindset, and why should I care?
- In what ways is *my* art interesting?
- How can I build a viable business/career/organizational model?
- What will it take to make the money work?
- Which tools help effectively manage projects and time?
- How might I/we leave a meaningful legacy?

Chapter 1
The Path to Remarkable Success

How do you know if you've made it as a musician? When someone reads your resume, website, or obituary, how will they determine if your existence constitutes one of success? When considering a few lines from the bio of fictional character Hugh Kileylee, most will immediately concede his story is one of respectable achievement.

> *Hugh Kileylee is an international sensation. Stunning audiences with his dizzying technique and high-energy presentations, he has performed more than 3,000 concerts worldwide. His 150 recording credits have earned a host of prestigious awards.*

WOW!!! This guy is hot! But bios tell only part of the tale. Consider the next paragraph of Hugh's story, one never included in his electronic press kit.

> *Due to demand for Kileylee's playing, he tours nonstop. Since he has spent precious few days with his three children, the oldest now refuses to acknowledge his existence. Two years ago, his wife left him for a restaurant employee who treats her extremely well. Most of Kileylee's friends have written him off, aside from the few who exploit his connections. Gradually, this musician's alcohol consumption has gotten out of control. Last year he was arrested for driving drunk and spent a week in jail.*

Oh my, how depressing! What a sad, sad story.

It's easy to buy into the myth that there are absolute determinants of success. We convince ourselves that a clarinet prodigy who winds up as a general music teacher or stockbroker has fallen short of their potential, or that winning that special competition/getting that special job/making that special connection will put a stamp of approval on our lives. Many musicians worry obsessively about how they will be judged, constantly comparing personal accomplishments with that of peers and industry superstars.

In truth, many variables contribute to success, both as an artist and as a human being. Savvy musicians understand that *finding a lifestyle that works is more important than fulfilling traditional benchmarks of accomplishment*. The ideal solution for one person might be the worst scenario for someone else. So stop worrying about how the world views you and which accolades will be boast-worthy at your

25-year reunion. Instead, discover a path that complements your unique dreams, skills, and goals. In other words... think like an entrepreneur.

> ### An Entrepreneurial Existence
>
> Growing up, Andrea Fisher aspired to become an orchestral flute player. Chasing that dream, she attended Juilliard and practiced long hours. But after witnessing talented friends audition and get eliminated, she forged her own path. "I really like being the first to do something unique and fun."
>
> Fisher created buzz by selling CDs while performing on the roof of an ice cream truck. She became the first classical musician ever to perform live with multiple holograms of herself. In the video "Dance Macabre," which amassed more than 2 million views, she plays flute (left hand), organ keyboard (right hand), and pedals (feet) in a glow-in-the-dark skeleton costume.
>
> Fisher's primary venture, Fluterscooter, sells instrument cases. Beginning small, it has since erupted, manufacturing accessories for flutes, clarinets, and guitars that often match marching band colors. One viral campaign invited clients to post photos with their Fluterscooter product plus a pet. Whoever posted the most "liked" image received a free instrument case. It turns out "fluters" love dogs, cats, horses, snakes, hedgehogs, frogs, even hermit crabs.
>
> During the height of COVID-19, musicians stopped buying instrument merchandise. "I thought, what am I going to do? I can't just sit around and not make money." Pursuing a need of the moment, she pivoted and imported masks from China. In total, this venture moved more than a quarter million units! Ah, the entrepreneurial existence...

THINKING LIKE AN ENTREPRENEUR

WHY BE ENTREPRENEURIAL?

The word *entrepreneur* has many definitions. For some, it is a business term, strictly reserved for those who found and run enterprises. Throughout this book, however, the expression is used liberally. It describes anyone who creates opportunities, thinks outside the box, gets the "big picture," and is unafraid to question conventional wisdom. Under this definition, entrepreneurial inclinations influence artistic, educational, financial, and personal decisions. *Entrepreneurship equals creativity—* it is as much an attitude as it is a business practice. Such a disposition can:

1. **Create freedom and gratification.** Entrepreneurs take control of their destiny, building frameworks that embrace "labors of love" and favorable conditions.

2. **Enhance financial gain.** Entrepreneurs amplify income, both personally and for their organizations.
3. **Stand out.** Entrepreneurs invent unique approaches, offering an edge over those who simply do the "normal thing."
4. **Address job demands.** Aspects of even the most traditional career paths require entrepreneurial solutions (recruiting students, attracting audiences, raising money, etc.).
5. **Increase relevance.** Entrepreneurial approaches ensure quality musical experiences maintain an important voice in society.
6. **Leave a legacy.** Meaningful entrepreneurial action can reverberate for years to come.

As a result of their inventiveness, entrepreneurial professionals often enjoy exciting successes. Employing innovative solutions, they create demand, pack venues, attract media, grow consumers, and earn respectable livings. Savvy entrepreneurs are revered and rewarded.

Having a vision and bringing it to fruition are not the same thing. Much of life is out of our control, making some ambitions impossible regardless of preparation, diligence, or wishful thinking. But entrepreneurs are not simply blessed with the mystifying ability to concoct one perfect, magical revelation. On the contrary, they constantly cook up exotic recipes. Though not every plan succeeds, the baking continues until delicious discoveries emerge.

What About Excellence?

The pursuit of excellence is a driving force for large swaths of the musical ecosystem. Competitions seek to identify the absolute best. "Blind" auditions behind a screen ensure that performance quality—and little else—impacts decision-making. Music educators employ powerful pedagogies that help students advance effectively and efficiently. In some communities, 3, 6, or even 10 hours of daily practice is commonplace.

There are now more great players and a higher overall level than ever, thanks partly to a proliferation of university programs, constantly improving learning methods, and online resources. This uncompromising value defines not only our industry at large but also the psyche of individuals. Many musicians become incredibly disciplined humans, expecting and accepting nothing less than high-quality output across the board.

We should be proud of this value. I am an unwavering advocate of excellence, with extremely high standards for my colleagues, students, and self. Recognize, however, that an obsessive focus here comes with risks when other critical values are neglected. Allow me to debunk several myths.

Myth #1: Excellence is enough
Many musicians mistakenly believe that excellence in art secures excellence in career. In reality, quality output is just one of many factors necessary for professional success. Other assets: vision, creativity, financial literacy, likeability, networking, technological fluency, time/life management.

> ### But What If I Just Want a Job?
>
> Suppose you aspire to win a top orchestra job. After landing this impressive position, the contract simply compels you to show up on time, be prepared, and play well. Literature is chosen by others, events are scheduled years in advance, administration is responsible for marketing. No entrepreneurship required!
>
> This argument comes with shortfalls. What if things don't work out? Not every worthy candidate obtains this employment, and few orchestras pay well enough to constitute full-time wages. Even if everything comes to fruition, supplementary opportunities may be helpful to augment income, variety, and fulfillment.
>
> Furthermore, *relinquishing responsibility for an organization's commercial success from its workers may be a flawed notion.* If orchestras are truly in dire straits, wouldn't they be well served by having members actively problem solve?
>
> Imagine a hypothetical model where great playing was only the starting point. Audition finalists face an interview round: "How might we attract new audiences? What education initiatives interest you? Which additional skills do you bring?" Each new hire then becomes responsible for fulfilling at least one nonperformance role that helps the organization thrive. This adjustment favors a different breed of musician. By incentivizing outstanding performers to take more ownership in their employer's success, an entrepreneurial structure might revolutionize even the orchestral world!

Myth #2: Excellence (alone) is marketable
Hopefully, everything you share or sell (be it a performance, recording session, music lesson, instrument, yourself as a job candidate, etc.) is high quality. But from a purely marketing standpoint, is the promise of excellence enough?

Many presenters allege to showcase "the planet's finest musicians!" Similarly, music schools promote their *world-class faculty*. Claims may well be true. The challenge is that most companies, products, and services across sectors assert excellence. Whether they are excellent is debatable; some are certainly better than others. (Can you imagine a business conceding, "Our products are—honestly—around the 65th percentile. But check us out anyway. We smell amazing!") As a result, merit-based declarations often get drowned out. Of course you say you're good. That's expected. What else do you have?

There is an element of subjectivity when defining *excellence*. Some attendees may be blown away by a particular performance, while questionable intonation and rhythmic sloppiness inflict horror upon others. Additionally, this term means different things to different people. What makes a great show? Zero mistakes? Varied repertoire? Other-worldly virtuosity? Players who smile? Ninety minutes instead of two hours? A famous soloist with great hair? If your messaging centers on excellence, be sure to define what that means.

Furthermore, audiences may not seek greater excellence. Some artists at the top of their game struggle to attract robust followings warranted by their achievement. If a major opera company got 10% better, would they sell even one more ticket? Perhaps not. How about 10% worse? The truth: Few devoted patrons would flee. The reason many arts entities fail to attract sufficient customers isn't because they aren't GOOD enough. *It's because they're not RELEVANT enough.* Or at least, that is the perception. When shaping your vision. make excellence the floor rather than the ceiling. Outstanding performance, plus...[1]

Marketing, a topic we will examine in depth, is largely about storytelling. Appealing to a potential audience member, student, customer, employer, donor, or grant agency will almost certainly require more than claiming you're good. What message will you send? (Oh, and once you've garnered attention, blow them away with top-notch art!)

Myth #3: Perfectionism is desirable

For many committed musicians, excellence is a gateway drug. The goal morphs into perfection. Flawless execution. Zero errors. While this insistence drives improvement, it also means that failure for mere mortals is guaranteed, every time.

Perfectionism is a brutal disease. It convinces our ego to tie self-esteem to artistic achievement. Worse yet, we don't just judge ourselves on overall ability but rather the most recent iteration. Riding a constant, emotional roller coaster, we beat ourselves up mercilessly when any performance feels subpar. Ironically, nerves are often paralyzed during moments when results matter most (e.g., the audition you desperately want to win).

Be careful not to conflate technical precision with overall worth as a human being.

Myth #4: Excellence and innovation are opposing forces

In a world of exponential change, innovation is essential. Businesses that fail to evolve are buried by those embracing the new rules of today and tomorrow. This brutal reality has reshaped essentially every industry: bookstores, newspapers, travel agencies, encyclopedias, the postal service, and essentially all music sectors. Expect developments with AI to turbocharge this phenomenon.

Unfortunately, too many contemporary musicians fail to view themselves as inspired changemakers. Why? Here's one possibility. We just addressed perfectionism. The archnemesis of *perfect* is a mistake. To minimize that probability, perfectionists (and even many "excellentists") shy away from the bold and

---

[1] This is the name and theme of Chapter 13.

uncommon. Regardless of potential reward, such risk taking feels too perilous. Status Quo and Safe Choices are the only characters permitted. It's not that they're inherently closed minded. They just don't want to risk making a mistake.

Our education system shapes the priorities of young people. Too often, scant time is devoted to creative problem solving and unapologetic exploration. When taught that success means scoring well on standardized tests, there is a danger of transforming students into obedient rule followers with the sole objective of identifying the singular "correct" answer. Similarly, music training focused disproportionately on technique and replication may discourage curiosity and experimentation. When that happens, not only aren't students being encouraged to innovate. They are taught to NOT innovate.

Are excellence and innovation inherently incompatible? On the contrary, music provides a spectacular playground for celebrating both. But that won't happen automatically. Attention to both sides of the equation is paramount. For example:

1. Music teachers can balance prescribed solutions and technical excellence with creative, personalized decision-making.
2. Virtuoso performers can radically reimagine repertoire or event design.
3. Arts organizations can showcase quality art through unique business models and unprecedented contexts.

Poorly executed innovation is every bit as problematic as obsolete excellence. Strive for artistic achievement AND relevant, entrepreneurial positioning. One without the other will not do. Savvy musicians achieve a balance.

> ### Excellence versus Entrepreneurship
>
> As an aspiring pianist, Susan Zhang was conflicted. On one hand, she believed success required the "traditional path" of winning prestigious competitions that reward excellence and lead to management. At the same time, she was entrepreneurially curious. "Becoming an entrepreneur made me double down on my love for music. To communicate authentically with donors, presenters, and audiences, I had to clarify why I play piano and the value of my art."
>
> After years of planning, Zhang and her partner unveiled The Concert Truck, a modified box truck with stage, lighting, and electric grand piano. This traveling music venue brought concerts to nontraditional spaces: parks, schools, town squares, homeless recovery centers, under a Boeing 747, anywhere a vehicle might be parked. While The Concert Truck generated excitement from day 1, her career took off during COVID-19.[2] Because socially distanced outdoor performance became the only safe way to share music, demand exploded.

---

[2] I have included stories around COVID-19 in the first two vignettes to demonstrate how even an international crisis impacting the entire music industry opened new doors for savvy musicians.

> Ironically, this unconventional business venture ultimately led to high-profile management.
>
> "The Concert Truck helped me understand myself as a performer in ways I hadn't in school. Playing 10 concerts weekly forced me to discover new methods to prepare, learn repertoire quickly, and improve technique. I've learned that entrepreneurship and excellence don't have to be competing goals. They can amplify one another."

A Success Formula

I would never tell someone how to live their life or design a career. The options are endless. What makes obvious sense to one person may feel ludicrous to another. Entrepreneurial journeying requires each individual to discover a unique path. But I have discovered a "success formula," something I consider when assessing my own projects and profile. Hopefully, it will help you too. I call it i^3, representing three intersecting concepts starting with the same letter.

One essential element is IMPACT. Most musicians pursue this career path to make a meaningful difference. Music has the power to build community, tell stories, inspire, educate, and create positive change in ways few other disciplines can.

Another is INCOME. Money is not everything, but it is important. If you want to record an album, propel an organization, repair your instrument, or raise a family, that costs something! Success requires making the money work.

Here's a savvy perspective. If you do things right, IMPACT and INCOME should be inextricably linked, growing together. To make more money, expand your footprint, either by reaching more people or affecting your current audience on a deeper level. If, on the hand, your scope of influence is already significant, be sure it is matched with a sound financial model.

The third aspect is INSPIRATION. Most people initially pursue music because it's something they love. The best professional frameworks continue to be personally fulfilling. It is hard to imagine a success model built around work you disdain. If you fall out of love with music, consider a change.

Similar I^3 considerations can be applied to music businesses and organizations. Successful entities balance important societal outcomes (IMPACT) with financial viability (INCOME) and a workforce boosted by soaring morale and passion (INSPIRATION).

To succeed, all three criteria must meet a certain threshold. Better yet is when they ascend together, in harmony. Unfortunately, few traditional opportunities offer this trifecta gift wrapped with a bow. Getting there typically requires a fourth *I*: INNOVATION. This is why savvy, entrepreneurial musicians have a distinct advantage.

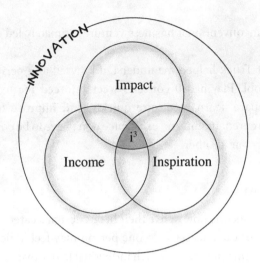

PROFESSIONAL FRAMEWORKS

THE THREE JOB TYPES

Day jobs are the ones you can't stand. (Please note: Musicians often use the term "day job" to describe all nonmusic work. That is not the intention here. My usage focuses on HOW employment impacts your life rather than WHAT specifically it entails.) Waking up each morning with a sense of dread, you impatiently count down the minutes until work is done and living begins. The gig is exhausting, zapping your vitality and sense of purpose. Each workday diminishes life expectancy, just a bit. What keeps you going, beyond the paychecks, are promises of a weekend or occasional holiday. Many day jobs—though not all—pay poorly.

Transition jobs are a means to an end. They advance your future in some meaningful way. Perhaps you learn new skills, make valuable connections, increase credibility, or line up for a promotion. Just be sure not to get trapped for the long run. Assign an expiration date.

Dream jobs are magic. Waking up each morning with a sense of excitement, you wonder how work minutes fly by so quickly. The gig is energizing, amplifying your vitality and sense of purpose. Each workday expands life expectancy, just a bit. Sometimes you pinch yourself—*I can't believe they're paying me to do this!* Dream jobs may pay well, but not always. Other factors may supersede compensation.

Interesting to note is that the same gig can shift positions over time. Maybe something that began as a day job winds up helping you advance to the next level. Or perhaps you ultimately fall in love with a transition job, turning it into the dream. Reality can traverse the other direction as well. There are musicians who spend years aspiring to secure an A-level gig only to discover it's not what they imagined. The fantasy plummets into a miserable, soul-sucking day job. Uck.

The Three Position Descriptions

Employees, whether full or part time, work consistently for someone else. Doing so offers predictability and security. They receive paychecks on a reliable schedule, negotiated at the point of hire or promotion. Income taxes are extracted, and a W-2 tax form (in the US) is issued annually. Employees report to a boss, who clarifies responsibilities and expectations.

Freelancers accept jobs on a case-by-case basis. Some opportunities are quickly completed (e.g., guest masterclass), while others require long commitments (composition commission). Pay is most often remitted when the work is complete. Income taxes are not withheld, requiring them to be paid independently. In the US, a 1099 tax form must be distributed for compensation over $600. Freelancers report to whomever hired them for the duration of the engagement. While contractors can pick and choose engagements, turning down opportunities may lead to future lost offers.

Though it takes time to build reputations and relationships, proactive freelancers often secure significant work within a few years. Employment can be unpredictable. Sometimes the phone rings off the hook, while other periods are painfully quiet. Certain periods tend to be more lucrative than others. For example, the holiday festivities of November and December and popular wedding months of April through June are often busier than January and the hot summer season. With such erratic conditions, freelancers must be particularly disciplined about saving money during lucrative times. When workload slows, pursue other income streams, revisit the business plan, update your website, network, and create new marketing tools.

Venture *owners* run their own enterprise. This role comes with significant responsibility. Owners have ultimate authority over the business model, day-to-day operations, products offered, customer relations, their own hired employees and/or contracted freelancers, and more. These positions offer the most likely path to earning big, but risk is inherent. Income is directly tied to an organization's short- and long-term success. When businesses thrive (and there is a sound financial model), profits accumulate. Those that struggle may bleed cash.

The Three Career Models

Portfolio careers entail two or more—sometimes many more—income streams. They are the most common career model for musicians and may even combine all three job descriptions. Perhaps someone works as a full-time recording engineer (employee), freelances with local ensembles (contractor), and self-publishes sheet music online (owner). This path offers a variety of activities/challenges and direct access to multiple communities. It also provides flexible options for realizing earning objectives. If one stream dries up, lean into others. For example, an independent teacher with few summer students might write method books during the slow season. The biggest challenge is time management. How can you keep so many balls in the air?

Basket careers draw from a single income stream, placing all eggs into one basket. (That said, even professionals with basket careers often find themselves managing a portfolio of projects.) For a certain kind of person, this focused approach is preferable to the constant juggling of the previous option. If work dries up, however, it can spell trouble.

Hat careers involve zero income streams, shy of proverbial panhandling with a fedora while pleading, "Can you spare some change?" This model is not recommended (unless you are independently wealthy or marry into money).

Setting Your Course

We have considered nine professional frameworks. Which are best for you? Anyone reading this book should banish the notion of a hat career. And one of the easiest decisions should be ditching any day job(s) (unless income is really high, which complicates the calculus. Even then, weigh paychecks against your career trajectory and mental health. There are almost always better options than a low-paying day job). The other seven pursuits are worthy of consideration. Design your path with intentionality.

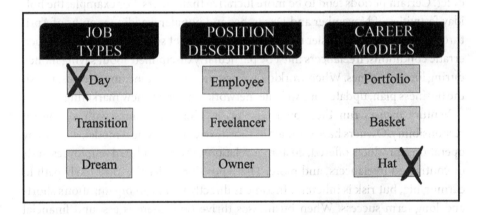

A SAVVY MUSICIAN'S "HOW TO" PRIMER

How to Win the Rat Race

Picture the music world as a skyscraper. The goal, called *Musical Success*, is located on the top-floor veranda. There is no elevator, only a narrow staircase. Thousands of individuals compete to make it there. Let's call them *The Musicians*. The Musicians pack themselves in the stairwell, pushing and pulling, hoping to progress upward. Some fall, some get trampled, others get stuck, still others quit. And every once in a while, a new champion makes it to the top.

Enter another character: *You*. You have a choice to make. You can join the rat race, take the same stairs, pass the same floors, face the same challenges, or . . .

... You could take a different approach. Might You crawl up the fire escape? Can a helicopter deliver You? How about ascending with the window washer? What if You go up the structure kitty-corner to this building and erect a bridge? Finally, why not seek Musical Success somewhere else? We define our own victories after all.

Each of these solutions introduces an element of risk. However, isn't there also danger in the heavily trafficked staircase? Many of The Musicians take these steps without considering alternatives. In fact, they believe there is only one route to Musical Success. The sad irony is that many will never make it there. Believe it or not, the staircase may be the most difficult route.

Being savvy doesn't mean you have to constantly reinvent the wheel! Make no mistake, entrepreneurial musicians absolutely embrace existing opportunities. If something comes along that fulfills your goals, *please* take it. Pursue all leads vigorously! Just understand that many such "goldmines" are cutthroat. The staircase is crowded.

There are vast audiences for every kind of music, though some potential enthusiasts may not know it yet. Art funders do exist for those creative enough to find them. A place for you to shine in the music industry is realistic. You just have to figure out a solution, like working through a puzzle. There may not be board-approved formulas in the music world, but many roads lead to prosperity. Ironically, people who take control of their own destiny often find themselves courted by pre-existing opportunities!

Flipping the Script

In part, oboist Phil Popham moved to Los Angeles to record movie music. What he found was that many film composers use only electronics. And big-budget films with full orchestras rely on a handful of contractors who repeatedly hire the same players. Breaking into the scene can take years. It may never pan out.

Following a soul-sucking process, Popham left the rat race and cofounded the nonprofit Helix Collective. Connecting with young film directors, they offer a novel proposal: "You have a unique film that deserves unique music. We will help you identify a great composer, record their soundtrack, and perform it live during a film festival premiere! Better yet, we will raise the funds," typically through sponsorships or grants.

Not surprisingly, Helix Collective is in demand. To date, Popham has more than 60 film credits to his name. Many relationships have blossomed, leading to bigger projects. "To realize my dream, I had to reject the 'right way' and flip the script!"

How to Get "Lucky"

All successful people and organizations have at least one thing in common—they experience fortunate breaks partially or completely out of their control. The lucky moment may have been getting a job offer (no one better happened to apply), winning an award (their aesthetic happened to suit the judges), or being signed by a record label (a talent scout happened to hear their demo).

A common contention is that some people are born lucky, while others get no breaks. Clearly, your childhood neighborhood, parents, and genetics are determined by fate. Yet there seems to be a science to striking gold. Certain individuals find treasure no matter what hurdles life throws. And lucky people usually only appear that way following years of diligence.

Perhaps luck is a skill. You don't just have to be in the right place at the right time—you must make good decisions along the way that place you there.

1. **Be good at what you do.** When you excel, word spreads and luck may come your way.
2. **Have a plan.** Take control of your life, define goals, and maneuver with intention.
3. **Schedule "luck time."** Regularly devote minutes to proactively promoting your vision.
4. **Build your network.** Serendipity increases when more people know and like you.
5. **Increase your "fame."** The perception of success attracts new opportunities.
6. **Be flexible.** When an opportunity falls outside the master plan, consider pivoting.
7. **Just say no.** Lucky people know the difference between a blessing and a distraction.
8. **Plant many seeds and see which ones grow.** Submitting 20 grants provides multiple shots at getting lucky. With just one, odds are greatly diminished.
9. **Plant better seeds.** Learn what is most likely to pay off and focus efforts there.
10. **Turn negatives into positives.** Luck is often a matter of perspective.

A Lucky Star

At 25, singer-songwriter Audrey Callahan forfeited her lofty dream of becoming a musician. Returning at 30, she was determined to succeed despite an industry claiming she was too old. To summon the strength, Callahan attended a personal development seminar alongside 4,000 others. "It suddenly dawned on me that my songs focus on self-empowerment. Though these events only feature speakers, I wondered how I might get showcased on that stage."

> In the following weeks, cold calls to gatekeepers were met with disappointment: *Sorry, we don't hire entertainers.* But one day, she got lucky. A curious staffer happened to open her "sizzle reel," inspiring a brilliant idea. *What if we add music?* Within months, she was offered the first of many gigs to perform for these types of sold-out crowds.
>
> Callahan attributes her triumphs to fearless proactivity. Seemingly out of the blue, she was asked to sing on a video game. A major corporation CEO invited her to perform at a personal event, covering full expenses plus a robust paycheck. A German amusement park began featuring her voice during nightly parades. Her epiphany? "The more hands I shake, the more money I make."

How to Deal with Rejection

When reading the bio of a thriving musician or organization, it is easy to be humbled by the weight and quantity of their accomplishments. Yet any successful artist can produce alternative accounts detailing failed ventures and dreams shot down. In almost all cases, this volume is significantly thicker than the "success showcase." Rejection is a major character in the life of all entrepreneurs. Those without substantial negative responses are likely playing it too safe.

Rejection has been known to trigger depression, low self-esteem, and angst. Fragile individuals who crumble at the hint of rejection are not healthy contenders to become professional musicians. While nobody likes getting turned down, thick skin is crucial.

Decisions often say more about external factors than the quality of your product. There may be internal candidates, aesthetic preferences, too many outstanding applicants, or other unpredictable issues. The same set of aspirants might be ranked differently by alternate jurors. Acceptance or rejection, in many cases, is largely a matter of opinion. Don't take them as personal indictments.

Some rejections, however, are the result of flawed or weak submissions. Detach your ego and search for ways to benefit from the experience. Consider which aspects might be improved. Try to obtain feedback. What you learn may be surprising.

To ease the sting, some entrepreneurs have an interesting ritual. Understanding that dismissals are an inevitable part of the game, each denial brings bragging rights. Rejection letters are proudly displayed for all to enjoy.

> **You Failed!**
>
> British composer Cheryl Frances-Hoad boasts a long list of successes. Her commission for a huge orchestra and choir, written to commemorate the late Queen Elizabeth, was televised internationally. The recipient of many fellowships, grants, and awards, she has been able to sustain the "rather stupid career model" of being a concert music composer.

> Her life, however, is not just a bed of roses. On average, every opportunity is counterbalanced by five rejections. She was denied one prize 13 times before getting a yes. Harder yet are "brutal, stinker" media reviews. One significant piece was written off as "hackneyed" and "almost hackneyed" by two critics. After ghosting Frances-Hoad for months, commissioners from one of her song cycles publicly decreed that this work was so boring they would never unleash it upon the public. (It has since been recorded, to great acclaim.)
>
> Frances-Hoad's website includes a *failure CV*, reminding others that achievement is never linear. "For every success, there are usually a LOT more failures nobody hears about. Though rejection stings, I learn from each situation and use it as motivation. Overall, I've been really lucky, and have gotten more strategic over time."

How to Become the Best in the World

Here's a success strategy: *What if you became the best in the world?* To be clear, you don't need a first-in-class trophy to make it in the music business. Few of us can claim that mantle. But imagine the immense benefits if you were known as a world champion. More demand, money, buzz, impact. Opportunities would fall into your lap.

How might you achieve such an aspiration? Any musician knows the answer: PRACTICE! I am a huge advocate of hard work, having spent many days logging 6, 8, or 12 hours on my instrument. Malcolm Gladwell's best-seller *Outliers* suggests that around 10,000 practice hours are required to master just about anything. So now we've got a vision (become the best in the world) and strategy for getting there (practice). Let's see how it holds up to scrutiny.

From where I stand, there are at least three glaring concerns. First, do you really think YOU have what it takes to become the best? I mean, let's get real. Suppose you take my advice and, starting tomorrow, commit to rehearsing 27 hours a day for the next 132 years. Even then, is this goal realistic? In a world oversaturated with talent, the only honest answer for most mere mortals? *Not a chance in Hades.*

Second, does this advice apply equally to organizations? Suppose a barber, café, university program, or musical museum decides they want to become the best in the world. Why haven't they achieved this status already? Is it simply because more practice is needed?

Finally, what exactly is meant by "world"? Clearly, many worlds are worthy of consideration: The Earth. Your state. A neighborhood. Some discipline at large. An online channel. Unfortunately, rather than upping their performance, too many folks narrowly define the scope to rig the game in their favor. *Our aspiration is to become ONE of the best in the world ... of direct competitors who hail from midsized northeastern suburbs starting with the letter K.* What happened to our sense of ambition?

Many musicians—and people from most fields for that matter—believe the key to success is being as good as possible at pretty much the same thing everyone else does. Their path is dictated by best practices and familiar practices (excuse the pun). Savvy musicians apply a different approach. Rather than "Which steps must I take to outperform the competition?", individuals might ask: "With my unique background, talents, and perspectives, what might I do better than anyone else?" Similarly, organizations can consider: "With our unique people, resources, and imaginations, how might we stand apart?" Changing the question changes the answer. Consider some of the many ways to dominate a category:

APPROACH	EXAMPLE
Combine musical skills	Harpist–bass trombonist (I know one!)
Combine various art forms	Clarinetist who dances while playing
Combine musical skill with hobby	Guitarist-swimmer doing poolside concerts
Find a niche/specialize	Sacred music composer for amateur choirs
Become an expert	Balinese music, dance, culture, all things related
Take a unique approach	Perform on newly invented instruments
Form unique collaborations	Band pairing with mimes, chefs, comedians, etc.
Champion a cause	Choir advocating hemophilia research
Invent a system	Your own teaching method

Every individual and organization has the potential to become the best in the world at something! Determining your area may require soul searching, but I guarantee this is possible *for you*. So for today, and maybe the next month, why not cut your practice short by an hour? During that time, determine what it will take to become the best.

Multiplicity

Gunhild Carling is a Swedish jazz musician who plays trombone. And recorder. And harmonica, bagpipes, piano, bass, ukulele, harp, flute, oboe, and trumpet (up to three at a time!). She also sings and tap dances. While each skill opens independent opportunities, it is the combination of talents that places this artist in a class of her own. In just three minutes, you can witness her playing 10 instruments in a video rendition of Pharell Williams's "Happy."

Chapter 2
Finding Your Voice

McDonald's. Nike. Oprah. Bezos. Juilliard. Steinway. Gaga. Yo-Yo. After hearing each name, a distinctive connotation probably arises, thanks to their strong *brand identity*. Branding entails more than a catchy name and logo. It is the sum total of what you do, how it's presented, and, most importantly, how others perceive your offerings.

When someone hears your name—or that of your organization/venture/project—what comes to mind? What do you hope to be known for? How will this unique identity help you thrive, both artistically and professionally? Most importantly, what makes you YOU? Savvy musicians discover their own, distinctive voice. Doing so clarifies which initiatives to pursue and how to approach them. What you say and how you say it matter!

CREATING DEMAND IN ANY ENVIRONMENT

To thrive professionally, there must be demand for what you do. Demand is essential for getting:

- A job
- Opportunities
- Clients
- Discovered
- Higher pay
- More work
- Attention
- Influence
- Marketing success
- Devoted fans
- Media coverage
- Connections
- Website traffic
- Negotiating power
- Bragging rights
- A strong reputation
- More demand

But what exactly does that take? Consider the three marketplaces for selling music-related products. Each requires different tactics, so be sure you analyze the environment in play.

Marketplace 1

How do you create demand when there's a lot of demand?
Hint: Easy, but not common.

When folks clamor for what you offer and competition is sparse, you've hit the jackpot. For example, suppose you live in an area with many regional choirs but few tenors. If that describes your specialty, it shouldn't be hard to seize opportunities.

But that won't happen automatically. First, people have to know (and remember) that you exist. Invisibility won't cut it. In other words, be seen, whether that entails physical presence or online activity. American filmmaker Woody Allen summed it up best with his renowned quote: "Eighty percent of success is showing up."

Second, be a pleasant team player. People don't like working with self-impressed narcissists, misanthropic gloom merchants, or other species of jerks. It can be preferable to leave a need unfilled rather than constantly nurturing migraines. To ensure the first call is yours, go out of your way to become an indispensable, likable collaborator.

Solution: Be PRESENT, and be COOL!

Marketplace 2

How do you create demand in a highly competitive environment?
Hint: Common, but not easy.

This is where most musicians live most of the time. Dozens—even hundreds—of eager competitors vie for the same limited opportunities. What is required to rise to the top?

Being *remarkable* is key to this puzzle. But what exactly does that entail? Bestselling author Seth Godin solves the riddle in his book *Purple Cow: Transform Your Business by Being Remarkable* during a passage titled "The Opposite of Remarkable." Before reading on, consider your definition of this term's antonym. Then brace yourself.

> *The opposite of remarkable is . . . "very good." Ideas that are remarkable are much more likely to spread than ideas that aren't. Yet so few brave people make remarkable stuff. Why? I think it's because they think the opposite is "bad" or "mediocre" or "poorly done." Thus, if they make something very good, they confuse it with being virus-worthy.[1] Yet this is not a discussion about quality at all.*
>
> *If you travel on an airline and they get you there safely, you don't tell anyone. That's what's supposed to happen. What makes it remarkable is if it's horrible beyond belief, or if the service is so unexpected that you need to share it: They were an hour early! They comped my ticket because I was cute! They served flaming crepes suzette!*

---

[1] *Purple Cow* was written years before COVID-19 redefined our worldview. The reference to *virus-worthy* here implies something that spreads quickly, traveling far and wide.

Factories set quality requirements and try to meet them. That's boring. "Very good" is an everyday occurrence hardly worth mentioning. Are you making very good stuff? How soon can you stop?[2]

This passage is particularly poignant for musicians whose obsessive pursuit of very good comes at the direct expense of remarkable. Yet it provides an opening for those willing to think creatively, challenge norms, and turn the status quo on its head.

What does it take to stand out? Context matters. The first time something is tried, it appears revolutionary. The 3rd repetition is fresh. The 10th example is trendy. The 100th is commonplace. The 1,000th is archaic. How different must something be? Minor surface tweaks are unlikely to do the trick. The eighth concert venue on a block may generate little buzz even if the walls are browner and ushers marginally taller. To make a splash, bold innovation must be dramatic, immediately igniting the imagination.

Solution: Be "PURPLE!"

MARKETPLACE 3

How do you create demand when there is no demand whatsoever?
Hint: Challenging, and likely where the most potential exists.

Imagine all the places where absolutely nobody cares about what you do. Your art form makes no blip on the radar whatsoever. It's not that they hate it; there are simply other priorities. Chances are this describes the majority of the world. If only an infinitesimal percentage developed an interest, your career profile would explode.

Consider this: With existing opportunities, there may be dozens or even hundreds of competitors. On the other hand, you are the only one in the running when proposing something unprecedented to a given audience. True, a compelling argument must be made. But you have an "attention monopoly." Invent new markets and reap the rewards.

Solving this puzzle involves *filling a gap, connecting with an interest, solving a problem*. Don't start with YOUR art, but rather THEIR passions and concerns. Then connect the dots. People will gladly try something new when it clearly adds value.

Solution: Be VALUABLE

Extreme demand, high competition, zero demand whatsoever. These three marketplaces are as different as Wagnerian tubas and '80s power ballads. However, combining their secrets leads to powerhouse positioning that thrives across the spectrum.

---

[2] Seth Godin, *Purple Cow: Transform Your Business by Being Remarkable* (Portfolio, 2009), 82–83.

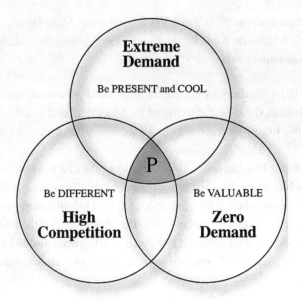

P = Powerhouse Positioning

WHAT MAKES YOU INTERESTING?

In my experience, asking a musician *What makes you good?* (or not good enough) commonly unleashes a detailed analysis of strengths and weaknesses. Inquiring *What makes you interesting?*, on the other hand, triggers a gawky, dear-in-the-headlights look of terror 97% of the time. How might a compelling reply catapult your career?

Spoiler alert: The answer probably isn't instrumentation. "I play violin!" "We're an a capella choir!!" "Check out our rhythm section!!!" While what you play provides clues about timbral output, chances are the market is flooded with others who share that specialty. And if you have a distinct makeup—say a voice/harpsichord/electric guitar trio—will people truly care? Is that what audiences seek? Probably not. Instrumentation should rarely receive top billing. In fact, it probably isn't simply WHAT you do on any level—at least, not in a competitive marketplace. Being a trumpet teacher, recording engineer, or piano technician gives clues about your output but not individuality (unless that thing is particularly unusual in a given situation).

> ### When Instrumentation Intrigues
>
> Invoke is the rare ensemble whose instrumentation provokes a double take. Being a string quartet gets them in the door, but their tagline captures imagination: *Bowed and fretted string quartet.* Collectively, the musicians play violin,

> five-string violin, viola, cello, six-string cello, banjo, mandolin, guitar, and banjo uke. (They also sing with barbershop quartet ranges, but that confuses the branding.)
>
> Invoke's instrumentation has catalyzed a unique repertoire. They perform originals by group members and commissioned composers. Additionally, standard works are reimagined. To celebrate Beethoven's 250th birthday, they recomposed Opus 131 as if "Uncle Ludwig" had written it specifically for them. "Upon request, we used to include some *bone throws*, or standard string quartet rep," explains violinist+ Zach Matteson. "But many other groups do that well. We proudly embrace the sound that is distinctly our own."

How about the scope of your repertoire? A common response: "I play everything!" That claim, though bold, is unlikely. Classical musicians touting this accolade often have repertoires limited to Baroque through contemporary Western classical. No jazz, salsa, samba, gospel, country, gamelan, ragas. Just a single genre. Nothing is wrong with such a confined focus, but its breadth is hardly Earth shattering. A similar argument can be made for many musicians with jazz, rock, or other backgrounds.

What makes a musical venture interesting in today's landscape? The best frames are simple to articulate, easy to understand, different from competitors, and thought provoking. They indicate what you stand for and—just as importantly—what you don't. Below are six approaches worthy of consideration.[3]

1 - GET NARROW (AND THEN GO BIG)

Specialists are often more compelling than generalists who happen to do that particular thing. A meaningful *niche* may clearly present itself or require soul searching. Examples include:

- Accompanying saxophonists
- Performing Venezuelan rock
- Composing comical numbers
- Addressing performance anxiety
- Recording folk singers
- Producing outlandish concerts
- Offering world music seminars
- Teaching corporate CEOs

How narrow should your sphere be? Consider the following continuum of specialties. The further to the right, the higher someone's perceived worth may be for related activities. However, fewer opportunities fall under that umbrella. The key is positioning yourself strategically.

---

[3] The vignettes in this section reference performers/performances, allowing readers to contrast similar entities. Lessons learned can be transferred to any type of venture.

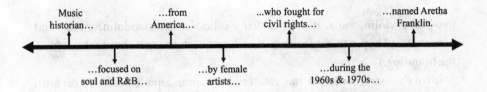

Not all niches present equal opportunities. The best examples (1) aren't oversaturated and (2) are in demand with a sizable audience. Becoming the world's leading scholar on Claudio Merulo's (1533–1604) Venetian polychoral stylings might be fascinating, but this focus is far too obscure to generate much following (unless you do a phenomenal job storytelling!).

After embracing a specialty, go big. Blow it up and build an empire. If your identity involves the tango, research every aspect of this genre: sociology, major figures, stylistic traditions, etc. Take up *bandoneón* and study the choreography. Travel to Argentina, master Spanish, learn to cook *matambre*. Start a blog. Film a documentary. Found a holiday. When it comes to this art form, look no further than Encyclopedia You!

Owning a Niche

Castle of Our Skins presents a wide range of concerts and educational initiatives that celebrate heritage and cultural exploration. Each year, their programming impacts thousands. "Edutainment" recitals, college residencies, and annual recordings infuse storytelling with performance. Several published anthologies feature over sixty 30-second compositions for a given instrumentation. Curriculum guides offer K–12 teachers highly engaging lecture notes, worksheets, and activities.

What unifies these projects is a focus on Black composers, past and present, typically classical rather than jazz or hip-hop. Embracing such a concentrated niche opens up a world of opportunity. "What amazes me is the sheer amount of repertoire available," reflects violist, artistic director, and cofounder Ashleigh Gordon. "We've barely scratched the surface."

2 - Go Broad (and Then Shrink)

In a marketplace jam-packed with single-area expertise, the secret sauce here involves fusing multiple traditions. An "everything bagel" approach requires always-expanding aptitudes. As the eternal explorer, push to see how far and wide the net may be cast. For performers, this might mean extreme stylistic inclusion. For educators, perhaps lessons from Suzuki, Gordon, Dalcroze, Kodály, and Orff are synthesized. Living up to this promise requires shrinking the scope of projects to those consistently embracing breadth.

> ### Expanding the Palette
>
> The a cappella, eight-voice "band" Roomful of Teeth is dedicated to reimagining expressive depths of the human voice. While all singers are classically trained, the group regularly studies wide-ranging traditions: alpine yodeling, Tuvan throat singing, Korean p'ansori, Persian tahrir, Sardinian cantu a tenòre, Broadway belting. Commissions then explicitly challenge composers to paint expansive sonic palettes that combine multiple techniques while highlighting the unique capabilities of each member.
>
> Something this ensemble never does: perform repertoire specific to a single historic tradition. "*Authenticity* is a problematic term for us," explains founding member Estelí Gomez. "We are careful to avoid cultural appropriation. Plenty of amazing groups specialize in these styles. Our priority is to weave musical tapestries that are distinctly authentic to us, combining various approaches in fresh and unprecedented ways."

3 - BLEND TALENTS

We live during an era where remarkable performance is oddly ... *unremarkable*. A lot of people do one thing well. Yet, multitalents fascinate. A music video is more likely to go viral if one person plays five instruments rather than five artists performing one apiece, even if audio is identical.

Consider the entire set of skills you bring to the table. Are there intriguing ways they might be combined? Package your unique mix of gifts as one. Blending talents is like going broad in that the fusion of multiple worlds becomes a focal point. Rather than occasional cameos, copresent these elements with regularity.

Unusual collaboration is another way to blend talents. For example, perhaps a summer music series always integrates visual art. A clarinetist could team up with a concessions stand. A music education curriculum might employ sports coaches once per month to teach transferable lessons.

> ### Breaking the Fourth Wall
>
> The *hybrid arts* Fourth Wall Ensemble includes a trio of musicians who are also dancers, actors, and acrobats. All skills are displayed equivalently, and often simultaneously.
>
> During the show finale of *Without a Net*, flutist Hilary Abigana plays upside down while executing aerial tricks on fabric sheets high in the air. Meanwhile, bass trombonist Neil Parsons and percussionist/accordionist Greg Jukes perform upon circling hoverboards, turning the silks. In their rendition of Erik Satie's *Gymnopédie*, two performers transform into a single, larger-than-life

six-legged insect, with slithering choreography that mirrors the music. "Audiences listen with more than their ears," explains Parsons. "We share personal, multisensory experiences that engage all the senses."

4 - Lean into Personality

Becoming known for an extreme personality allows the pursuit of any artistic scope as long as the character remains intact. This approach isn't about being nice—hopefully that's already the case—but rather embracing a persona around some eccentricity or ethos. Humor is an obvious example, but it is also possible to become known for compelling storytelling, awkwardness, vulgarities, or extraordinary empathy.

> **Suppose Pavarotti and Jack Black Birthed an Adorable Man Child**
>
> Robert McPherson's robust resume boasts of major opera performances. But his alter ego, the Drunken Tenor, "brings low comedy to new heights." Whether presenting *A Very Drunken Christmas Carol*, solo standup in comedy clubs, or GeekWire Awards through song, he is a virtuoso diva known for screwing up. Wearing a tuxedo T-shirt and Converse sneakers, he forgets lyrics, performs while riding an inflatable dinosaur, and works up the courage to reach for "money notes" while gulping martinis.
>
> This persona has catapulted McPherson's career. He also solves a problem for opera companies, providing small-cast, low-budget, mainstage productions that thrill. Why does he do it? "When the world looks like it's going to burn, you re-evaluate. There is a great need for laughter and levity at this moment." What does the future hold? "Robert has more to say as an artist. The Drunken Tenor has more to do as a brand."

5 - Adopt a Mission

"People don't buy what you do, they buy why you do it," argues American writer Simon Sinek in his book *Start with Why*. What do you stand for, and how might that be placed at the heart of professional activity? Causes like climate change, cancer prevention, and social justice not only have the potential to make a positive impact but also come with armies of devoted supporters. Such a focus is a great way to reach ever-elusive "nontraditional audiences." Of course, an issue mustn't be serious to garner attention. Imagine the cult following a quirky cause around "hedgehog empathy" or "the profound dangers of corn dogs" might engender.

Many people find their calling despite—or thanks to—the tough hand they've been dealt. When searching for meaningful causes, consider significant obstacles you have faced. Doing so not only helps connect to a sense of purpose but also makes you a credible messenger.

There are several ways to tie a cause to your business model. Examples include:

1. **Financial support.** A recording studio contributes 5% of profits to a homeless shelter.
2. **Target audience.** Music lessons impact students with autism.
3. **Artistic creation.** A battle-of-the-bands concert centers on social justice themes.

> ### Compassion and Purpose
>
> Concerts for Compassion (CFC), a nonprofit cofounded by violinist Jocelyn Zhu, facilitates cultural integration by bringing music and education to displaced peoples and their local communities. As a second-generation immigrant from China and Taiwan who grew up in Mississippi, Zhu understands firsthand how disorienting it can be when lives are uprooted to confront a new language, culture, and reality. CFC pursues three types of projects:
>
> 1. **Refugee camp concerts.** Presented across North America, Central America, Europe, and the Middle East, often in collaboration with humanitarian aid organizations. Events feature carefully curated repertoire while inviting attendees to sing, share meaningful recordings, and dialogue openly.
> 2. **Benefit concerts.** Scheduled in partnership with refugee-centric charities. One hundred percent of donations support targeted communities.
> 3. **Educational workshops.** Geared toward new migrants and local neighbors. These programs work on soft skills through the language of music.
>
> "I wanted to build something that went beyond my own career success. This gratifying work fills me with a sense of purpose."

6 - Subtract a Vision

In theory, *vision statements* describe the unique goals of a person, organization, or project. In reality, the vast majority use flowery mumbo jumbo that is neither distinctive nor substantiated. If 10 direct competitors were presented with these proclamations (names blotted out), most would be hard-pressed to identify their own tribe.

Effective visioning clarifies what you stand for and what you don't. A *negative vision statement* presents a powerful framework. This two-part declaration identifies a commonplace tradition you reject, followed by the embraced alternative thanks to freed resources.

> _____ commits to NOT _____.
> *(project/business name)*   *(something competitors do)*
> Instead, _____.
>   *(something unique to you)*

Pinpointing near-ubiquitous features across your specialty shouldn't be hard, since most individuals and organizations in any sector approach things similarly. The more obvious, the better. For example:

Music Conference X commits to NOT presenting lectures. Instead, all sessions will be interactive and team based.

It is also possible to disallow traditional rituals a percentage of the time. For example:

Violin Teacher Y commits to NOT incorporating music stands/notated music at least 50% of the time. Instead, students develop their ears and improvisational abilities.

The Death of Classical

"There's nothing wrong with traditional venues," explains Andrew Ousley, founder of the concert series Death of Classical (DOC). "But I find unusual spaces focus people's attention." His events take place in crypts, catacombs, and cemeteries. A host of other common conventions are also banned: intermissions, long performances (one-hour cap strictly enforced), traditional program notes, and music served without anything to taste.

The popularity of DOC has exploded. From an initial season with 8 shows, there are now 60 to 70 per year, ranging from intimate salons to massive gatherings attracting thousands. With titles like *Burgers, Bourbon, & Beethoven* and *Hot Dogs, Hooch, & Handel*, the attire is "catacomb chic." Evenings commonly open with food, libations, and socializing, followed by a community hike through the graveyard, and then the music—performed with purity and excellence. "My goal was to design high-quality experiences so moving that even friends who didn't give a $h!t about classical music would beg me to attend. It turns out, the plan worked!"

Chapter 3
Mind Your Own Business

Successful music careers require concept development, strategic planning, marketing, financial management, and other aspects of being a #SavvyMusician. Do you have what it takes? The answer is almost certainly affirmative. Thriving at the business of being a musician requires many of the same skills as becoming a great artist: attention to detail, ironclad work ethic, short- and long-term planning, creative problem solving, finding your own voice. Musicians often make outstanding businesspeople once they take the leap. In fact, many come to love the intersection of art and commerce.

This chapter provides frameworks for developing an entrepreneurial project. It might be a business *venture*, organizational *model*, standalone *product*,[1] or artistic *statement*. In fact, it could even encompass your entire *career*. I encourage you to trust the process that follows. As a savvy musician, be open to the possibility that treasure may be buried in the strangest of places.

ENTREPRENEURIAL INSIGHTS

Before strategizing, step into your entrepreneurial skin. Embrace the adventure, and get out of your own way.

Insight #1: Allow Yourself to Dream BIG
Too many of us halt BIG thinking before it is even permitted to start. We sabotage the inclination to fantasize, paralyzed by lacking resources or repressive permission structures. Try a different approach. Put aside realities, at least upfront. Start with the best-case scenario. If a vision is truly remarkable, there is almost always a way to bring some version to life given the resources at hand.

Dreams first, then logistics.

Insight #2: Your First Idea is Rarely the Best
Too many of us pursue the original thing that comes to mind, the solution dictated by conventional wisdom, the low-hanging fruit. While not inherently wrong, obvious choices are unlikely powerhouses. Start with a blank slate and an open mind. Weigh many options before choosing a direction.

Explore before committing.

---

[1] I use *product* as a blanket term to describe any physical item, virtual resource, or service that commands a price tag.

Insight #3: Allow Concepts to Evolve

The goal should not be to realize visions as they initially appear. Like a baby, entrepreneurial ideas should be permitted to grow and change. Such flexibility is tricky for many. Even flashing yellow signs screaming, "THERE IS A BETTER WAY..." are promptly ignored. The next time someone asks, "Have you considered this?," resist urges to respond, "No, let me explain the original plan!" Instead, embrace clues that invariably emerge. Be open to what might well be superior solutions. There is no one right way, but there is often a better way.

Beware of ending where you started.

Insight #4: Messy is OK

The entrepreneurial journey is never a straight line. Without an answer key, there will be unexpected developments, discord, and the need to backtrack. Things that go wrong are not indictments of your direction. Rather, they are inevitable, necessary hiccups that make you stronger.

Embrace uncertainty.

Insight #5: Just About Every Puzzle Can be Solved

With enough creativity and grit, almost every challenge can be conquered. There is a way to exponentially amplify earnings, make logistics work, grow your reputation, increase demand. In fact, there are probably scores of solutions, though not all are equivalent. Instead of asking, "Is this possible?," start with, "How can I/we make this happen?"

Opportunities are everywhere. But opportunities only belong to people who take them.

PROJECTS THAT MATTER

What does it take to design an in-demand project that makes a difference?

WHAT'S YOUR PROBLEM?

Savvy musicians know a secret. For a venture or product to have any chance at large-scale success, it must solve a meaningful *problem*—serious or fun, big or small. Rather than starting with WHAT you plan to sell, identify an important pain point for your target audience and focus energy accordingly. Be mindful not to prescribe solutions at this point.

As a community, we are far too unimaginative when it comes to identifying compelling problems. In my experience working with literally hundreds of musicians on entrepreneurial projects, the most commonly cited examples are:

1. Issues for musicians like *me* (i.e., oboist concerned about lack of quality double reeds)
2. Teaching music to kids

Clearly, musicians are real people with real problems that deserve solutions. And readers are unlikely to refute the immense value of childhood music education. But do they represent the majority of what music projects can impact? Who else might be helped, and how? (After hearing many competing proposals on educating youth, an exasperated wealthy woman shared: "I have money and love music, yet nobody seems interested in teaching me!")

Summarize the most important challenge your project attempts to solve in a single-sentence *problem statement*. These can be negative (e.g., "Audiences *hate* this"; "There *isn't* enough of that") or positive ("Kids crave more *fun*!"). Be sure to write it down, ensuring the concept is fixed rather than a moving target. Framing is critical—altering just a word or two may lead to drastically different solutions. The best examples are:

1. **Concise.** Typically 10 words or less, and easy to comprehend.
2. **Specific.** Focused problems are better than generalities. (Don't attempt to boil the ocean!)
3. **Targeted.** Clarify the audience who cares deeply about this conundrum.
4. **Fundable.** Compelling issues are so relevant that consumers or third parties (or both) will gladly pay for a powerhouse solution.

The next chart introduces actual statements I have encountered. After explaining the potential shortcomings of each, a more compelling framework is proposed.

PROBLEM	The PROBLEM's Problem	A Better PROBLEM
People want to have a good time and meet others.	Undoubtedly! But it's hard to market to all "people." A specific audience might inspire a more targeted solution.	*Young adults want to have a good time and meet others.*
In rural communities, music therapy is difficult to access.	Makes sense. But how many people are motivated by this issue? Most folks don't even know what music therapy is. This feels like more of a solution than a problem. What is the core issue?	*In rural communities, residents struggle with mental health care.*
Musicians don't have enough money.	Amen! However, is it likely that broke musicians will pay for your solution? Why not flip the model?	*People with money don't have enough music.*
There aren't enough local venues for jazz musicians to perform in.	This may be true. But once again, is it likely that musicians will pay for your solution to this problem?	*There aren't enough venues to satisfy the demand of local audiences.*

| Having cultural awareness while recognizing there is no comparison of quality of life. | While the intent resonates, this sentence is confusing. Be clear and concise. | Residents are ignorant of their neighbors' cultures. |

A dozen additional problem statements follow. What other pain points, annoyances, or desires might you add to this list?

1. Halloween parties are boring.
2. Senior citizens love concerts, but the music is too loud.
3. A successful corporation has a dysfunctional employee culture.
4. Independent films need better soundtracks.
5. Many singles want to meet people but hate dating apps.
6. A politician has been unsuccessful getting out her message about an important issue.
7. Learning new languages is hard.
8. The incarcerated face abysmal conditions.
9. Business meetings are boring and largely unproductive.
10. Funerals are depressing.
11. A rural town wants to increase its number of tourists to stimulate economic development.
12. All banks are similar, making it difficult to stand out and attract new clients.

Before becoming emotionally invested in a particular solution, *fall in love with the problem.*

What's Your Solution?

An entrepreneurial idea should directly address the stated problem. When there isn't alignment, change either the problem or the solution. Otherwise, you may suffer the same fate as the musical comedian Victor Borges's grandfather, who "invented the cure for which there is no disease. (Unfortunately, his wife later caught the cure, and died.)"[2] After articulating a consequential problem statement, brainstorm various solutions. Perhaps your project incorporates:

- **Performances.** Traditional concerts, house concerts, streamed events, background music, installations, customized shows.
- **Compositions.** New works, songwriting, arrangement, transcriptions, lyrics.
- **Education.** Private lessons, group lessons, classes, camps, workshops, eCourses.
- **Physical items.** Instruments, accessories, wearables, books, swag, furniture.
- **Physical spaces.** Venues for performing, working, rehearsing, creating, recording, networking, socializing, listening.

[2] Signature line in his standup act.

- **Services.** Streaming, booking, consulting, marketing, licensing, restoration, curation.
- **Technology.** Recordings, videos, blogs, podcasts, online resources, virtual reality, augmented reality, artificial intelligence, robots.

To exercise your creative muscles, consider how various musical solutions might tackle issues highlighted previously. In fact, savvy musicians often develop multiple products approaching the same challenge.

PROBLEM	Potential SOLUTIONS
Senior citizens love concerts, but the music is too loud.	1. High-end earplugs that don't diminish clarity 2. "Quiet concerts" marketed to seniors 3. "Silent concerts" where everyone wears headphones and adjusts volume individually 4. Concerts broadcast to multiple salons with different volume levels 5. Virtual reality concerts where users control the loudness
Learning a new language is hard.	1. Vocabulary songs 2. Workshops where musical activities facilitate language learning 3. eCourses or camps that combine language learning with culture 4. Concerts that teach foreign language musical terms 5. Language textbook paired with musical recordings
A rural town wants to increase tourists to stimulate economic development.	1. Concert series in a barn 2. Local band of "musical ambassadors" who spread the word about that village while on tour 3. Catchy town jingle for tourists, intended to go viral 4. Musical museum that shares Indigenous art forms 5. Major national talent competition, hosted annually

It is sometimes necessary to work backward. For example, if you already offer private lessons, determine the most important issue your sessions solve (or might in the future). Is it to prepare future professionals, build self-esteem, create a sense of belonging, ignite creative potential, propel musical culture, strengthen bonds within families, or something else altogether?

Freedom

The incarcerated face abysmal conditions. Relegated to cramped, dystopian quarters, they lack sufficient healthy food, natural light, fresh air, or mental stimulation.

Decoda, a chamber music collective and affiliate ensemble at Carnegie Hall, is committed to making a difference. Their biannual songwriting workshops at a South Carolina maximum-security prison facilitate musical creation and

> collaboration among 30 to 50 inmates (ranging from former music professionals to those who struggle with matching pitch). First as a full community and then in smaller groups, they compose lyrics, melodies, and harmonies. After rehearsing on donated instruments alongside Decoda performers, they conclude the week with a public performance for other detainees, prison staff, VIP guests, even family members. Since the project began, more than 200 songs have been penned, including a Hamilton-inspired musical about Abraham Lincoln.
>
> "Creativity is a human right," explains bassoonist Brad Balliett, a founding ensemble member. "Our program may not fix fundamental problems with the US incarceration system, but it makes life a little less bad for people society has forgotten." This approach to music making rehabilitates, fostering beauty, excitement, and other positive mental health outcomes. In the words of one contributor, "While I'm doing this, I'm really not in prison. I'm free."

Entrepreneurial ventures must generate revenue. Otherwise, they are passion projects rather than business propositions. Who will pay for your outstanding solution? Most items are purchased by the user. For example, mops are likely to be procured by home dwellers with dirty floors. Sometimes, however, a third party makes the investment. An initiative that elevates underserved youth might be funded by grants or businesses who care deeply about that cause.

What's Your Difference?

Many music products compete in cutthroat marketplaces. As we have learned, getting more than a small slice of that professional pie requires being remarkably differentiated, or *purple* (Chapter 2). That leaves room for creativity to thrive.

It's shocking how little diversity exists across most sectors (great news for savvy musicians!). True, surface details vary. Quality level spans the equator, from mind-blowing excellence to borderline negligence. But it often seems that at least 97% of core features are strikingly similar. I call this phenomenon the *97% rule*.

At least 97% of American middle schools teach the same topics, meet morning to midafternoon, schedule long summer breaks, use "A" to "F" letter grades. At least 97% of professional orchestra concerts feature formal-attire musicians sitting behind music stands, with thunderous applause appreciated (but never between movements). At least 97% of university music programs offer similar majors, faculty lines, ensembles, audition days, course requirements, graduation rituals. Consider three meaningful takeaways:

1. "Normal" doesn't mean that something lacks value. A successful history is a primary reason 97% adopt similar paths. (Another is lack of imagination.)
2. Limited available options offer a great opportunity to those with the vision to join the exceptional 3% of outliers.
3. There is no need to change everything. Transforming even a single aspect may be enough (e.g., a traditional music school that radically reimagines juries or senior recitals).

The following innovation tools can help turn your concept purple.[3]

Strategy A: Feature Tweaking

Innovation is contextual. To stand out, it is essential to analyze the status quo and choose another direction. Suppose a string quartet aims to secure more performance opportunities, but competition is stiff.

Step 1: **Identify TRADITIONS.** The more obvious, the better. Words used here become instrumental in the next steps, so be specific.

Step 2: **Imagine TWEAKS.** Dream up at least three alternatives to each tradition.

Step 3: **ADOPT something!** This is just a brainstorm, and not all concepts rise to the top. Embracing just one or two points can dramatically differentiate your work.

CLASSICAL CONCERTS	
TRADITIONS	TWEAKS
Duration is 1 to 2 hours	• 30-minute concerts • 10 minutes or less • 12- to 24-hour drop-in events
Players dress formally	• Informal dress • Irreverent attire • Costumes relevant to the theme • Uniform with a strong vibe • Boas and fedoras
Players read from music stands	• Music is memorized • Music projected onto wall • Music adhered to various places onstage, allowing performers to move • Players (and audience?) wear virtual reality goggles that share the score
Visual stimulus limited to musicians on chairs, center stage	• Perform offstage at times • Stand, lay down, choreograph • Sit on couch, ladder, instrument cases • Audience center stage, musicians in the hall • Cameos by local celebs • Collaborate with dancers and painters • Video projection • Build a sophisticated set, players move as if in a play

Strategy B: Concept Collision

Most of us seek guidance from same-sector relatives. Orchestras mimic orchestras. Vocalists apprentice with singers. Recording engineers attend conferences for

---

[3] For more creative idea generation techniques, see my visual book *The GAME of Innovation*.

like-minded professionals. But breakthrough solutions are exponentially more likely to occur when one world bumps into another. Suppose you run a brick-and-mortar retail music store, but customers are buying online. How might you turn more into loyal patrons?

Step 1: **Identify noncompeting ENTITIES.** Choose organizations and experiences significantly different from yours.
Step 2: **Consider THEIR SUCCESS strategies.** What do they do well?
Step 3: **Imagine how to ADAPT.** How might those concepts be applied to your product?

MUSIC RETAIL STORE		
ENTITIES	THEIR SUCCESS	ADAPT
Food trucks	Mobile restaurants for lunch	Mobile instrument showcases
Olympics	Televised, skill-based competitions	Locally televised event from store where musicians compete in skill-based competitions
Sushi	Chef prepares delicious food at a sushi bar	Once a month, sushi chef prepares delicious food in the store, served to look like a bar of music
Bowling league	Bowlers compete on teams; top season scorer gets a trophy	Music theory students play relevant video games in store on teams; top season scorer gets a trophy
Kindergarten	Student artwork showcased on walls, fostering community pride	Local musician compositions showcased on walls, fostering community pride
Airlines	Loyalty points unlock benefits	Loyalty points unlock benefits

Strategy C: Value Amplification
Existing models already do certain things well. How might you catapult these concepts to the next level? Suppose most student recitals are predictable and lack engagement, yet you want to generate buzz.

Step 1: **Identify current PRIORITIES.** What general categories are already valued?
Step 2: **Describe TRADITIONAL role(s).** How does the typical model address them?
Step 3: **Imagine AMPLIFIED roles(s).** How might you go further yet?

STUDENT RECITALS	
	**PRIORITY: Student Involvement**
TRADITIONAL Students: • Play instrument/sing for an audience	AMPLIFIED Students: • Write program notes • Provide verbal intros to music they perform • Provide verbal intros to music OTHER students perform • Film video intros • Design the "set," program order, reception, etc.
	**PRIORITY: Flexibility in the Moment**
TRADITIONAL • Operate in a new venue • Adopt to new performance conditions • Adjust if memory slip/mistake occurs	AMPLIFIED • Program order drawn from hat • Improvisations • Audience members suggest parameters (loud, slow, high, etc.) • Sight-reading recitals
	**PRIORITY: Community Building**
TRADITIONAL Audience: • Sits together to enjoy event • Mingles before and after, possibly at reception • Applauds as a group	AMPLIFIED Audience: • Dresses in costumes related to theme • Participates (sing-along, clapping in time, call and response) • Adult vs. kids "cheering" competition (hint: kids will win) • Family members introduce performers (hobbies, anecdotes) • Studio cookbook features favorite family recipes paired with QR codes to student musical recordings

What's Your Scope?

Most entrepreneurial ventures, arts organizations, and musical careers offer an array of products that provide multiple income streams. What's the best mix? Ideally, all items in your portfolio should fall under the same umbrella concept. Perhaps they consistently address a given problem or audience, or emphasize whatever makes you most interesting. Aligned efforts strengthen brand and reputation.

When that doesn't happen, overall success may be diluted. This trap seizes many artists and businesses who are spread too thin, pursuing too many competing directions. If products aren't conceptually connected, consider whether you should be running multiple ventures with independent websites and business plans.

What's Your Model?

There are two overarching business models: for-profits and nonprofits. Many musical organizations operate as nonprofits. In fact, musicians often view this as a foregone conclusion. One executive director who asked to remain anonymous explained, "Audiences don't support our kind of art in substantial numbers. The only conceivable option is to be nonprofit." Do not be fooled by the misleading descriptor. One thing for-profits and nonprofits have in common: *they MUST generate a profit*. Failure to bring in more money than you spend over the long haul also has a name—a failing business!

Nonprofits, officially designated by the US Internal Revenue Service as *501c3s*, receive several significant financial benefits:

1. **Tax-deductible donations.** The ability to accept contributions creates a win-win. The business generates new revenue; the donor receives a tax write-off.
2. **Grants.** A majority of grants require nonprofit status to be eligible.[4]
3. **No income tax.** Nonprofits aren't required to pay income tax, allowing more earnings to support programming and overhead.

Accessing these benefits, however, comes with strings attached. Stringent regulations cost time, money, and flexibility. It typically takes at least six months to be processed and approved as a nonprofit. To apply, you must write a mission statement, establish a board, prepare articles of incorporation, incorporate, draft bylaws describing how the organization will be run, and complete the Internal Revenue Service's form 1023. Organizations commonly hire an attorney to help navigate this complex, time-consuming document.

Needless to say, this is not the most efficient way to launch a venture, sometimes requiring more expenses than it is worth. But the clear advantages make this structure worthwhile for some ventures.

NONPROFIT	FOR-PROFIT
Donors can make tax-deductible donations	Donations are not tax deductible
Many grants are open only to nonprofits	Not eligible for those grants (may be allowed to partner with a nonprofit)
No income taxes must be paid	Income taxes must be paid
Though allowed to pay "reasonable" salaries, surplus must be reinvested into the nonprofit	Any amount may be earned, and it can be spent as owners/shareholders wish

---

[4] There is, however, a creative workaround when engaging a "fiscal sponsor," described in Chapter 10.

All activities must help achieve a mission statement, which describes how the nonprofit contributes to the "public good"	Can have any mission it wants, including simply earning a high profit margin
Excellent records must be kept of all finances and activities	Keeping excellent records has many benefits, but legal requirements are not as stringent
Must maintain a board of directors	Not required to have a board but can opt to
If going out of business, assets must be donated to another nonprofit	If going out of business, assets may be distributed among owners/shareholders

Transitioning the Business Model

Offering an alternative to clubs with smoky halls, nasty bar food, and shows way too late, Hal Real launched World Cafe Live (WCL). His goal was to create a "*listening room* big enough to matter, small enough to care." With two performance spaces and a full-service restaurant/bar, this for-profit venture generated revenue through (1) ticketing, (2) food and beverage sales, and (3) private event rentals.

A few years later, Real created a separate but related 501c3 called Live Connections (LC). Their signature Bridge Sessions, held in WCL for groups of 100, empowers 7th through 12th graders to empathize, lead, listen, and participate in live performances. "Because programming is so meaningful and different, raising $500,000 a year was manageable." Operating for- and nonprofit businesses that intersect, however, requires independent boards and extreme caution to ensure finances do not mix.

Running an independent venue with fewer than 1,000 seats is tough to sustain. Following an international pandemic and disruptive market changes, Real and his investors confronted a consequential decision: close shop or transform into a nonprofit. Choosing the latter, WCL was legally folded into LC. Doing so allowed them to amplify fundraising, and programming became more accessible. "Today, 80% of our revenue is earned and 20% contributed. That's healthy, and the inverse of so many music nonprofits."

POWERHOUSE PROPOSALS

Time and again, you will be required to articulate your value, whether applying for jobs, soliciting donors, marketing to clients, crafting a website, pitching ventures, or describing what you do to a fresh face. Messaging matters, since communication may lead to "yes," "maybe later," or "no." Most descriptions are adequate, providing a laundry list of fine features, lovely yet hardly mind blowing. The marketplace responds accordingly. Don't expect miracles.

How might you increase the odds of success? *Powerhouse proposals*, a term I coined to describe a specific framework for designing and pitching initiatives, break through the noise and ignite imaginations. While there are many recipes for success, this formula consistently delivers.

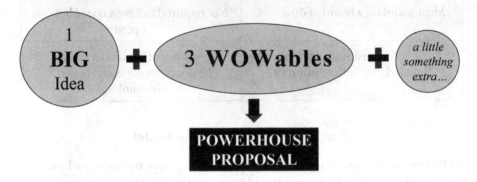

Powerhouse proposals are more than exercises in creative storytelling. As you design a vision, build projects with intention on the front end rather than attempting to reverse-engineer the appearance of innovation down the road.

BIG Idea

A *BIG idea* is the central organizing principle that defines and propels a vision. It often clarifies WHAT you do plus a top-level priority (astrology-based concerts, record label for healthy living, leadership training through music, etc.). Boiling down goals to a single top-level concept is not easy but can be transformative. The best examples are:

1. **Simple.** Catchy hooks are easily explained in minimal words.
2. **Specific.** Concrete rather than fluffy, they clarify your unique priority.
3. **Singular.** Two or more BIG ideas should never battle for attention.
4. **Surprising.** Unexpected elements are more likely to stick.
5. **Stressed.** This element should be consistently emphasized.

In Chapter 2, we considered "What makes you interesting?" A strong answer is likely a great candidate for a BIG idea.

WOWABLES

Major innovations are typically offered as second-level features that support a BIG idea. I call them *WOWables* because great examples elicit the response "WOW!!!," often unprompted.

Each WOWable should clearly reinforce your umbrella concept. Those that compete against it dilute the power of a proposition. For example, if your BIG idea is astrology-inspired concerts, WOWables might be (1) "planetarium events," (2) "horoscope projections coordinated with music," and (3) "intermission tarot card readings." "Supermarket performances" may also intrigue, but connecting grocery stores to astrology is illogical and confusing. If a BIG idea and WOWable feel unrelated, adjust one side of the equation to foster alignment.

A simple rubric immediately clarifies how *WOW-worthy* an idea is. After describing a proposed WOWable to others, invite a one-word reaction:

Achieving a WOW!!! is no easy task. Consistently receiving this assessment means your approach is truly inspired. Interestingly, the second-best grade is often BOO!!! True hatred indicates direct emotional resonance. Others will likely counterbalance the other extreme. MEHs and HMMs are the most common feedback, and problematic. They suggest you have more work to do, at least if the goal is to stand out and attract considerable demand.

Three is an ideal number of WOWables. More can overwhelm, while less feels empty. Consider the order in which they are presented. Try to add razzle dazzle with each subsequent unveiling. "BIG idea X incorporates (1) this (wow!), (2) that (Wow!!), and (3) the other thing (SUPER WOW!!!)."

A LITTLE SOMETHING EXTRA

If the previous steps are effective, your proposal is likely already a hit. To ensure a home run, however, *a little something extra* provides insurance. This is a "but wait, there's more . . ." statement. As if that ice cream sundae weren't sweet enough, add a cherry on top. This final feature typically explores another direction, adding a different type of perceived value. Continuing with astrology-inspired concerts, perhaps a local newspaper plans to showcase a writeup about your series in the horoscope section.

> **Powerhouse Performance**
>
> Moab Music Festival (MMF), cofounded by pianist Michael Barrett and violist Leslie Tomkins, is an annual, two-week summer music festival like no other. It is no wonder this has become a bucket-list priority for so many.
>
> ### *The BIG Idea*: "Music in Concert with the Landscape"
> MMF's six-word tagline sums up their BIG idea.
>
> ### *WOWable 1*: Nature shows
> Moab's other-worldly magnificence encompasses two national parks and the Colorado River. Performances, scheduled in breathtaking locations, offer a "moveable feast." There are grotto, ranch, house, and river concerts, even musical hikes!
>
> ### *WOWable 2*: Diverse, curated programming
> Music is as varied and gorgeous as the surroundings. Events draw from a vast array of styles: classical, jazz, ragtime, tango, Native American songs, Asian folk tunes, and more. Every program is carefully curated, often around themes matched to their location.
>
> ### *WOWable 3*: Musical raft trips
> Bookending the festival are four-day/three-night rafting adventures down the Colorado River, offering an exclusive group of 18 guests and 4 musicians an experience like no other. There are onshore cocktail party recitals each night and daily "floating concerts" where musicians play from boats while guests gliding in the water (wearing life jackets) listen and levitate.
>
> ### *A Little Something Extra*: Befriend the talent!
> At MMF, you don't simply see musicians from afar. Get to know these performers as you explore the wilderness, side by side!

Chapter 4
Sharpen Your Vision

Developing a career model, business concept, entrepreneurial framework, or other creative project is no small feat. As the structure comes together, hopefully your enthusiasm grows. (If not, perhaps it's back to the drawing board.) Of course, concocting a brilliant idea and bringing it to life are not the same thing. Will aspects actually work as they do in your mind? Which features must be included? How much will folks pay for your WOWables (Chapter 3)?

This chapter introduces six tools that help sharpen the vision. Of course, understanding how each works is only the first step. It's what you build that counts.

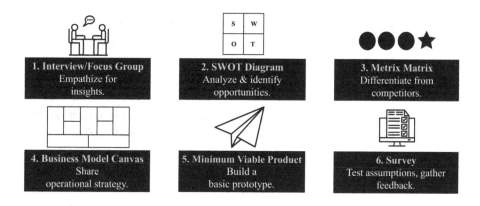

Savvy musicians are more than dreamers. They are committed doers who see things through.

Empathize for Insights

Human-centered design is a problem-solving approach that starts with detective work, seeking insights from actual people before drawing conclusions. What reliable information can human subjects disclose? Apple's cofounder Steve Jobs argued: "Henry Ford once said, 'If I'd ask customers what they wanted, they would've told me a faster horse.' People don't know what they want until you show it to them." If you expect interview subjects to prophesize brilliant innovations for your new idea, prepare to be disappointed. However, people can accurately describe how they feel—what resonates, excites, repels. They can address *empathy points*:

Tool: Interview/Focus Group

Before designing—or even beginning to imagine—entrepreneurial solutions, conduct a research phase. An incredible amount can be learned from interviews and focus groups with *target users*, the people you hope to impact.

Prior to meeting, compile a rough series of questions. Sequence them logically. Consider what you most hope to learn and the best strategy for uncovering that narrative. Determine how many positive versus negative queries make sense (i.e., *What were your **favorite** musical experiences growing up? Which aspects of lessons did you like the least?*). Also weigh the psychological impact of each query, particularly when exploring emotionally charged topics.

During conversation, listen more than you talk. Resist the temptation to overshare personal information or in-depth explanations about your project. Using your question list as a roadmap, adjust as necessary, allowing for meaningful follow-ups. Keep eyes on the clock, forecasting clues on the depth of answers sought (detailed analysis or two-sentence headline?).

Document conversations rather than relying on memory alone. Some skilled interviewers are adept at taking notes as they listen, but others quickly become overwhelmed by this multitasking. Alternatives include video or audio recording—always request permission—or engaging a separate *scribe* to take notes in real time.

Following each session, hunt for *insights*. Insights are not facts, data, or statistics. Rather, they are shocking "a-ha" revelations that catalyze breakthrough thinking. As you analyze findings, pay particular attention to elation, fantasy, and pain points. What do folks love? What would they love? What can't they love? Use these lessons to inform decisions when ideating solutions and mapping features.

Listen to This

When oboist Karisa Antonio became Detroit Symphony Orchestra's director of social innovation, her job description could be boiled down to a single sentence: *Help us become a better neighbor and community member.* From the start, Antonio proceeded with intention and respect. "As arts organizations, we often view communities through a deficit lens, in need of our help and our culture. A more powerful approach involves centering neighbors as experts in their own experience."

> Scheduling listening sessions, Antonio cast a wide net involving local parents, schools, businesses, block clubs, anyone willing to meet. Three overarching questions shaped conversations:
>
> 1. What is your dream?
> 2. What challenges stand between you and your goal?
> 3. How might we celebrate together while addressing challenges in your way?
>
> Important insights emerged from hundreds of meetings: The rich local legacy of diverse cultural traditions should be championed; programming should take place in our own neighborhoods; students deserve high-quality arts experiences. Initially, Antonio's mindset involved discovering actionable strategies for the Detroit Symphony Orchestra. What she learned was that they can't do it alone. Being responsive to the listening process would require many partners and a cross-sectoral effort. The result? The Detroit Neighborhood Initiative. *Continued later in this chapter...*

Assess Your Positioning

Whether examining your career model, existing venture, or fresh project, take a 360-degree look at the hand you've been dealt. Using that as a starting point, identify prospective clues that might amplify success.

Tool: SWOT Diagram

A SWOT analysis is a traditional but powerful approach to examining a situation's realities. Though the letters stand for **S**trengths, **W**eaknesses, **O**pportunities, and **T**hreats, all four point to opportunity when approached strategically. The first two areas address issues internal to you and your business. *What are our Strengths and Weaknesses?* The latter pair references external elements out of your control. *Which Opportunities and Threats are emerging in the world today?* A SWOT analysis for a hypothetical performing ensemble might look as follows:

S	W	O	T
Great players	Not enough products	Publishing market	Economic downturn
Great music	Fan base too small	Education partners	Arts funding cuts
Entertaining shows	Outdated website	News item: Olympics	Fierce competition
Strong brand identity	Too few East Coast connections	Growing interest in multiculturalism	AI may take over

After completing the analysis, turn SWOT points to your advantage.

What to do with STRENGTHS. Strengths are your best features, so make them count.	
MENTION	It is shockingly common for people/organizations to neglect mentioning strengths while highlighting their weaknesses. Proudly share your assets!
EXPLOIT	Place important strengths at the heart of your project.
AMPLIFY	Make strengths stronger yet. How might you become "the best in the world" (Chapter 1) by leaning into these aspects?
What to do with WEAKNESSES. Weaknesses are every bit as valuable as strengths.	
OVERCOME	Develop shortcomings so they no longer drag you down.
OUTSOURCE	Hire someone to assist.
PURGE	Remove them from your model altogether, turning focus elsewhere.
OWN	Many people find their calling in response to challenges/adversity (e.g., if you've always struggled with stage fright, make this obstacle central to your identity).
What to do with OPPORTUNITIES and THREATS. Interestingly, opportunities and threats can be synonyms. It's largely a matter of perspective.	
RESEARCH	Learn more about the opportunity or threat.
EMBRACE	Might an element somehow become part of your framework?
PARTNER	Embrace the development through meaningful alliances.
PIVOT	When external forces are strong, it may make sense to change directions, either running toward or away from the issue.
FLIP	Use threats to uncover better solutions (e.g., COVID was a catastrophe, yet it helped many savvy musicians think differently and open new doors).

Distinguish from Competition

Regardless of specialty, there will be competitors. Understanding their model provides clues on what to do and, just as importantly, what to avoid. Interestingly, innovators and imitators often reach opposite conclusions.

Tool: Competitive Array

A great vehicle for working through your distinctive value involves a *competitive array*. Create a grid, say 5 × 6. Across the top, list your venture—first or last—alongside "direct competitors" (addressing the same problem through a comparable solution), "indirect competitors" (offering contrasting products that target a similar problem/audience), or a combination. Choose entities that offer meaningful points of comparison.

Going down the left, add consequential elements to be examined, such as pricing, features, user experience, location, loyalty program, space design, etc. Favor aspects that clarify your unique marketplace positioning.

	Comp 1	Comp 2	Comp 3	YOU
Element 1				
Element 2				
Element 3				
Element 4				
Element 5				

In the remaining fields, concisely capture how elements are approached by each venture. A great matrix illuminates your competitive advantage in at least a few ways, highlighting what makes you better, different, and/or more compelling (or will in the future). If you struggle to identify meaningful points of differentiation, revisit creativity lessons from Chapter 3 such as *feature tweaking* and *concept collision*.

Keynote Concerts

Singer-songwriter Tiamo De Vettori began his career like so many, playing coffee shops, bars, restaurants, farmers markets. With no viable career path in sight, he attended personal growth and business seminars to figure out what to do. Noting that each featured a keynote, he thought, "These speakers are just storytellers with a message, exactly what I do at my live gigs!" That spark led him to develop *keynote concerts*—talks around themes like "Luminary Leadership" that integrate his original songs. Careful to position himself as a speaker rather than musician, De Vettori's clearly differentiated product has unlocked scores of presentations for groups of up to 15,000, earning him as much as $20,000 per gig.

	TRADITIONAL Keynotes	TIAMO'S Keynote Concerts
Conference types	Seminar, association, corporate, academic	Seminar, association, corporate
Audience size	50–5,000+	50–5,000+
Fee	$$$	$$$ + upgrades (e.g., custom conference songs, VIP concert, digital album sales)
Stage setup	Podium, PowerPoint, mic	Guitar on guitar stand, mic, NO/minimal slide projection
Content	1 overarching message	3 stories + 3 lessons + 3 songs
Impact	Emotional experience drawn from words/message	Emotional experience drawn from stories/live music/lyrics
Audience role	Listen, watch projections	Listen, interact during exercises, sing along, dance
End	Final thought, clapping	Final upbeat song, people on feet cheering

Design the Business Model

To bring any project to life, you must architect a viable framework. One possibility involves drafting a traditional *business plan*. Typically 30 to 100+ pages, these documents include an executive summary, product/service overview, competitive analysis, marketing strategy, financial projections, and more. While thinking through the model in such detail is helpful, business plans are time consuming to create and often loaded with inaccuracies. Elements may contradict one another rather than contributing to a unified, cohesive plan. Analyzing its essence requires extensive digging through endless prose. I recommend a leaner methodology.

Tool: Business Model Canvas
In their groundbreaking book *Business Model Generation*,[1] authors Alexander Osterwalder and Yves Pigneur propose a radical alternative. What if you capture the essence of an entire business model on a single page? Their "Business Model

---

[1] Alexander Osterwalder and Yves Pigneur, *Business Model Generation: A Handbook for Visionaries, Game Changers, and Challengers* (John Wiley and Sons, 2010).

Canvas" (BMC) can be downloaded for free (www.strategyzer.com). I recommend printing it on large paper, typically 24 × 36 inches or larger.

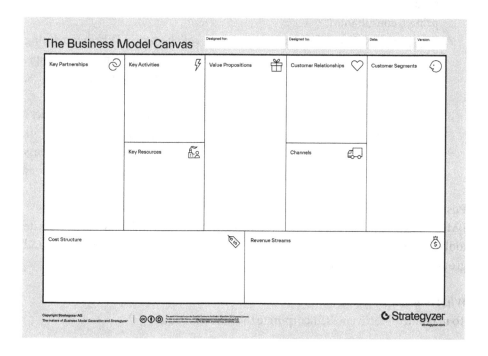

A BMC contains nine fields.

1. **Value proposition.** *What are your most compelling benefits?* Which pain points do you solve? What exciting features should be prominently showcased?
2. **Customer segments.** *Who will buy?* Consider primary and secondary audiences.
3. **Customer relationships.** *How do you communicate with clients?* Website? Phone? Newsletters? Physical location?
4. **Channels.** *How is your value delivered to clients?* In other words, how/where will consumers get your stuff? Are products shipped through the postal service? Can they be accessed through a virtual platform? Do you maintain a physical storefront or studio?
5. **Key activities.** *What are the most important tasks your business does?* What requires time and energy from employees? Building curriculum? Manufacturing? Practicing? Planning logistics? Running the festival? "Marketing" almost always appears.

6. **Key resources.** *What are the most important assets your business needs?* Consider human, physical, financial, and intellectual resources. Do you require an office, musical instruments, recording gear, computer, tour bus, 3D printer, consultants?
7. **Key partnerships.** *Who are your primary collaborators?* Whether naming individuals, companies, or industries, identify true win-win relationships. Consider what they can do for you and vice versa: spread buzz, increase sales, split costs, amplify mission, etc.
8. **Cost structure.** *How do you spend money?* What are major expense categories? Hint: Personnel almost always represents the largest expenditure.
9. **Revenue streams.** *How do you earn money?* Be creative. Sustainable business models generate more than they spend!

Post-it Strategy
BMCs are often completed with 3 × 3 inch Post-it notes. "Stickies" are a favorite tool for innovators because of their flexibility. Easy to sort, swap, remove, add, and group, this tool allows various solutions to be tested.

What makes a great Post-it?
To maximize effectiveness, incorporate the following rules:

Does color matter?
Post-it notes span the rainbow. Take advantage of this opportunity by using different colors for specific purposes, further emphasizing your strategy. Be sure to include a legend. For example, different colors might be used to indicate items like:

| Short-, medium-, or long-term goal | Who is in charge of each task? | If there are 2+ main things you sell, show connections with colors | If there are 2+ customer groups, show connections with colors |

How many Post-its per field should be included?
As with any brainstorm, begin by notating everything and anything that comes to mind. Quantity over quality. Then, after all potential solutions have been documented, whittle down the realm of possibility. Edit, combine, and tighten entries until the strategy is just right.

Think of each Post-it in your ultimate solution as a project, requiring unique time and resources. Too many create an overwhelming, impossible model. Too few make it difficult to realize goals and may indicate overlooked essentials. Aim to include just the right amount. Typically, this means two to five entries per field, though that is a guide rather than inflexible dogma.

How should Post-its be organized?
Indicate priority order. In each field of the canvas, show the most important point on top, second most important below, etc.

What else goes on a Post-it?
Quantify entries when helpful. For example, how many customers must be reached? Another option involves clarifying details. If one value proposition indicates "weekend fun!," add specifics with a different writing utensil, clarifying which elements will be pleasing.

The Business of Groupmusing

Groupmuse, a musician-owned co-op cofounded by Sam Bodkin, has instigated more than 10,000 house concerts in multiple cities. With the mission of hosting "a concert on every corner," much of this nonprofit's energy is spent recruiting and preparing "hosts" who present "groupmuses" in their living room or backyard. Events combine performances with plenty of mingle time. "It's about making new friends, building community, and being transported through the beauty of live music."

Groupmuse generates revenue in several ways. Each Groupmuse attendee must RSVP through their website, paying either a $5 flat fee or $9/month Supermuser subscription. (Performers are compensated through additional contributions/ticket fees.) They self-produce Massivemuse performances in nontraditional spaces and also sell donated, otherwise nonpurchased tickets to performances by partner organizations (e.g., symphony concerts) through their Night Out initiative.

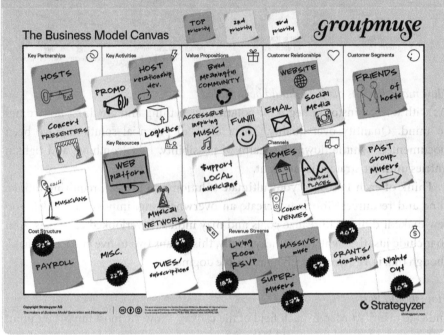

BUILD A PROTOTYPE

Mental visioning is helpful to a point. But for any concept to work, it is necessary to think through specifics and solidify design elements. As they say, the devil is in the ~~details~~ sixteenth notes. Start with a large-scale framework and work inward. Consider the what, where, when, who, how, how much, how long. For example:

- **Music lessons.** How long? Sessions per term? Location? Piano available?
- **Live performance.** Who plays? How long? What repertoire? Technical requirements?
- **Café with performance stage.** Dimensions? Food/drinks? Hours? Number of tables?
- **Recording studio.** Major equipment? Styles of music? Services provided?
- **Instrument accessory.** What does it look like? How does it feel? Does it work?

To test and demonstrate your approach, build a *prototype* that can be touched, viewed, heard, and critiqued. Doing so forces you to wrestle with any number of pertinent issues.

Tool: Minimum Viable Product

A common mistake made by musicians: Identify a project, toil for months, share it publicly only after it's been rehearsed to perfection (literally or metaphorically). If it turns out people don't love the vision—or fail to show up—too bad. The investment of time, energy, and money has been spent.

A much better approach involves building a *minimum viable product*, or *MVP*.[2] In other words, what is the LEAST you can do before collecting feedback and evaluating whether your vision is what people actually want? Prototyping an MVP offers the opportunity to quickly work through specifics and solidify design elements. The following chart suggests possible MVPs for a variety of musical products:

PRODUCT	MINIMUM VIABLE PRODUCT (example)
Concert	Paragraph overview, full-typed program, demo recording featuring excerpts of each piece (even if other artists are performing)
Online course	Course description, curriculum overview, one to two sample video lessons (partial or full) so viewers can evaluate the general approach
Summer camp	Powerhouse proposal, rough schedule, spec sheet (describing cost, number of students/faculty, location, etc.), 2-minute marketing video
Venue	Blueprint sketch, feature sheet, proposed menu, basic website
Book	Table of contents, back cover copy, one sample chapter, marketing plan
Physical product	For a guitar: Product overview, drawing (or better yet crude 3D model), features list
App	Map of activities to be featured, graphic design showcasing various pages (does not need to be functional)

Many items can be constructed with readily available free software. I'm also a fan of kindergarten art supplies. Crayons, Legos, pipe cleaners, Post-its, wood, milk cartons, and action figures can ignite creativity while effectively conveying ideas.

BINGO!!!

Following decades of frustration in the tech sector, Canadian drummer Sean Wallbridge yearned to pursue music full time. Though his cover band sounded great, how could they generate demand? All members were introverts, and

---

[2] This term was coined by Frank Robinson and popularized in Eric Ries's book *Lean Startup*.

without originals, their product was similar to a thousand others. Then he got an idea: *What if we play 30-second snippets and attendees mark bingo cards until someone gets five in a row?*

Determined to quickly test "Rockstar Bingo," Wallbridge built an MVP. Within a week, he and a talented friend had engineered a crude app that generated unique bingo cards listing song titles in lieu of numbers. It wasn't pretty or perfect, but functioned. The band quickly decided where to start and stop each song. (The top? The chorus? The end?) For a quarter of the tunes, they simply played recordings. The beta test engaged a small audience via Zoom.

There were hiccups, to be sure, but people seemed to like it. Wallbridge listened to feedback, steadily improved the platform, grew the rep list, and watched buzz spread. Within a year, audiences regularly topped 600. Other groups asked to license the platform. Today, Rockstar Bingo has a devoted following in 14 countries.

Gather Feedback

Feedback, collected during different phases of the design process, is invaluable. During initial ideation, it offers clues on demand, which features resonate, the ideal audience, and how much to charge. After sharing an MVP prototype or refined product, testers can offer insights on what works and what does not.

Tool: Survey

Where interviews allow for deep digging, surveys track trends by collating feedback from many people. The point is to collect honest responses and learn. It is NOT to provide superficial validation. Though affirmation feels great, insights about weaknesses or incorrect expectations are often more instructive.

Assumption Identification

In life and business, we must rely upon assumptions. Something as basic as crossing the street requires faith you won't be struck by a falling anvil. Since beliefs may or may not reflect reality, test their merits early on to avoid wasting time, money, or resources if calculations are off. When developing a survey, begin by identifying the **8 to 12 most important hypotheses** in one concise sentence each, considering issues like:

- **Demographics.** Who is your ideal customer (age/background/economic profile, etc.)?
- **Demand.** How much do they care about the problem you solve?
- **Habits.** Which solutions do they currently use, and how do they feel about them?
- **Persuadability.** How open are they to trying new solutions?
- **Features.** What would they like to see? Are they excited about your proposed specifics?

- **WOWables.** Do innovations truly WOW?
- **Impact.** How effective are various elements? What might be improved?
- **Price.** How much are consumers willing to pay?

Survey Design

A great survey accomplishes several goals. Ask a few *demographic* questions (if you assume middle-class, suburban women are your primary customer, gather data on income, neighborhood, and gender) to understand more about each respondent before examining elements relevant to your project. Always include an *overview paragraph* clarifying the vision.

What is the best way to frame a question? Many options exist: *fill in the blank, binary, scales, multiple choice, drop-down menu, ranking*, etc. *Open-ended* inquiries allow for personalized insights, but including more than one or two may decrease the completion rate since responses demand more from the taker. The wording of each question has psychological implications that affect answers and can skew results. Consider five ways to test a pricing assumption. Which option do you believe is most likely to generate accurate data?

QUESTION	IMPLICATIONS
I would pay $____ for this product.	While this *fill-in-the-blank* allows any response, it lacks context. Respondents may be unable to assess if this is a cheap (e.g., $10), average ($50), or luxury ($1,000) product.
I would pay $150 for this product. *(yes/no)*	*Binary questions* are easy to answer but offer little nuance. I rarely recommend this approach.
How likely are you to pay $300 for this product? *(1–5 scale, extremely unlikely to extremely likely)*	*Scales* test relative interest. Odd-numbered rating systems have a "neutral" option in the middle. Even-numbered scales force respondents to choose if they are more positive or negative.
How much would you pay for this product? *(a) $10–20, (b) $25–50, (c) $75–100, (d) $125–150*	*Multiple choice* presents various options. Introduce all conceivable preferences. This question does not allow for the possibility of respondents who wouldn't pay anything or might spend more than $150. Also, be aware that people often choose the second-lowest number so they don't appear cheap, whether or not that reflects reality.
What is the maximum you would pay for this product? *(a) $150 or less, (b) $300, (c) $500, (d) $1,000+, (e) I would not buy*	This *multiple-choice* variation introduces a different set of price points. It also provides an out for those who are disinterested.

How many questions should be incorporated? The more you ask, the more you can learn. However, people are quickly spooked by long forms. Typically, 7 to 12 feels reasonable. Ask only what is most illuminating.

Common Survey Shortcomings

Make every question count! Don't fall into the trap of asking for:

1. **Insights without explanation.** "How likely are you to use our product?" is useless if people don't clearly understand what you offer.
2. **Obvious reactions.** "Do you ever feel stress?" is likely to receive a 100% "yes" vote. Be wary of meaningless, unanimous responses.
3. **Unlikely expertise.** Only ask what survey takers are likely to know. A potential client can share how much they might pay but should not be expected to predict manufacturing costs.
4. **Innovative visioning.** It is unlikely respondents will have breakthrough ideas about what your business should do. Instead, invite them to examine the plan/proposal you have imagined.
5. **Nonaligned perspectives.** If some questions are geared toward potential clients but others are for partners, distribute independent surveys to each audience.

Every survey question should test a stated assumption. If one does not, either change/delete the inquiry or update your assumption list.

Suppose your project involves short lunchtime concerts for small audiences. The beliefs that follow are specific and often measurable, allowing each point to be evaluated through carefully worded questions:

1. Our primary audience is successful businesspeople who work downtown.
2. This audience will love the idea of personalized, intimate 15-minute performances.
3. The experience should include 10 minutes of music plus 5 minutes of conversation.
4. The ideal audience size is 6 to 10 people.
5. Customers will gladly pay $30 to attend.
6. Attendees will want some kind of souvenir. (But what?)

A hypothetical survey for this venture follows. As you read through it, *compare each question with the corresponding assumption being referenced* (shown in the "#" column).

> **Survey for Bite-Sized Beats**
>
> *Bite-Sized Beats* offers super-short concerts to super-small audiences, conveniently arranged during lunchtime in your own office building! Witness world-class performances for an awe-inspiring experience you will never forget!!!
>
> | Question | Answer Type | # |
> |---|---|---|
> | 1. What sector do you work in? | Drop-down with relevant options | 1 |
> | 2. How exciting is this concept? | 7-point scale: 1 = indifferent; 7 = ecstatic | 2 |
> | 3. To maintain an intimate vibe, how many people should attend? | (a) just me!, (b) 3–5, (c) 6–10, (d) 11–15, (e) 16–25, (f) 26–40+ | 4 |
> | 4. The ideal experience incorporates: | (Select all that apply): (a) music only, (b) dialogue, (c) informational slides, (d) bring your own lunch, (e) snacks provided, (f) alcohol | 3 |
> | 5. How long should our intentionally short concerts last? | (a) 5 min, (b) 10 min, (c) 15 min, (d) other_____ | 2 |
> | 6. Is it important to take home a souvenir? If so, what? | Ranking: (a) recording, (b) printed program, (c) polaroid with artist, (d) T-shirt, (e) the experience is enough! | 6 |
> | 7. I would pay $____ to attend this kind of event | Fill in the blank | 5 |
> | 8. Any suggestions? | Open ended | — |

Like any important document, proofread extensively and run it by others before releasing. The quality of writing directly impacts the value of data received.

Distribution and Analysis
Collect a critical mass of responses. At the least, aim for 25, though (many) more are often desirable. Depending on the audience, determine the best way to circulate this form. Does it make sense to share with the masses through social media or to distribute a QR code within a closed community (hospital, school, conference, etc.).

Once a survey has closed, analyze its data. Seek takeaways, paying attention to unexpected results. If signs challenge your thinking, resist the temptation to discount responses or get defensive. Savvy musicians, well aware that assumptions might be off, pivot when necessary. At the least, use these data points to prompt further research.

> ### Did We Hear You Right?
>
> Guided by an intensive engagement process, Karisa Antonio (from this chapter's opening) and Detroit Symphony Orchestra launched the Detroit Neighborhood Initiative. To date, this project has engaged 233 partner organizations and over 7,000 people in local neighborhoods, cocreating daylong arts festivals with food, activities, booths, tons of resources, and performances featuring Detroit Neighborhood Initiative members and local artists. All events are free and open to the public.
>
> Significantly, the initiative is not about what the orchestra does *for* or *to* their audience but rather *with* them. The engagement process involves five principles: (1) listening, (2) responsiveness, (3) codesign, (4) coimplementation, and (5) evaluation. This framework has since been applied across the organization, whether considering artistic projects, internal collaboration, or paths for elevating underrepresented voices.
>
> The necessity of phase five (evaluation) should not be discounted. Antonio distributes separate customer and partner surveys (in English and Spanish) to identify what went well and opportunities for improvement. Specifically, this tool examines three aspects:
>
> 1. **Quantity.** How many visitors attended various activities and performances?
> 2. **Quality.** What are we doing well and what should be improved (accessibility, timeliness, communication, etc.)?
> 3. **Impact.** Are people better off as a result of our work?

Chapter 5
Marketing Is Everything

Marketing shapes how people think and feel by directing priorities, perceptions, and attitudes. Used to increase demand (get more gigs, clients, notoriety, votes), it has three overriding goals:

1. Keep past customers engaged.
2. Attract new fans.
3. Increase name recognition.

Savvy musicians embrace the opportunity of proactive marketing. But what does it take to run an effective campaign?

EIGHT MARKETING MYTHS

Myth #1: People Care
It often seems musicians believe audiences are sitting around, bored to tears, twiddling their thumbs, struggling to figure out what to do with their abundant free time. When they run across a poster, ad, or social media post, it'll hit them like a ton of tubas. "Of course! I should do that!"

People are busy—busier than ever. They're busy with jobs, families, and hobbies. They're busy exercising, watching Netflix, commuting, texting, eating out, devouring social media, vacationing, networking, watching news, cooking, reading, gaming, procrastinating, vacuuming, and stopping by Starbucks to caffeinate themselves enough to survive it all. This hectic schedule spans 8 days a week, 462 days a year. Argh—there's no relief in sight.

When most folks consider attending a show, they're not just weighing it against comparable events during the same time slot, or even that month. Instead, they subconsciously ask, "In my crazy life, already overflowing with urgent stuff, is it worth two hours to experience *this*?" Long drives, parking expenses, or babysitting needs fuel further complications. That's a tall order. Which leads to the most common answer. "No!"

Myth #2: Traditional Advertising Works
Ads today are in full assault from every direction: search engines, email, apps, TV, magazines, billboards, and branding on everything from buses to T-shirts to mugs.

Some companies print messages on eggs! The battle for consumers is raging, with no place to hide.

What are the results of such brutal combat? The vast majority of ads are tuned out. Forgotten. Hardly noticed. For a message to break through, it must be extreme, outrageous, or utterly unusual in some way. And repeated. To have a fighting chance, multiple exposures are necessary. The *rule of seven*, a term coined by 1930s TV/radio advertising executives, suggested that consumers must see a message seven times before taking note. In today's digital era, that number is much higher. Such a massive campaign is out of the question for many musicians.

Ads reaching the wrong people do little more than annoy. This is particularly true with commercials that interrupt your favorite activity (whether or not you have restless leg syndrome or any interest in the arts). Then there's the issue of credibility. Consumers don't believe ads. They're too smart for that. Too much advertising overhypes and underdelivers.

And now for the biggie: Advertisements are expensive! True, those selling the space will present a forceful case. Yes, it only costs $50 (or $500, or $5,000) for a beautiful half page with a trapezoidal border. Yes, the magazine has 3,247 devoted readers. But if the rate of return is 0%—not uncommon for isolated ads—how valuable are even a million viewers ignoring your message? Expensive and ineffective is not a great combination.

Of course, some ads work wonders. But there are less expensive, more powerful marketing solutions for cash-strapped ventures. Proceed with caution.

Myth #3: Social Media Will Save You
Hallelujah, hallelujah! The Great Redeemer has arrived!!! Naturally, we're talking about social media. Publications revere its supernatural power. This, they argue, is the secret to all professional success. Social media is free (except most companies now are pay-to-play). And it targets "friends" and specific audiences, rather than spamming the world at large.

True, most successful marketing campaigns today employ social media in some way. Also true, however, is that most *unsuccessful* efforts utilize it. Unfortunately, there are many more examples of the latter. The potency of social media, like any other tool, depends on what you are building and the method for getting there.

Myth #4: Marketing is Expensive
Many musicians believe marketing requires big money. The larger the budget, the better. Luckily, no such ratio exists. In fact, hefty cash reserves often have a negative effect. They can obstruct creativity, promote waste, and encourage marketers to adopt simple solutions with limited efficacy. Far more valuable are *time, energy,* and *imagination.* Jay Conrad Levinson's term *guerilla marketing* describes an approach that not only is valuable to those with small budgets but also can yield superior results to organizations blessed (cursed) with mountains of cash.

Guer·ril·la Mar·ket·ing

Noun: Low-cost, high-commitment, high-creativity promotional approach.

Myth #5: Audiences Attend Concerts for the Music
This folklore used to be the case. In 1843, if you wanted to hear a great performance, how else would that happen? But today, if the primary aim is to experience outstanding audio, why not save money and check out the perfectly mixed, digitally edited recording from the comfort of your earbuds? True, a few people attend concerts just for music (you, me, and that fellow in the green hat). But capturing their imagination often requires something else.

Myth #6: High Prices Deter Audiences
In this economy, consumers pinch every penny. Unfortunately, most people aren't willing to pay much for music, right? Well . . . I recently opted for the "cheapest available tickets" when attending a Cirque du Soleil show, nominally priced at $170 apiece (!). This theater presents 10 sold-out performances per week to a hall seating 1,800. It seems many people are in fact willing to pay exorbitant prices, at least for certain experiences. (BTW, it was well worth the cost.) On the other hand, there are wonderful performances that struggle to gain traction at $5 to $20.

If you're worried high ticket prices deter the audience, try lowering them to $1 and note the difference. If attendance booms, you've uncovered the culprit. If there's still room for cows to graze, perhaps the challenge is something else altogether.

Of course, the opposite can also be true. Low prices may dissuade audiences. Many people assume a correlation between quality and cost. In this case, small numbers do not bode well. When demand lags, *perhaps the rate simply isn't high enough.*

Myth #7: Marketing is Not *Your* Job
Some musicians are passionately disinterested in marketing. They'd rather practice. Or compose. Or fish. Or anything else. In fact, they long for the day when a record label, publishing company, artist manager, or some other noble savior does it for them. Reality check—that's not how the game is played! To begin with, nobody understands your art as well as you. Few will be as invested either. This is not to suggest that artists must always oversee all marketing. But no matter how famous you become, savvy musicians take responsibility for their own success. Even superstars collaborate closely with management to control their image.

Myth #8: You Know What Marketing Means
This chapter is about *marketing*. In a word, what does that mean? It's a question I've asked many audiences. The vast majority suggest "advertising." In fact, they use the terms interchangeably. A second common answer: "sales." With such perceptions,

it's no wonder so many arts marketers limit efforts to ads, posters, and social media. These sailors are missing the boat.

Marketing is an attitude, a way of life. It encompasses everything that impacts how people perceive you (positively or negatively):

The brand you build, and how others view your work.
The products you produce, and the problems they solve.
The relationships you cultivate, because success goes both ways.
The web presence you maintain, showing up and offering value.
The persistence you show, not giving up after three attempts.
The customer service you demonstrate, particularly when there's a problem.
The loyalty you cultivate, because business is about relationships.
The look you wear, including expressions on your face.
The attitude projected, even on your worst day.

A bio or resume doesn't just state what you've done; it's marketing. Volunteering for a great cause isn't just charitable; it's marketing. Showing up late isn't just unprofessional; it's *demarketing*. Your events, products, lessons, communications, and interactions are far more than just that: They're all marketing!

ARTS MARKETING A-LIST

Effective marketing requires a comprehensive, multidimensional plan. Business schools teach the four Ps—product, price, place, and promotion[1]—but this may not go far enough. A more powerful approach for savvy musicians involves what I call the *arts marketing A-List*. (which can be downloaded and reprinted from: **www.savvymusician.com/alist.**

---

[1] Variations on this system may also include concepts like people, process, positioning, packaging, or physical evidence.

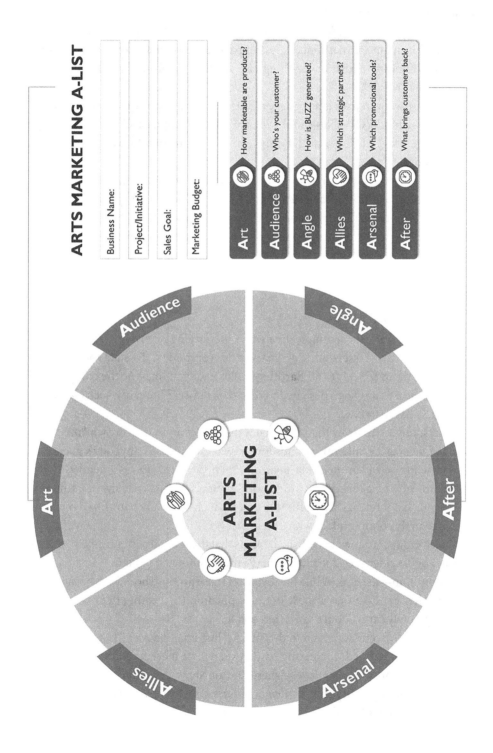

ART

How marketable are products?
At the core of every marketing campaign should be ART, the product(s) being offered. This might mean a concert, lesson package, instrument repair, audio services, crowdfunding effort, or anything else warranting promotion. (A plumber's ART is sewage repair.)

Any first-time purchase is a mystery of sorts. Customers are driven by a *promise*. What compelling WOWables should your marketing emphasize? Resist the temptation to get bogged down in details. Keep this list to two to five points. More overwhelms.

Some ART simply doesn't have the potential to attract a sizable following. No amount of promotion can save projects with inadequate appeal. With that in mind, design ART that is so compelling, so meaningful, that even obsessive, type A, do-aholics with way too much on their plates will move mountains to embrace it.

AUDIENCE

Who's your customer?
Musicians are notoriously uncreative when identifying AUDIENCE. A common—and cringeworthy—assertion: "We market to everybody!" To state the painfully obvious, nothing appeals to all Earthlings. Plus, can you imagine the complexities and expense of a campaign designed to reach the masses? In reality, such claims are code for, "I haven't a clue."

Others, hoping to grow the pie, discuss their sincere desire to reach "nontraditional audiences." While this sounds lovely, what it means is anybody's guess. No human being self-identifies as a *nontraditional* (at least, not as intended here). There are no social media or in-person channels for this elusive community. Everything is contextual. An AUDIENCE that hasn't historically patronized one type of ART is surely commonplace with others.

A third group, resigned to realism, laments that the limited roster of likely patrons consists of (1) elderly, established fans; (2) music students; (3) family and friends; and (4) hmmm—the end. While the loyalty of these groups should not be taken for granted, they bemoan that just 3% of the population (or another depressingly low figure) remotely cares about the art they create.

There is a different approach to this puzzle. Just imagine . . . 97% of the population has been untapped! Increasing market share by a mere fraction could change the game. Opportunities are everywhere and music is a superpower. It is important, however, to identify specific *demographics*, or *customer segments*. The list of possibilities is literally endless.

POTENTIAL AUDIENCES			
Age	Social status/ gender	Ethnicity/origin	Career
College students Grandparents Kids Parents Retirees Millennials Teenagers Working age Young adults	Colleagues Divorcees Families LGBTQIA Men Personal friends Single moms Singles Women	Asians Blacks Foreigners Hispanics Immigrants Indigenous Tourists Various nationalities Various regions	Arts Business Education Financial Law enforcement Legal Medical Military Transportation
Education	Hobby	Community	VIPs
Alumni College students Elementary students Junior/senior high students Music majors	Amateur artists Arts lovers Aspiring artists Associations/ guilds Fans of other arts Sports	Local Political Religious Special needs Underserved Wealthy	Community leaders Donors Influential voices Politicians Press Thought leaders

Some products are limited to a single segment (e.g., music theater camp for high schoolers from three school districts), while others pursue several. Targeting multiple AUDIENCE groups is a double-edged sword. Doing so increases the pool of consumers, yet unique resources and strategies are required to reach each population.

For best results: *Identify the biggest, littlest niche(s)*. The more sizable a group (biggest), the larger the customer pool available. The more specific this demographic (littlest), the easier it will be to design highly targeted, relevant campaigns.

Music To My Eyes!

Perhaps no AUDIENCE is more overlooked by musicians than the Deaf. Yet this group is hungry for meaningful artistic engagement. True, they could watch a musical and read subtitles. But so much gets lost. Captions are grossly oversimplified. It's hard to understand who is saying what, or the intent—*was that line angry or sarcastic?* "We get crumbs at the kids' table while hearing people enjoy the feast," reflects Garrett Zuercher, who has been profoundly Deaf from birth.

Deaf Broadway, a troupe he cofounded, is made up of nonhearing performers, directors, and creatives. Their productions of shows like *Sweeney Todd*, *Into*

> *the Woods*, and *Rent* are fully choreographed on top of original soundtrack recordings, as actors "sing" through American Sign Language (ASL). Rather than traditional subtitles, *dynamic captions* convey the music's spirit by integrating color, movement, and size.
>
> The reaction has been overwhelming, with a tsunami of interest from schools, teachers, and organizations. Quickly converted superfans are mesmerized by this "authentically Deaf" entertainment featuring their own people, culture, and language. "We never intended to start a theater company. But the giant hole it filled created such demand, we had to keep going."

Angle

How is BUZZ generated?
Get people talking. Word of mouth (whether spoken or online) is the best form of marketing, and not just because it's free. If your message goes viral, rest assured that sales will follow. A potent ANGLE, or *BUZZ hook*, captures attention and imagination. Providing journalists, podcasters, thought leaders, and loquacious gossipers with powerful capital, they offer fascinating openers for the dinner table, social media, and bowling night.

In a world of endless messages, what does it take to trigger dialogue? According to Mark Hughes's book *Buzzmarketing*,[2] there are six catalysts for BUZZ. "Push any of these buttons," he explains, "and you'll give people the currency to start a conversation."

Be careful not to confuse BUZZ hooks with themes. "Female Franco-Flemish composers" may be a fascinating recital unifier, but it's unlikely to become the talk of the town. "Songs at the cemetery" is so bizarre that it might just catch fire.

---

[2] Mark Huges, *Buzzmarketing: Getting People to Talk about Your Stuff* (Portfolio, 2005).

Some BUZZ hooks pinpoint aspects of the ART. Others highlight a related backstory (one performer survived a plane crash, caught on tape!). Also possible is making the publicity campaign itself buzzworthy: a wild video, controversial rumor, tantalizing mystery.

> **Handel at the Piano**
>
> Dutch pianist Daria Van Den Bercken made a startling discovery. While the keyboard works of George Frederic Handel are typically performed on harpsichord, they sound fantastic on piano! Problem is, most folks don't care much about this 18th-century composer, or classical music at all for that matter. What ANGLE might create buzz?
>
> Bercken filmed an impromptu tour, playing a piano hitched to a slow-driving car. "If I had performed anything from my rep, it would just be a gimmick. *Look, that car piano girl!* Placing the spotlight squarely on Handel's Suites was critical." Two important things happened. First, random people started chatting in ways that "gray mass" concert audiences never do. "It was inspiring, changing how I thought about engagement." Second, the video went viral, leading to media interviews, gigs, a TED Talk, even a record deal with Sony Classical.
>
> Six months later, Bercken reversed the experiment. Strangers on the street were invited to attend a 20-minute apartment concert "right now." Such an unusual proposition caught fire. After one guest asked, "Are you afraid of heights?" (and she said "no"), he invited her to perform in Brazil. Once there, she found herself hanging from a crane, suspended by bungee cord, performing to an ecstatic crowd of thousands below. The whole ordeal was broadcast to millions on a popular primetime TV show. "The Handel performance was all people would talk about!"

ALLIES

Which strategic partners?
You can't do this alone. Build a messaging army. Few tactics carry the potency of a trusted leader, colleague, or friend strongly sanctioning your project. The most effective ALLIES are prominent figures trusted by your target AUDIENCE. They might have leadership roles (pastors, teachers, managers), visible communication platforms (radio hosts, journalists, podcasters), or lots of friends. These individuals are not charged with selling. Rather, they become part of a marketing machine that generates BUZZ.

Logical candidates are family members, close friends, active donors, board members, superfans, collaborators, and those aligned with your cause. Why would someone expend energy on your behalf? Sometimes, all it takes is a simple ask. The first to share big news gains personal capital. Sweeten the deal with incentives, whether financial (i.e., $3 per ticket sold, discounts, free services) or nonmonetary (gifts, public gratitude).

> **Building Together**
>
> During the first Covid winter, when Manhattan became a ghost town, hornist–turned–executive director Kate Sheeran pursued a crazy idea. What if her organization, Kaufman Music Center, hosted concerts in a vacant storefront? How might they offer solid artist pay while allowing neighbors to safely encounter desperately missed live music? Ultimately hosting 107 events showcasing 202 artists over four months, this initiative required strong, win-win partnerships. These ALLIES were crucial to orchestrating logistics, yet their value went further. Partners helped spread word-of-mouth BUZZ. Partly as a result, an audience of more than 31,000 showed up. Additionally, the "Musical Storefronts" story was featured by 60 media outlets in 17 countries.
>
> | PARTNER | WHAT THEY GAVE | WHAT THEY GOT |
> |---|---|---|
> | Foundation | Financial contribution and visioning assistance | Fulfilling their mission of supporting artists and those who alleviate poverty |
> | Business improvement district | Connections to real estate, police department, local businesses | More people and economic development in their area when most residents were staying home |
> | Real estate developer | Storefront access, maintaining the space, shoveling sidewalk snow | Great press, positive branding, happy residents (who enjoyed the music) |
> | Instrument company | Grand piano loan | Highly visible logo placement |
> | Next-door bakery | Huge, full bag of food to every performer | Store traffic and sales from individuals watching shows |

ARSENAL

Which promotional tools?
This is where many arts marketers spend most or all of their energy. An ARSENAL includes tactics like ads, posters, and social media. While these weapons in isolation may not be enough to win the battle for consumers, incorporating them into comprehensive campaigns maximizes impact. Here's a partial list of available artillery:

- Advertisements (print, online)
- Articles
- Audio postcards
- Billboards
- Blog posts
- Brochures (bifold, trifold, multipage)
- Bumper stickers
- Business cards
- Calendar listings
- Cards (handwritten?)
- Chalking
- Coupons

- Direct calls
- Direct mail
- Email blasts
- Email signatures
- Flyers
- Free incentives
- Giveaways
- Greeting cards
- Handwritten notes
- Invitations
- Letterhead
- Letters to the editor
- Magnets
- Media interviews
- Merchandise
- News releases
- Newsletters
- Podcasts
- Postcards
- Posters
- PR (media)
- Preconcert performances
- Radio
- Raffle prizes
- Recordings
- Reviews
- Social media
- Social media ads
- Stationary
- Street marketing
- Swag (Frisbees, mugs, magnets, etc.)
- T-shirts
- Video statements
- Websites
- Window displays

American Screams

The Canadian rock band Arkells erected a billboard reading, "Can't sleep off those AMERICAN SCREAMS?," followed by a toll-free phone number. Callers heard the message "Hey, you've reached the American Screams hotline. If you'd like to hear our new song, please Press 1. If you'd like to leave a message for the Arkells, Press 2." Thousands of fans and curious onlookers flooded the line, generating sales, demand, and BUZZ.

Consider a range of issues when designing publicity tools. How do they reinforce your brand? What is the most important message? Do a series of items reference similar themes? Will there be a funny, informative, or emotional approach? Which fonts and colors are best? Weigh the importance of every word. Too much information overwhelms, while omitted essentials can frustrate or even lose sales. Always get feedback before sharing elements widely. Some pointers:

1. **Choose "weapons" carefully.** Weigh cost, time, and energy against likely impact.
2. **Spread the BUZZ.** Use your ARSENAL to get people talking.
3. **Focus on benefits.** Stress the value your product offers.

Features versus Benefits

Too many marketing messages emphasize only *features*. An event poster might detail repertoire, instrumentation, performers, date and time, location, ticket instructions. While such factoids may be important, be careful not to neglect a product's *benefits*. What's in it for the audience? Does this show provide rollicking fun? Build social capital? Champion a cause? Break a Guinness Book World Record?

4. **Provide a call to action.** Every marketing item should prompt one action, whether visiting a website, buying a ticket, or something else.
5. **Limit text to bare necessities.** Make every word count. Omit nonessential passages.
6. **Prioritize content AND presentation.** Perfectly compiled text that looks like a disaster and beautiful designs that fail to convey your message both fail.
7. **Maximize web presence.** If you can't be found online, you won't be taken seriously.
8. **Blow away the competition by every metric.** Be more personal, meaningful, beautiful, witty, funny, shocking, or otherwise noteworthy.
9. **Repeat.** An old business adage claims it requires seven marketing encounters before a message begins to stick, let alone sell. It may require more.[3]

"I May Be The Most Successful Failure in Music You've Ever Met"

Though aspirations to become the next Jimmy Page never panned out, guitarist Mike Grande owns *Rock Out Loud* music schools in three states, serving 500 eager students. Currently, his only online marketing weapon is Google My Business, used to boost citings when locals search for "music lessons near me." Messaging is crucial. "I provide value, tackling relevant topics such as navigating lessons around sports schedules, or how to build resilience in bullied children [through music]."

Most of Grande's ARSENAL involves win-win partnerships with noncompeting businesses that serve similar customers (children). For example, free napkins with his logo and contact info were gifted to local ice cream shops. Pizza boxes were inscribed with "Save some dough… when you book a free music lesson," followed by a QR code. He even gave branded capes to barbers, generating a haircut talking point. Better yet, when someone expressed interest, stylists could offer a *backstage pass* (aka free lesson). "All these strategies offer ALLIES social capital while saving them money. Meanwhile, they direct more clients to my business than social media ever could. The pizza promotion alone recruited 60 kids in four weeks!"

When a new student arrives, there is no pricing discussion. "Instead, we reframe the conversation, exploring how this experience is an investment in a child's future. Our *coaches* (as opposed to teachers) don't execute immovable curricula. Rather, they connect with each individual, building on personal interests."

AFTER

What brings customers back?
Attracting new clients is harder and more expensive (money, time, creativity) than re-engaging past ones. AFTER getting someone "in the door," work proactively to ensure this is no isolated incident. What will it take to convert "newbies" into superfans? The first step is the ART itself. At the least, deliver on promises. Better yet, exceed them.

---
[3] I mentioned this earlier in the chapter. Did it register?

Do you know who customers are? Collect contact information or risk losing connection. Then determine mechanisms likely to build trust and engagement. This might mean highly relevant newsletters or throwing a wine and cheese party celebrating "new friends." The worst idea is losing contact.

Building a Comprehensive Plan

Hopefully, the interconnectedness of arts marketing A-list elements is apparent. Understanding your AUDIENCE is critical when considering which ARSENAL weapons will most likely reach them. The ART and ANGLE provide clues on what to emphasize in messaging. Spreading the word requires commitment and enthusiasm from strategic ALLIES.

Piecing together a comprehensive marketing plan requires intentional design. A great way to do this involves mapping your strategy onto an A-list canvas. A copy can be downloaded from **www.savvymusician.com/alist**, ideally to be printed on paper 24" × 36" or larger.

When designing your campaign, begin by brainstorming solutions. Each idea is written on an independent sticky note (see Chapter 4 for Post-it strategy), adhered to the appropriate field. Don't edit or critique, just ideate. At this stage, the canvas may start to look like a dense shaggy rug. After exhausting the realm of possibility, whittle down entries. Test various combinations, moving sticky notes off, on, or around the board. Make decisions about what is most important. Create a plan that is ambitious but doable. Discard everything else (or save for later reference).

It is possible to move freely through the canvas as the muse hits. Another approach involves prescribing a specific sequence. For example, suppose you hope to design a high-impact event or other kind of product. Consider how processes beginning with various combinations might result with different marketing strategies. In fact, why not turn it into a game?

Sequence A	Sequence B	Sequence C
1. ALLIES. Who are great strategic partners? 2. AUDIENCE. Which groups can they easily reach? 3. ART. What kind of musical product would they love?	1. ANGLE. How might we create HUGE buzz? 2. ALLIES. Which partners will best amplify that message? 3. ART. What event features might emphasize our buzz?	1. ART. What compelling theme should drive our project? 2. ARSENAL. Which tools best propel that idea? 3. AUDIENCE. With which audiences will this resonate?

A-List Marketing

Chicago Philharmonic (CP), a musician-governed organization, is not your average orchestra. Known for championing wide-ranging genres, personnel for each of 35 events per year are selected from an invitation-only roster of 200 based on availability and fit. Shows featuring video game or film music consistently sell out within the hour. Other events require more proactive creativity.

Consider *Improvisations on EO9066*, featuring singer-songwriter-violinist Kishi Bashi (KB). "This six-movement multimedia piece for KB, full orchestra, recordings, and imagery grapples with the legacy of an Executive Order placed in WWII that incarcerated over 120,000 Japanese-Americans." The soloist's respectable following was not enough to fill their 1,500-seat hall. Given a limited marketing budget, augmenting demand involved a powerful video trailer, community partners, and "insane availability" to any and every media source.

"The AFTER phase is particularly important," explains Lydia Penningroth, director of marketing. "Opposite most orchestras, 96% of our attendees are first-timers. Retaining them is arguably the most important objective. *How might we transform diehard KB fans into diehard CP fans?*" A taiko drum opening act was added after the show had sold out to "exceed expectations." An AFTER party and content-rich email campaign also helped. While conversion based on a single encounter is never easy, around 200 new visitors from this performance have subsequently returned. It also generated several board members without prior CP relationships.

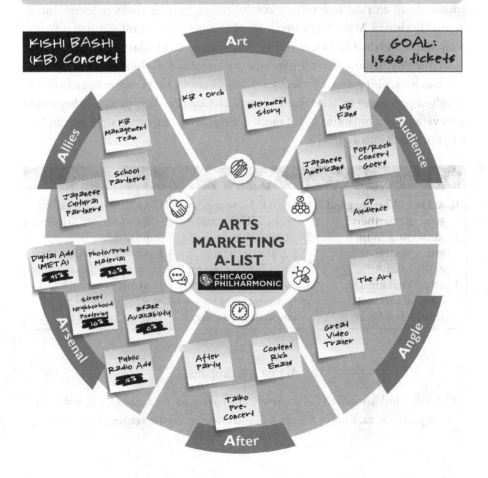

MARKETING CONSIDERATIONS

The Goal

How many customers do you aim to attract?[4] An all too common response: *as many as possible*. Wonderful enthusiasm, indeed, but oh how problematic! For starters, failure is guaranteed. Every time. No matter how successful the effort, there's always at least one more person who could have been swayed. Such statements often serve as an excuse. Fuzzy objectives eliminate the hard work of thinking things through and setting firm ambitions. Perhaps the 8,000, or 337, or 12 ticket buyers that emerged were all that could have been interested.

Get specific and measurable. In precise whole numbers, how many visitors constitute success? If your goal is 175 but only 168 arrive, the verdict is clear. Marketing fell short (though just slightly). Bringing in 177, on the other hand, is cause for celebration. Expectations exceeded!

Low Expectations?

During a recent workshop, I asked if anyone was planning an event. One hand shot up. She raved about her "amazing" show. To the question "How many people do you hope to attract?," I was delighted to hear a specific figure. Unfortunately, it was specifically low: 75 (in a huge hall). "That's much better than my last show," she confided, "which brought just *14*" (!). For an outstanding performance, surely more than 75 individuals from this large urban metropolis could be interested. If not, something is severely wrong. Artists often have too little ambition when it comes to securing an audience. True, marketing is hard. But don't let yourself off the hook. Sharing your gifts while increasing the payoff is a win-win!

Quantifying a marketing goal is a great start, but don't stop there. Break down numbers further. When hoping to sell 225 tickets, divide that figure into smaller, digestible bites. Though the outcome is unlikely to perfectly mirror projections, this process offers several advantages. Smaller numbers feel less overwhelming than bigger ones. Micro-projections allow you to plan accordingly (i.e., how exactly will you interest 90 members of the *niche* group?). And estimates provide further metrics by which success or failure can be measured.

---

[4] Another great question: How much money do you hope to generate?

Tickets	Demographic
90	Identified *niche* group
60	Established fans of our genre
35	Family and friends of the group
25	Professional artist colleagues
15	VIPs (important community members receiving personalized invitations)
225	TOTAL

To increase the likelihood of success, *oversolve your objective*. Perhaps it makes sense to map a path to 300 when the aim is 225. That way, you can meet/beat the overall goal even if several submetrics fall short.

In the end, marketing is about results. When a campaign pursues all the "right" tactics but too few consumers bite, reflect on what went wrong and pivot future efforts. And if you blow past expectations, congratulations. Mission accomplished!

The Lists

In my opinion, *spreadsheets* are among the greatest inventions for savvy musicians (rivaled only by the Post-it). This tool allows various data to be placed into distinct cells that can be easily sorted. It is possible to automatically tabulate mathematical formulas (like adding earnings or tickets sold), view only some information while temporarily hiding others, and more. They can aid every aspect of your campaign, whether brainstorming ideas, sorting the timeline, budgeting expenses, projecting incomes, detailing interactions, or organizing an afterparty. When marketing, track everything.

First Name	Last Name	Organization	Email	Contact	Reply?	Notes
Tim	Panny	SuperHuman Percussion	TimPanny@SHP.com	3/13	Y	Bought a ticket!
May	Jorskell	Neighbor	FGABbCDEF@yahoo.com	2/26	—	
Sir	Clophiths	Kitchen Depot	FCGDAEB@FatherCharles.org	3/17	Y	Possibly interested, asked to write back next week
Abe	Forforty	Edgerton Symphony	abe@tuning.music	3/14	Y	Will be out of town, try next time

The Timeline

Marketing takes time to plan and time to work. Though some musicians pray for quick results, don't hold your breath. Map a timeline and stick to it.

Timeline	Activities
3–6 months prior	Draft publicity plan Compile media list Organize/update guest mailing list Website announcement Mail press releases to quarterly/monthly publications*
2–3 months prior	Invitations to critics* Develop group sales campaign
1–2 months prior	Press releases to local radio/television producers* Press releases to weekly publications* Save-the-date invitations Register performance information with various calendar listings
3–4 weeks prior	Ticket sales go live Begin poster/flyer campaign Press releases to daily publications* Reminder notice to critics
1–2 weeks prior	Ratchet up poster/flier campaign Invitations to guests Generate BUZZ Other promotional strategies
1–3 days prior	Reminder emails
1 week after	Thank you notes to critics, helpers, and guests Collect all media coverage for event Finally ... sleep

*When appropriate, follow up to confirm receipt.

The Words

Musicians are regularly responsible for crafting written documents: press releases, website content, bios, grant proposals, brochures, program notes, business plans. Do not underestimate the power of strong prose. A well-crafted statement persuasively promotes your message, while consumers assume that poor writing parallels inferior workmanship. Even carefully "wordsmithed" emails can unlock huge opportunities. If your writing abilities aren't up to par, consider employing a publicist or working with a coach. This is a skill worth mastering. The most effective writing captures four critical elements:

1. Relevant message
2. Fascinating angle
3. Effective style
4. Free of errors

Though strong writing will take you far, it requires imagination to draft memorable, captivating text. Embrace a personalized voice appropriate to your brand identity. Present messages with clarity, avoiding jargon, fancy acronyms, or other insider talk. Find a distinctive hook that immediately draws in readers. An attention-grabbing opening is essential, since it's difficult to recover after a weak start. Keep content relevant throughout, and always end strong. Just as the final sounds of a composition disproportionately affect a listener's reaction, conclusions should make a powerful impression.

Use short, readable statements. Brevity beats rambling. Eliminate nonessential words. Long multiclause sentences (more than three) are difficult to navigate. ~~Why not~~ make it into a game, seeing how few words can ~~be used in order to~~ convey your message ~~effectively~~[5]? Break up paragraphs into digestible bites. Too much information is overwhelming.

Omissions, incorrect information, and careless mistakes bias others against you. Use spell check, but beware that even AI can miss errors. Proofread at least three times, hunting for typos, grammatical inaccuracies, or awkward writing. Read text aloud, ensuring that passages flow naturally. Return for another pass later with fresh eyes. Once satisfied, have a colleague take a look. Make no mistake: Writing is serious business.

THE LOOK

Great news: It is easier than ever to make materials sparkle. Even free software comes loaded with fonts galore, sophisticated templates, and user-friendly graphic editing. *Tough news*: Everyone has access. Audiences expect beauty. Documents that aren't visually striking, from large-scale layout to minute details, fall flat.

Though some businesses pay thousands to hire graphic designers, effective artwork can be acquired on a shoestring. Printing companies often offer design assistance as part of package deals. Friends, students, or local artists may be willing to contribute for a small fee. If you are visually inclined, do it yourself. Savvy musicians with even basic design skills are well served.

Too many fonts make a document cluttered and unprofessional. With the exception of special effects, limit this count to two or three. It is, however, often appropriate to establish visual hierarchy with different styles and sizes. Make text large enough to be easily deciphered from a likely viewing distance. Color adds zest and interest, highlighting key points while adding variety. Consider the psychological impact of a color scheme, limiting and unifying hues.

---

[5] I recommend reading *Several Short Sentences about Writing*, by Verlyn Klinkenborg. This book teaches the value of making every word count.

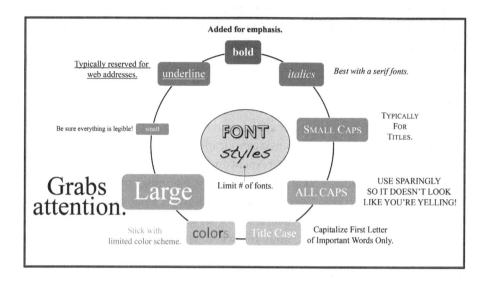

Employ clean, clear formatting. Create easy-to-navigate layouts, ensuring important elements pop. Lists, bullets, charts, and graphics are effective when used appropriately. Consider density—words per line, spacing between lines, width of margins, lengths of paragraphs. Well-placed, visually appealing graphics like logos, photographs, drawings, paintings, sketches, and AI-generated images bring a level of interest that no amount of text can capture.

Content versus Presentation

All marketing materials, or anything you share for that matter, should balance two overriding elements: *content* and *presentation*. In most cases, excellence in both is critical to success.

CONTENT: The ideas, words, and sequence
PRESENTATION: How something is designed, packaged, and delivered

Some musicians discount the necessity of stunning presentation, arguing that it distracts from what matters most. While high-quality content should be nonnegotiable—whether delivering music, words, an experience, or anything else—it is rarely enough.

Presentation is often the first test. People assume that stunning visual appeal equates to excellence; sloppiness means substandard. Many observers take little from a poorly delivered lecture, regardless of its profundity. Grant committees dismiss ugly applications from even ultra-qualified candidates. Conductors veto compositions because of sloppy notation. This may not seem "fair," but it represents reality. On the flip side, flashy materials with limited depth will eventually be dropped under the pretext of superficiality.

> That said, you don't need to devote equal time to these elements. It may take weeks to craft the details of a resume but just hours to adjust the look, or months to learn a program and 10 minutes to select an outfit.

The Investment

Some musicians believe they can't afford to market. The opposite may be true—anyone serious about a career in music cannot afford to *not* market. However, there is no fixed correlation between dollars spent and business earned.

Successful marketing necessitates time, energy, planning, and follow-through, but not a second mortgage. Savvy musicians with limited budgets may be ideally positioned, forced to invent creative, low-cost solutions. Trial and error, as well as ever-evolving creativity, is key. Study the scene, target populations, deliver clear messaging, design effective materials, and employ a comprehensive A-list approach. It need not take an enormous operation to get noticed. It does, however, require a smart one.

Chapter 6
Promotional Storytelling

Once upon a time, there was a musician with superb talent and big dreams. Let's call him Barry Sacks. Barry seemed to have it all. He went to the best schools, got the best grades, won all sorts of awards. He felt he was doing what it takes to become a celebrated professional.

But following graduation, Barry confronted a grave challenge. Everywhere he looked, there were hoards of competitors just as gifted, vying for the same opportunities. Getting noticed, let alone breaking through the clutter, felt impossible. Despite doing all the "right" things—writing a bio, scripting a cover letter, launching a website—nothing gained traction. Barry got discouraged. He almost quit.

Then, in a last-ditch attempt, our protagonist discovered a secret weapon. Transforming materials into more than mere fact-sharing dissemination, Barry began placing audiences under the spell of magical *storytelling*. Suddenly, his unique voice mesmerized, and opportunities followed. Today, he enjoys a thriving career as a savvy musician, even coaching others to amplify success by weaving captivating narratives throughout promotional documents.

STORYTELLING TOOLS

Promotional materials are the public face of your career, business, and products. Prime marketing real estate—an entry point for new clients and a reminder of your existence to existing ones—they make the case for what you do. Stellar documents tilt the scale in your favor. To prove effective, they must:

- **Get noticed.** Boring is never acceptable!
- **Inform.** Provide critical details with carefully chosen words.
- **Reinforce brand.** Strengthen the core image/value you aim to convey.

As Barry learned in this chapter's intro, promotional documents are not merely for data sharing. The best examples tell carefully architected stories that capture the imagination. With a clearly delineated beginning, middle, and end, they take listeners/readers on a journey that educates and inspires.

Whether applying for a job or promoting a product, consider the image you hope to convey. "Hip and modern," or "traditional and sophisticated"? "Professional but personable," or "fun and user-friendly"? Brainstorm adjectives illustrating the essence of your work and reinforce that aura. Decisions should affect everything from product name to marketing materials to the atmosphere of events.

Why are some messages more memorable than others? In their book *Made to Stick: Why Some Ideas Survive and Others Die*, authors Chip and Dan Heath discuss six compelling traits, represented by the acronym SUCCESs: Simple, Unexpected, Concrete, Credible, Emotional, Stories. For best results, integrate these principles when crafting your message.

Simple
Unexpected
Concrete
Credible
Emotional
Stories
(s)

Name, Slogan, Logo

"Names have power," explains American author Rick Riordan. They create a first impression and project an image, whether intentional or not. Yours may attract curiosity, turn folks off, or (problematically) generate apathy. Great names intrigue; complex or generic ones make little impact. Avoid difficult-to-spell words and overly common phrases that get buried online. *Southwest Iowa Euphonium Quartet* offers specifics but feels regional and amateurish. Consider whether business titles should incorporate your name (e.g., David Cutler), a pseudonym (Davey Crotchet), or something epitomizing your work (The Savvy Musician).

Slogans are short, memorable phrases. They can describe product benefits, scope of work, or company spirit. Fast-food chain Wendy's shares, "It's waaay better than fast food." Whether or not you agree, they aim to distinguish themselves. The best taglines:

- Clarify what you do, or why you do it.
- Are concise (usually seven words or less) and "sticky."
- Avoid reusing words from the title.
- May incorporate alliterations, rhymes, or other poetic devices.

A logo is a visual element representing your venture. At the least, it presents your name in a special font. Also consider graphic elements that convey your mission, services offered, or an attitude. A number of AI platforms quickly produce attractive, sophisticated logos, to be used as is or provide direction for a professional designer. Include your logo on appropriate materials including business cards, letterheads, posters, brochures, contracts, and websites.[1]

Elevator Pitch

60, 59, 58, 57 . . . You walk into an elevator and guess who's there? A VIP who could propel your dreams: funder, presenter, manager, employer, collaborator, client, influencer. While the lift ascends, you have the rare blessing of undivided attention for 60 sacred seconds.

. . . 56, 55, 54 . . . Throughout your career, there will be numerous opportunities (rarely on an elevator) to convey your value, be they formal presentations or chance encounters. What will you say? In one minute, most speakers convey around 140 words. Using thoughtful storytelling, clarify your value and call to action, whether it's for a purchase, donation, introduction, follow-up, or partnership plea. Since listeners quickly form slow-to-change opinions, immediately ignite the imagination. Open with a provocative question, problem statement, or humorous anecdote. Spin a logical narrative and meaningful conclusion.

Practice your pitch! Rehearse with a timer in front of a mirror or video camera. Get the message and delivery just right. Because one minute just might change your life . . . 3, 2, 1.

Elevator Music

"How do you get someone who never thought about opera to give it a try?" That question drove tenor Josh Shaw to found Pacific Opera Project, for which he directs four to six productions a year. Note how the following 141-word pitch uses the powerhouse proposal framework, including a BIG idea, three WOWables, and a little something extra.

. . .

[**BIG idea**] Pacific Opera Project presents reimagined opera-tainment.
[**WOWable 1**] We set Mozart's *Abduction from the Seraglio* as a Star Trek

---

[1] Arbutus Records logo designed by Emily Kai Bock. Friends of Chamber Music Kansas City logo designed by Mikaela Garrett, Rival Designs. SAVVY Arts Venture Challenge logo designed by David Hunt Creative. Miss April's Clarinet Studio logo designed by MadhyaDesign. Greenville Jazz Fest logo designed by Caroline Black, City of Greenville Parks, Recreation, and Tourism.

> episode; *Magic Flute* takes place in the world of 1990s Nintendo video games. You'll be blown away by the uber-talented cast (we are in Hollywood, after all…), though they aren't your grandmother's divas. [**WOWable 2**] Chosen in part because they "fit the playbill," our hipster *La Boheme* even featured real-life hipsters, man buns included! [**WOWable 3**] The audience also dresses in costume—you should have seen all the RBG's during our *Scalia/Ginsburg* production—to face off during an intermission contest.
>
> Clearly, this experience is like no other. But can you afford it? [**A little something extra**] Remarkably, tickets start at just $15! So whether you're a seasoned connoisseur or Netflix junkie who believes operas are best served with soap, prepare to POP your mind with Pacific Opera Project.

Bio

Far too many artist bios look like uninspired brag lists. There is no reason for this statement to read like a Wikipedia entry! Think of it as a short story summarizing your journey. In fact, I recommend titling the piece (whether this is printed or not), emphasizing the BIG idea you hope to convey. Bios have three primary goals:

1. **Unique value.** This comes back to the question: *What makes you interesting?* Be sure to include some WOWables.
2. **Credibility.** Share specific achievements like awards, premieres, and publications.
3. **Connection.** Intrigue readers with language and examples that connect emotionally.

Lead with an attention-grabber and maintain interest throughout. Emphasize the two to three points you hope will break through, omitting unnecessary details. Place compelling information early on, not only to quickly connect but also because some editors shorten writing by eliminating final paragraphs. Making a strong impression with fewer points is better than overwhelming readers with facts. Consider the "voice" of your statement. Various literary styles are possible: character pieces, comedic accounts, performer "trivia" lists, poems, etc. Consider the audience, as some constituents are turned off by straying too far from the norm while others love it.

Various lengths may be requested. Standard word counts include 50, 100, 250, and full page. Conclude with your web address for further information. Update at least once a year.

> ### Biofeedback
>
> Feedback on potential lines from a fictional musician's bio:
>
> *Guitarist Murray McPickens recently graduated with his doctoral degree from Heaven University.* Never open with educational pedigree. There has to be something more interesting about you than having studied somewhere, even if it's a great place.
>
> *Murray McPickens is one of the top guitarists of his generation.* Avoid hyperbolic, self-impressed judgments. Substantiate!
>
> *According to the* New York Times, *Murray McPickens is "one of the top guitarists of his generation."* More credible, since the opinion was expressed externally.
>
> *Murray McPickens has distinguished himself by winning many awards, including the prestigious International Bar Chord Prize in 1984.* Don't present yourself as a has-been. When including accomplishments from long ago, highlight recent activity as well.
>
> *Dr. McPickens has performed extensively throughout the United States.* Support with specifics. Also, think twice before including titles like "Dr.," since people may assume that overt academics are weak players.
>
> *Ever since laying eyes on a guitar at the age of seven, I have been addicted to this instrument.* With few exceptions, bios are written in the third person.
>
> *Truly an international musician, Murray McPickens's playing spans from Cuban salsa and American jazz to Spanish flamenco and Italian Baroque.* A pretty good opener, especially if your brand involves versatility. However, this sentence fails to mention WHAT Murray actually does (plays guitar)—include expertise early on.
>
> *One windy afternoon, Murray McPickens found himself stranded in Mexico City with nothing but a toothbrush and a guitar.* Wow, you have my attention!

Publicity Photo

A photograph in itself may not generate work (though that has happened!) but can pique interest or lead to disqualification. Photos, like bios, make a statement. When people see your image, how will they complete the sentence "This artist seems so _____"?

When possible, employ a photographer who has previously worked with musicians. Ask for referrals. View work samples. Get pricing upfront, and fully comprehend what that includes. How many prints does it buy? Can you obtain the digital files? Do you have permission to reprint without additional fees?

Some musicians eliminate expenses by having a friend take the pictures. Think twice before traveling this route. Expectations run high, and amateurish shots count against you. If you're in a pinch, approach a photography student. They may need portfolio subjects, and work is generally done under the supervision of a teacher.

> **Getting Shot**
>
> When strategizing with a photographer, share existing photos that demonstrate the spirit desired. On the day of the shoot, pack several outfits including performance attire, instruments, makeup, hair products, jewelry, accessories such as hats or scarves, and other props. Sessions typically involve two to four hours and hundreds of shots. Posing can be exhausting! Conserve energy, drink plenty of water, and trust your photographer.

What makes a great publicity photo?

1. **Strong impression.** Make a statement, stir an emotion, reinforce your brand.
2. **Appropriate location.** Photographer's studio, concert venue, beach, train station, etc.
3. **Characteristic.** A super old photo that does not resemble you today is false advertising.
4. **Focus.** Have a single focal point rather than multiple elements competing for attention. Many sources require *headshots*, which may expand to include the upper torso and a portion of your instrument. Full body *artistic shots* can be cropped.
5. **Simplicity.** Prevent unnecessary clutter from muddling up the shot, such as electrical outlets, cords, random objects or people, etc.
6. **Spontaneity.** Try to look natural. Overly posed shots convey insincerity.
7. **Contrasts.** Varying colors, textures, and images sharpen photos. This becomes more important with black-and-white photos. Beware of outfits too close to your skin tone and other elements that camouflage rather than distinguish.
8. **Good lighting.** Successful shots are not dark or overexposed.
9. **High res.** For reproducible digital images, supply the highest available resolution. At a minimum, it should be one megabyte.

For physical prints, black-and-white 8 × 10 shots with a glossy finish are the industry standard, though color is increasingly popular. An image may span from edge to edge, or a white border can frame the periphery. Your name, contact information, website, and instrument/voice type can be imprinted toward the bottom or backside of the portrait. Another possibility is typing onto an adhesive label, affixed to the back. Do not write on photos! Not only does this look unprofessional, but also the impression of a pen can seep through.

Steampunk, Sunrise, and Saltwater

The time for new publicity photos had come. David Cutler, author of *The Savvy Musician 2.0*—the book you are holding—wanted something striking. Unfortunately, most photographers specialize in normal headshots. Few demonstrated the level of creativity sought. And then he discovered an anomaly in Scott Pardue, whose otherworldly images suggest sci-fi magic.

Cutler shared the BIG idea behind his professional identity: music + innovation. To his wonderful dismay, Pardue replied with increasingly preposterous WOWables. *What if we try a steampunk look? With a piano, at sunrise? In the ocean...?* Later, he asked about a little something extra. *If you could transform your instrument, what would it become?* Cutler responded confidently: "My compositions fuse wide-ranging musical traditions. Let's make it a teleporter!" Working through complex logistics, they planned an early morning beach shoot, two hours away. No Photoshop tricks. To view it, please see this book's author bio page.

ELECTRONIC PRESS KITS

Think of electronic press kits (EPKs) as interactive digital brochures. Typically presented as a single PDF or webpage, they are shared with presenters, managers, agents, record labels, contractors, clients, and of course the press. EPKs include some combination of the following: pitch paragraph; highlights/achievements/services; bio or company history; frequently asked questions; quotes and testimonials; press clippings, including articles and/or reviews; embedded audio/video; high-res photos and other meaningful imagery; social media links; contact info; additional relevant content (tech rider, tour schedule, rep list, etc.).

Do not include all of the above! An effective package provides just enough information. The more material, the less likely each will be studied. Make your EPK easy to navigate, beautiful to view, and rich with substance.

Press Kit Power

What if Louis XIV were living today and curated his court composers with musicians like Beyoncé, Lana Del Rey, or Adele? So begins an EPK of Emi Ferguson, a singer and flutist who "blurs the lines between classical and pop music." Toward the top of the page, boxes navigate to various elements such as recordings, videos, bio, project descriptions, reviews, photos (high resolution once clicked), and contact details. There are also buttons for connecting via seven social media channels, and a link to download the PDF version. What makes this statement so potent, beyond the music itself, is its attention to detail.

> A logical design balances striking drawings, evocative photographs, additional visuals, and just the right amount of text.
>
> Ferguson creates separate EPKs for each project, housed in a Dropbox folder easily shared with publicists, presenters, media, and the public. "These documents help people who don't know much about a program quickly understand its scope and locate relevant assets. I love graphic design and determining interesting angles that make my work pop."

WORKING WITH MEDIA

The media needs compelling, entertaining stories to keep its audience engaged. You want publicity to bring attention to projects. In this light, become a mutually beneficial partner. Any and all coverage can be helpful to your cause, either directly or indirectly. Even better—much publicity is free. Learn how the industry operates and use it to your advantage.

The Media Circus

People consume news, information, and entertainment from a huge variety of sources. There are likely more accessible sources than you realize to help spread intriguing messages.

SOURCE	DESCRIPTION
NEWSPAPERS Major	It is extremely difficult to get covered by major newspapers, particularly for positive stories. If you can, the impact may be huge.
Suburban daily/weekly	More likely to show interest, especially during early phases of your career, and likelier to reach your target audience.
School	College or high school papers connect with young people.
Special interest	Tabloid-sized papers targeting specific segments. Find an appropriate angle that connects with their mission.
MAGAZINES Trade	Examples such as *Jazziz*, *Opera News*, and *Modern Drummer*, written by and geared toward musicians. Articles and reviews circulate to colleagues with similar interests and backgrounds.
Scholarly	Academic journals for peer-reviewed articles.
Nonmusic	Intriguing potential for musicians tying their art to their focus.
City guides/ entertainment	Published monthly or quarterly, reach locals and tourists.

NEWSLETTERS Print	Covering every interest imaginable. Published monthly, quarterly, or annually. Most are short (two to eight pages) and printed on standard paper, though larger organizations may use magazine-like formats. Smaller distribution makes it realistically attainable to get featured.
School	Elementary through university levels. Provides alumni/faculty updates and relevant stories on current events and education trends.
Community	Sent to residents to spread the word about local happenings and issues.
Special interest	Clubs, religious associations, and other special interest groups consider stories related to their mission.
Music	Numerous music organizations and individuals produce digital newsletters—in fact, you may want to distribute your own.
BROADCAST Commercial radio and TV stations	Dependent on advertisers to pay bills—the wider the audience, the more they can charge. Most are interested only in famous artists or newsworthy stories. Competition for airtime is intense, but coverage reaches vast audiences.
Community supported	Most specializing in classical/jazz are nonprofits dependent on donations. Part of their mission is to promote local artists.
College	Another great source to target students.
Public access	Community members broadcast for free. With a limited audience, they nonetheless provide publicity and media experience.
Podcasts	Typically run by one or two individuals, most serve a highly specialized niche. Some have zero listenership; others build a devoted following. Podcasters constantly seek meaningful stories.

IN THE NAME OF PUBLICITY

Each establishment has its own submission rules, often laid out on the company website. Follow guidelines religiously, as many stories are rejected solely because of logistical inconsistencies. When is the submission cutoff? Should proposals be shared via email or another format? What length, and which content? Follow through if additional information is requested, and be flexible in terms of scheduling interviews.

For print media, proposals can be submitted to multiple writers/editors who deal with music or local news stories. For broadcast media, target producers and hosts of appropriate programs. These representatives are constantly under the gun to meet deadlines, so keep correspondence brief.

If you don't have the bandwidth, consider hiring a publicist. Strong candidates are outstanding storytellers, good writers, well connected, and persistent. Beyond determining buzzworthy angles, they write press releases and pursue media opportunities. Note that publicists are not advertisers. It may be difficult to draw a straight line between the coverage generated and direct sales. However, building credibility and getting your name out offer numerous benefits. Expect to pay a retainer of $1,500 to 3,000+ per month for a minimum of three to six months.

After someone brings you positive press, send a note of gratitude. This fosters a healthy relationship and encourages future coverage. Archive all media mentions to extract quotes, include in press kits, and reflect upon your impact.

On Becoming Newsworthy

Let's begin by discussing what does NOT fall into this category—the fact that your product is outstanding. *Excellence does not an interesting story make.* Other unnewsworthy items: standard literature presented in typical ways, musically technical descriptions, advertisements.

Something becomes newsworthy when it has an interesting BUZZ hook, good or bad, heartwarming or terrifying. In many cases, the wackier the story, the more likely it will be picked up. For example, it is near impossible for an unknown ensemble to be featured in a music magazine. Yet the same group backpacking across the country on trains might attract attention from travel magazines (that have not previously covered musicians). Potential angles:

- The FIRST. Premiere performance, initial use of Chinese instruments with a local band, inaugural Pizzicato-Only Convention.
- The NEW. Commissions, freshly discovered works, recently invented instruments.
- The UNUSUAL. Atypical presentations (interdisciplinary, multimedia, multicultural, themed) or venues (museums, bowling alleys, highways).
- The CONTROVERSIAL. The media loves contention.
- The INTERESTING. Intriguing stories about how music was composed, where it was recorded, the life struggles of an artist.
- The MEANINGFUL. Community issues may be positive (e.g., a veteran's musical memorial) or negative (music funding cuts threatened by a school board).
- The FAMOUS. Cameos with a local celebrity.
- The EDUCATIONAL. Consequential ways in which musicians teach the public.
- The CHARITABLE. Benefit events for worthy causes.
- The LOCAL. Neighborhood guitarist reaches a major milestone.

> **Multimedia Coverage**
>
> Years in the trenches as a music critic and radio host/producer prepared "recovering bassoonist" Gail Wein to thrive as a music publicist. Beyond a business contact list thousands strong, she has a keen understanding of what motivates the media. When working with clients—performers, composers, presenters, venues, labels—her first priority always involves clarifying goals. *What do you truly hope to achieve, and why?* The next step is identifying newsworthy angles. Examples of her projects that have generated big coverage include:
> 1. A concert-drama with narration and video about courageous Jewish prisoners who performed in a concentration camp.
>   - Angles: Jewish, refugee, oppression, overcoming adversity.
>   - Coverage: Three-page *Chicago Tribune* spread, *LA Times* preview, podcast interviews across country.
> 2. A song cycle by an African American composer/poet to commemorate Tomb of the Unknown Soldier's 100th anniversary.
>   - Angles: Tomb centennial, veterans, military, war, Arlington cemetery, Black artists.
>   - Coverage: Nationally broadcast TV show "News Hour" (six-minute segment), locally broadcast arts TV (30-minute episode), *Washington Post* article.
> 3. A renowned pianist performing interactive concerts for kids aged three to six, held at a bar (!).
>   - Angles: Underserved age population, interactive music making, listening skills.
>   - Coverage: Prominent *Wall Street Journal* story, radio segments, concert broadcasts.

Pressing Release

Press releases are short news stories sent to the media, booking agents, presenters, clients, and others. Media organizations receive far more leads than are publishable, so be sure yours merits attention. An interested editor may choose to print it word for word, pare down content, or have a staff writer conduct supplementary interviews/research.

Press releases are not advertisements but rather human interest stories. Why should someone pay attention to your news? Boil that information down to a single, sharp, focused sentence and *voilà*, you have a hook. Create a thought-provoking title and opening paragraph that (1) intrigues the reader and answers (2) who, (3) what, (4) where, (5) when, and (6) why. If these six crucial elements do not appear early on, assume your release will be unsuccessful.

> ### Press Release Checklist
>
> Write "FOR IMMEDIATE RELEASE" or a relevant date on top of the page. Include all pertinent information, since omitted details lose opportunities. Did you include:
>
> - ❑ Project description and title?
> - ❑ Location and directions?
> - ❑ Date and time?
> - ❑ Names of people involved?
> - ❑ Background information?
> - ❑ Ticket prices/purchase information?
> - ❑ Web address with more info?
> - ❑ An intriguing, compelling angle?
> - ❑ Reasons people should care?
> - ❑ Contact information?

Use a journalistic writing style with short sentences and paragraphs. Provide additional details in *descending* order of importance. This way, if an editor whittles off the last few paragraphs, key material still appears. Effective content includes information about contributors, relevant quotes, and supporting details. Point to your website for further information. The length should never exceed 500 to 700 words. Less is better.

Upon receiving a release, reporters first assess timeliness. Does this require prompt attention or can it wait? Most media contacts prefer that press releases be placed in the body of an email. Attachments are generally frowned upon since they can be large, sifted out by spam filters, or infected with viruses. Alternatively, link to a *media resources* webpage. Another option is employing a company like Artspromo.org, which distributes press releases of touring acts to newspapers, radio, TV, internet bulletins, and blogs.

> ### Pressing the Release
>
> The document that follows, written by British publicist Frances Wilson, is the first page of a press release promoting a sacred music choral album. Page two includes a list of the recording's 21 tracks, along with photos/brief bios of the composer, conductor, and organist.

PRESS RELEASE

HEAVEN TO EARTH
Joanna Forbes L'Estrange, composer
London Voices
Ben Parry, conductor
Andreana Chan, organist

RELEASE DATE: 12 January 2024
Signum Classics SIGCD790

"This is simply beautiful choral writing by someone who knows, from a singer's perspective, how to compose music which every choir will want to sing."
John Rutter CBE

Heaven to Earth is a collection of singable, accessible, sacred choral music by the best-selling choral composer and multi-faceted musician **Joanna Forbes L'Estrange**.

The album comprises introits, anthems, canticles, a set of Preces and Responses, and a congregational mass setting, and the 17 pieces display a range of styles, from traditional, church choral music to gospel- and jazz-influenced. Each piece sits comfortably within the SATB vocal ranges, the organ accompaniments are designed to support the choir, there is minimal division within the parts, and the harmonies are attractive and approachable. The texts are drawn from the Bible, the Psalms, The Book of Common Prayer, Holy Communion, writers including St Richard of Chichester, Phineas Fletcher, Jane Austen, and the composer herself, and all of the pieces are suitable for church services: Eucharist, Choral Evensong, weddings and funerals. The settings are written with the intention of enhancing the meaning of the words, both for those who sing them and for those who hear them.

Joanna Forbes L'Estrange says, '*I'm a great believer in the power of a melody to elevate words.... I aim to set the words in such a way that congregations are drawn in, not alienated. I want to write uplifting, prayerful, tuneful pieces which are musically interesting enough for choirs to enjoy singing, whilst always remaining accessible and approachable to church choirs of all sizes and abilities.*'

Sample track: *Drop, Drop, Slow Tears* https://youtu.be/OUIzXssKc3M?si=tBVUDv89xIeHYFVM

Heaven to Earth is a collection of contemporary church music which has been composed with *all* choirs in mind, from small church/community choirs to professional ones. Having began her musical life as a chorister in her local parish church choir of Bisley and West End in Surrey, Joanna became a professional singer (The Swingles, Tenebrae, London Voices) but, as a composer, feels a strong connection with her musical roots. Her first piece to be published was *The St Helen's Service*, a congregational setting of the mass which has since been adopted by many church choirs as their weekly setting.

"This music is simply heavenly, and no choir, church or performance venue should miss out on the blessing this music brings. Through beautifully crafted accessible melodies, glorious harmonies, and a real ability to convey the sense of meaning of the text, this richly varied repertoire goes straight to the heart."
Ken Burton, conductor, composer, arranger & performer

Many of the pieces on this album were specially commissioned by, amongst others, the Royal School of Church Music (RSCM), Ben Parry for King's Voices Cambridge, a number of American choirs, composer and organist Philip Moore, and by friends and family for specific occasions. *The Mountains Shall Bring Peace* (Track 20) was commissioned by the RSCM to mark the Coronation of King Charles III in 2023.

The sheet music for all the pieces on this album is available from RSCM Music Direct and L'Estrange Music. The album was recorded at St Barnabas Church, Ealing, on June 19th and 20th 2023, engineered by Al Forbes and edited and produced by Alexander L'Estrange.

Heaven to Earth is dedicated to the memory Reverend Richard Abbott (1943-2022). He was Joanna Forbes L'Estrange's foster father and encouraged her to become a composer.

"Joanna's choral music is truly sublime. It was a pleasure and honour to sing on this recording. Each piece brings a fresh approach to familiar church texts."
Louise Clare Marshall, singer

"I commend most warmly this CD of Joanna Forbes L'Estrange's choral music. She has a gift for melody and for setting words with great sensitivity. Above all, choirs universally enjoy performing her music."
Philip Moore, composer & organist

Chapter 7
Pounding the Virtual Pavement

The internet shapes every aspect of our lives. It democratizes art, makes geography largely irrelevant, and places superstars and emerging artists on somewhat equal footing. What an opportunity for savvy musicians! Of course, technology changes at breakneck speeds. Hip fads today fade into oblivion tomorrow, overtaken by new crazes. Staying relevant requires adapting to a quickly changing landscape.

In the eyes of many, something not easily found online does not exist. By extension, musicians without strong web representation have no serious career. Obviously, this logic is flawed, but perception is everything. Suppose you have two referrals. A keyword search for the first turns up three peripheral listings, but 130 unique hits for the second. It may be impossible to assess the better performer from this exercise, but contestant #2 certainly has more "fame." How successful have you been? Google your name to find out. You can never be too rich, be too good looking, or have too much web presence!

YOUR PROFESSIONAL WEBSITE

A website is arguably the most important online tool. Unlike social media platforms, you have complete control over its messaging and design and can maintain full ownership forever. Think of this as your digital storefront. What do you want people to find? Which takeaways will be emphasized? How does it reinforce your brand identity and larger marketing strategy? An effective URL delivers results and advances your cause. If you defy all suggestions below and business booms, something is going right!

STEP 1: SET THE SCOPE/DOMAIN

Building an effective website requires careful planning. Moving through the process forces consideration of your messaging, image, and value. Begin by defining what the site will represent. Everything you do? Just one aspect? A comprehensive resource? Your venture?

Another task during this early phase involves choosing the URL. Will you incorporate your name (e.g., **www.davidcutler.net**) or brand title (**www.savvymusician.com**)? Where you purchase this domain is largely irrelevant. However, some platforms offer additional benefits, so shop around to find the desired price and features.

STEP 2: SKETCH THE MAP

A *sitemap*, equivalent to a book's table of contents, diagrams the navigational structure. Create an outline indicating top-level *mastheads* and second-level *subpages*. Some musicians prefer standard page titles like *home, about, media, calendar, services, projects, reviews, store, contact*. Others get more creative. As a rule of thumb, limit these to one to two words apiece.

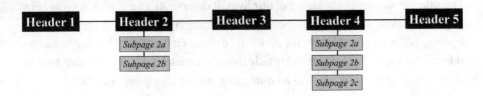

As you sketch the map, consider what to include or omit. Visitors spend shockingly little time browsing websites. Those who don't immediately spot what they want may zip away. While there is no "correct" number of mastheads, aim for seven or fewer. More can intimidate. If significant content must appear, add subpages. Possibilities include:

PAGE/ITEM	TIPS
Audio	No music site should be devoid of audio. However, nothing is more irksome than unwanted music—a sonic assault on the hapless visitor with speaker volume up! Pause and stop buttons should be easy to locate. Avoid extraordinarily large files.
Bio	Make it compelling! (See Chapter 6.) Include downloadable bios of various lengths. Word processing formats allow editors to copy and paste without risking typos. These often appear within an electronic press kit.
Blogs	Anything from a personal diary to a public forum. May incorporate links, audio files, graphics, or even video.
Calendar	Include location, time, repertoire, cost, ticketing, and links. Update regularly or avoid. Nothing looks sadder than an empty calendar.
Composition list	Include duration, instrumentation, year, premiere info, awards, program notes, audio/score samples, purchase instructions.
Contact	Make it easy for people to reach you. You may or may not want to include a phone number. Think twice before placing a home address online.
Description of services	Clearly outline products offered, how they benefit clients, and distinguishing features. Address likely questions.

Electronic press kit	A downloadable press kit makes it easy for presenters, clients, and reviewers to learn about your offerings. (See Chapter 6.)
Home page	Every site must have a landing page. Make yours pop!
Links	Links drive traffic to other great sites, and there is a fabulous fringe benefit. Your site may emerge from keyword searches for those entities.
Merchandise	Recordings, scores, books, T-shirts, bumper stickers, and additional merch may be sold. Include pertinent purchasing details. Make shopping easy—many people flee cumbersome ordering processes.
Miscellaneous	Practice tips, trivia, music jokes, special fonts, details about unusual instruments, artist passions, other nonstandard pages. If anything is irrelevant to your audience or brand identity, take it out.
News	Keep updated or risk looking like you are plagued by a drought. An alternative, compelling option involves a "NOW" heading.
Newsletter	Make it easy for fans to opt in.
Photos/graphics	I cannot overstate the importance of visual appeal. Every page should include at least one powerful image.
Podcasts	Interview musicians, talk about creativity, air recordings, or provide additional value to your audience.
Reviews/testimonials	Praise from external sources, such as newspaper/magazine reviews, satisfied customers, teachers, and colleagues.
Repertoire list	Demonstrate versatility and promote programs. In some cases, it makes sense to allow clients to build setlists (i.e., wedding bands).
Video	Performance/promotional videos add pizzazz and impact. Embedded links don't bog down load time (important to Google's algorithm), with the added bonus of drawing attention to your YouTube channel.

STEP 3: COMPILE THE CONTENT

The most time-consuming step of website construction involves content compiling: text, graphics, audio, and video. It may take weeks or months to create/organize this information. On the front end, it is hard to predict exactly what will be required or where it goes. The important thing is to get started. Collect more than is needed, to be whittled down later. At the least, pull together enough to avoid constantly inventing new material during the design phase.

How much should ultimately be included? *Enough to address what visitors need and not a kilobyte more.* The purpose of a business site is not showing off impressive but irrelevant side projects or photos of your pet reptile (unless that reinforces identity). Focus on the core message.

Begin by drafting everything you might want to say. Then edit, edit, edit. Make sure your "voice" consistently projects the optimal image, be it professional, silly, or inspirational. Critical information should be easily findable. Omitted essentials such as contact details or geography (when relevant) cause viewers to become frustrated and leave. A more common problem, however, is overloading. Visitors don't know where to begin. Have you ever been handed an overstuffed 24-page restaurant menu? Despite heaps of nifty recipes, narrowing choices down to a single selection can be stressful. If you aim to sell apple pie, just place that on the menu. And unlike the eatery, where entering customers almost always stay, websites have a lower success rate. If someone becomes confused, overwhelmed, or annoyed, they'll leave more quickly than you can say "mp3." Keep things succinct, simple, and clear.

There's No Place Like Home

A homepage sets a website's tone, so get this right. Many people decide whether to stay based on a two-second impression. Great examples immediately WOW. They look great, illustrate purpose, and engage. Do not overload. Instead, provide just enough to intrigue, including:

1. A singular, spectacular graphic.
2. Name, logo, and slogan showcased prominently.
3. Essentials such as geography served or contact info.
4. Compelling single paragraph articulating unique value and/or philosophy.
5. Pithy testimonial that amplifies social proof.
6. If more must appear, have graphics and keywords point to other site highlights.
7. That's it!

Create a folder to store graphics worthy of consideration: headshots, band portraits, professional photos, live performance shots, personal pictures, instrument images, posters, caricatures, relevant artwork. Once website design begins, having a large library to choose from is better than constantly searching. Small resolution sizes under 50k will load quickly and appear adequately online. Contrastingly, reproducible publicity photos must be large, at least a megabyte. Be sure all graphics are legal (images discovered online can only be shared with permission).

Audio/video recordings clearly add value to music websites. Professionally produced artifacts are best, but consider live performances and raw footage as well.

Be sure the quality accurately represents your talent. You may wish to film fresh content, such as a brief welcome video. Since people are unlikely to listen to/watch long clips, one question is whether to present full takes or excerpts only of performances. At a minimum, eliminate pauses. Rather than uploading unique audio or video clips, which can slow down your site, consider embedding links from external sources like YouTube, Spotify, or Apple Music. You may also direct visitors to those platforms, but beware that they may not return once leaving. Set links to open a new window rather than migrating the current one so your site doesn't disappear!

> **Stunning and Effective**
>
> For a masterclass on website design, look no further than Katherine Emeneth. Her KE Creative URL features beautiful imagery, sharply contrasting fonts, varied layouts, and just the right amount of text. "Early on, my cookie-cutter website was similar to everyone else's from my 'bubble.' Embarrassingly, the tagline was *Flutist. Educator. Artist.* Fortunately, I learned that if something can be copied and pasted to someone else's page, it's not specific enough. The point is to paint an authentic picture." Some noteworthy elements:
>
> - Homepage begins with a four-word *BIG idea* headline, followed by a single-sentence "Let me show you..." value proposition.
> - Three short, quote-bubbled testimonials display satisfied clients' headshots. Notably, these appear *before* the first mention of Emeneth.
> - "Are you a *music teacher*...," followed by three checkmarked questions (e.g., "...looking for ideas?"), clarifies Emeneth's audience and expertise.
> - About page begins with a provocative question: "Have you ever felt so frustrated...?"
> - Rather than a traditional bio, relevant history unfolds like a storybook tale.
> - Long text blocks are divided into short paragraphs and lists, framed with white space.
>
> All product descriptions, including *freebies*, feature (1) a powerful image, (2) a **bolded title**, (3) a single-sentence overview, and (4) an "I need it!" button.

STEP 4: DESIGN THE SITE

There are many paths to creating a website. Ask a friend in exchange for a year's worth of music lessons. Employ a high school student for a small fee and the promise of a "great resume builder." Outsource the task to AI. Or do it yourself. *Website builders* like Wix and GoDaddy offer templates that are easy to use, flexible, and quite beautiful. For our purposes, the road traveled is inconsequential. More important are results.

Produce a website nothing less than visually stunning. This in no way suggests that overly complex graphics greet visitors at every turn! Avoid a *splash page* (initial entry screen), streams of floating notes that chase the cursor, or other frenetic metamorphoses. If you have to ask whether a feature is annoying, the answer is probably "yes."

Create an intuitive, user-friendly domain, with consistent navigational tools on every page. Never require visitors to hit a browser's back button. Because it is tiring to read endless prose on a screen, divide large text blocks into short paragraphs separated by white space (press return), and long passages into separate pages. In fact, single-sentence "paragraphs" are often ideal, particularly for smartphone viewing. Delete anything that's less than your best material.

Stick to a limited number of standard fonts. Systems arbitrarily choose substitutes for those not in their font folder, changing the look and spacing. Make sure text is large enough to be read on computers at a number of resolutions. Choose an attractive, brand-appropriate color scheme, typically limited to two to three primary hues. Be sure text is easy to decipher. Dark writing over dark images and light writing over light images are hard to read.

The eventual design of your site will evolve through trial and error. Your final product should be outstanding across the board, since visitors will assume a direct correlation between its quality and your professional workmanship.

Step 5: Test and Revise

Chapter 4 introduced the concept of a *minimum viable product* (MVP). *What is the least you can do before testing an idea?* Rather than spending months on development only to discover that your website concept fails to resonate, collect feedback early and often. The most important comments are likely to come from members of your target audience. Address valid concerns.

Proof content thoroughly. Triple check that all pages, graphics, links, and audio/video files open accurately. Test from multiple browsers, devices, and operating systems. For example, phones may display elements differently than laptops.

Constructing an effective platform requires an iterative process. Even "completed" websites are works in progress rather than masterpieces frozen in time. Regular tweaks, updates, or even significant revision will be needed on occasion. Fortunately, unlike printed documents, changes can be made at any time.

Frequently Asked Questions (FAQs)

Will a website make me more successful?
Without a website, your product may be invisible. Without a great one, sales potential is crippled. This is the ultimate marketing tool. However, its mere existence doesn't guarantee stardom. In fact, many music sites do little to help their cause.

> *Is it too early in my career to have a website?*
> If you work professionally, you can probably benefit. Cast yourself as a professional, since changing perceptions down the road is difficult.
>
> *Can a website hurt my career?*
> Indeed, it can. Poor-quality recordings, weak content, sloppy writing, and irritating design all count against you. Visitors quickly form an opinion. Be sure it's a good one.
>
> *Which is more important, a personal website or social media presence?*
> Each forum offers unique advantages, with the potential to reach different communities in different ways. Most savvy musicians maintain multiple platforms. Some use secondary pages to direct traffic to their primary URL or vice versa. If you have to pick one, choose a website.

STEP 6: ATTRACT ATTENTION

You are now the proud owner of one of the world's great websites! Only one problem . . . nobody knows about it. The next trick is getting people to visit—you must market this marketing tool! Share newsletters and social media updates celebrating your new domain. Ask contacts to kindly forward the link. Include your web address on everything. Mention it during media stories and proudly plug during performances. Heck, affix it on a tattoo. For more ideas, visit The Savvy Musician: **www.savvymusician.com**. (I couldn't resist.)

The web is a viral place where visitors stumble upon information. If you've done things wisely, the uniqueness and quality of content alone will be enough to attract some guests. Be sure to embed appropriate *meta tags* (keywords) so your site pops up for relevant keyword searches. Links from secondary sources can drive traffic to your domain.

NINE REASONS MOST WEBSITES FAIL

Browsing an assortment of websites is likely to highlight numerous mistakes: too much text, not enough visuals, missing vitals, counterintuitive navigation, no art, irritating elements. But even beautiful URLs following all the "rules" may fail to advance careers and organizations. Why?

#1: Most Websites Are GENERIC

Bio—check! Calendar—check! Contact—check! Links—check! Most artists follow a formula. It's as if they ask, "What is typical?" and do just that. Blending in is a huge threat. Here's a better question: *What will immediately distinguish my presence?*

#2: Most Websites Are BORING

No jokes. No anecdotes. No warmth. No eccentricity. No character whatsoever beyond, perhaps, remarkable lackluster. Just fact, fact, fact . . . brag, brag, brag . . . award, schooling, accomplishment. A website is not the place to demonstrate what makes you most like a robot. Instead, celebrate your delightful, intriguing, quirky personality!

#3: Most Websites Are SELF-ABSORBED
A bio of *me*, photos of *me*, news about *me*. The most common word: *I*. Of course, websites should describe your background and credibility. But an unapologetic focus on the first person appears narcissistic. Demonstrate genuine interest in others. Potent words: *you, we, community, collaboration, team, together, clients, eggplant (just because), students, friends, colleagues*.

#4: Most Websites Are REPELLANT
When approached like a lecture, the protagonist is a talking head expecting others to sit in awe, listen passively, and somehow be moved. There is no opportunity for participation or discourse. If you want to cultivate relationships, reject this unidirectional approach. Build a magnetic field. Ignite an online community.

#5: Most Websites Are POINTLESS
After asking artists about their website's primary objective, a common response is: "To get hired." *Doing what?* "Well, anything . . ." In other words, they expect viewers to dream up possible employment opportunities. That's unlikely. Clarify what you sell, how it works, and the call to action.

#6: Most Websites Are AGNOSTIC
Sure, we understand what you've done. But what do you believe? Why does your artistry matter? What problems do you work tirelessly to solve? Accomplished artists are a dime a dozen. Those who stand for something—now that matters.

#7: Most Websites Are SCATTERED
Musicians live complicated lives with multiple income streams. To reflect that reality, websites often feature various things we do. But when too many unrelated projects vie for attention, it gives a jack-of-all-trades, master-of-none impression. Visitors wonder, "Is this person a serious teacher or mainly a performer who teaches?" (Or vice versa?) *Each site should have a single BIG idea.* WOWables should support that vision rather than complicating the message. A broad umbrella theme may weave together various activities.

#8: Most Websites Are PROMISCUOUS
In an attempt to be all things to all people, the audience is *everyone*: kids, adults, seniors, professionals, amateurs, nature lovers, teachers, firefighters, "nontraditional audiences" (whatever that means). As a result, nothing feels particularly relevant to anyone. Instead, identify target users, empowering those segments to feel "WOW, this is tailored to me!!" In fact, broadcast who your audience isn't. "If you are NOT looking for the best-dressed, most polished wedding band around, please shop elsewhere!"

#9: Most Websites Are WIMPY
Sure, you play mandolin, teach piano, or compose (like 1,000 others). But in which way(s) are you best in the world? What uncommon aspirations do you chase?

How do your products make a remarkable impact? Don't focus all your energy on pitching features and proving competence! Instead, demonstrate what makes you a bold, impactful, differentiated leader.

And Now the GLORIOUS NEWS!!!
Because these points aren't subjective, it is easy to analyze any site to determine which pitfalls are in place. This brings us to the glorious news: Passing even a few tests rises above the fray. A little creativity goes a long way.

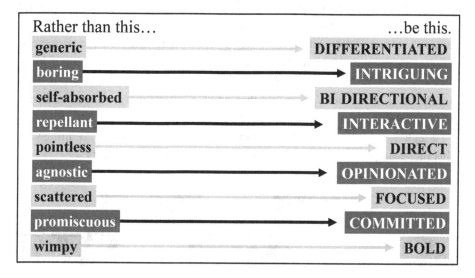

A website is not a resume. *It's the soul of your business*, open to the public. Make every word, image, and media clip count. Be clear. And be interesting!

YOUR DIGITAL FOOTPRINT

While websites are crucial for active musicians and organizations, they are not enough. A vast array of digital tools expand reach and deepen audience commitment.

24/7 Customer Service

To recruit students, guitarist Dereck Johnson tried everything. He once invested $700 into social media ads, A/B testing which of eight images performed best. (The ordeal netted just two clients.) But his creation of an AI assistant transformed marketing efforts. "It is critical to engage clients within 60 seconds, when interest is at its peak." After someone shares contact information, they instantly receive a text message from a named chatbot. Intelligent conversation builds rapport when sharing studio benefits, answering questions, and ultimately scheduling a call. "I love how this approach is active 24/7, even when I'm asleep or eating with family. AI can be trained with different personalities and functions, helping to engage, nurture, or even reactivate leads."

Platforms

For better and worse, social media has become an inescapable part of our lives. Much has been said about its addictive and destructive aspects: fake news, AI bots, trolling, annoying ads, cyberbullying, privacy concerns. At the same time, social media offers essential tools for individuals/organizations to connect, communicate, share, empathize, and inspire.

The number of social media platforms is mind-blowing. Rather than trying to be everywhere and failing, commit to a handful of relevant communities. Better yet, go all in on one, committing for at least six months before expanding further. Become a respected voice where it matters most. Determining which to pursue can be a strategic dilemma. It seems logical to go where the most people are. But if doing so competes against deafening noise, your message may get drowned out. Less gargantuan channels hold promise if they reach a critical mass of target audience members while permitting your voice to break through.

Though most platforms are "free," they are certainly not charities. Gaining visibility increasingly requires paying to play. Weigh benefits against costs.

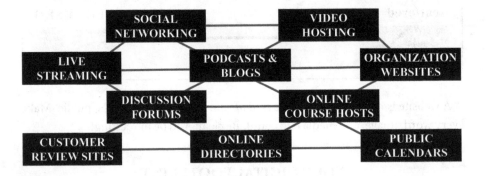

Perspectives

To effectively propel your professional reputation, messaging should consistently address a unified theme, however narrowly or broadly defined. Present yourself as a reliable authority in an area related to whatever makes you most interesting.

One important consideration is the intersection between *you* the person and *you* the brand. People like doing business with friends and "friends," trusted human beings even if they haven't met offline. People who always "sell" may do less well than those offering a balance between the personal and professional.

Social Media Mastermind

Being featured in the documentary *Uncharted: Detroit's Percussionist Mastermind* helped Joshua Jones discover his social media persona. Establishing himself as a practice guru, he began releasing one video per day via

Instagram, YouTube, and Facebook in his "Padding with Josh" series. During "Ask Me a Question" campaigns, fans can gain insights on technique-, wellness-, or preparation-related topics. Messaging sometimes incorporates his dog, scenes around town, and other things he likes or learns.

"I never had the intention of becoming famous, just helpful." But producing so much authentic, quality content has generated devotees. On Instagram alone, his 20,000 followers have generated unexpected gigs, collaborations, and connections. After Jones announced he needed help with health insurance, his online community set up a GoFundMe page, which raised $20,000 in two weeks.

Protocols

A treasure trove of resources reveal tricks of the social media trade: search engine optimization, algorithmic manipulation, analytics, hashtag protocols, which days of the week to post, specific tactics relevant to each platform. Because the rate of change is so fast, many are practically obsolete by release date. To become a social media superstar, stay on top of trends and policies. The following protocols, however, are unlikely to change:

1. **Show up.** Online karma is real. If you want people to care about you, show you care about them.
2. **Define your scope.** Be intentional when determining the types of messages shared. To get known as an authority or influencer, people expect consistency. Do you share personal posts from time to time or stick strictly to business?
3. **Don't just sell.** The vast majority of content should engage, intrigue, and provide true value. When it's time to promote something, be sure people are already hooked.
4. **Post regularly.** This may mean five times a day or twice a week depending on your platforms and commitment level.
5. **Amplify engagement.** The best posts generate reaction. If entries consistently fail to elicit responses or reposts, consider altering the approach.
6. **Answer quickly.** If somebody comments, thank them or continue the thread.
7. **Engage others.** Ask questions, comment, start and continue conversations.
8. **Write well.** Represent yourself in relatable ways that reinforce brand identity.
9. **Make it pretty.** Photos, videos, and other images get noticed more than text alone.
10. **Be positive.** Assume that anything posted can be seen by anybody until the end of time. Negativity in almost any form will come back to haunt you. When taking a deliberate stand against something, think through ramifications and prepare for potential backlash. While there is truth to P. T. Barnum's quote "There's no such thing as bad publicity," be sure you are committed to the fight before jumping in the ring.

> ### Fostering Community
>
> Though Nathan Chan serves as assistant principal cellist with Seattle Symphony, he is more widely known as a social media personality. Racking up more than 35 million views (!) between YouTube, Instagram, Facebook, and TikTok, he shares performances, pop tune arrangements, behind-the-scenes footage, and commentary on the struggles/joys of being a musician. A favorite posting features Chan performing all four parts of Debussy's *La Mer* (translation: the sea), filmed aboard a cruise ship, constructed as a multiscreen video.
>
> Chan's extraordinary visibility has led to numerous professional opportunities: gigs, collaborations, students, sponsorships, even a showcase at Google's Zeitgeist conference. Why does he do it? "Going viral shouldn't be the point. Social media is more about building a fan base, developing a persona, and inspiring others. My primary goal is fostering a community of music makers and lovers."

Permission

Beyond websites and social media, the third rail of a communication strategy involves landing correspondence in an inbox. Email newsletters are distributed to individuals who have opted into your mailing list. Significantly, you own this directory (as opposed to social media multinational conglomerates that may share whatever they want with your contacts in the name of maximizing profits). Services like Mailchimp and Constant Contact offer beautifully designed templates, a mechanism for distribution, detailed metric analysis (open rates, clicks, etc.), and easy opt-out options. These platforms require monthly or annual subscriptions, though free alternatives exist.

In his groundbreaking book *Permission Marketing: Turning Strangers into Friends and Friends into Customers*, Seth Godin articulates the importance of reaching clients who are eager to receive your communications. Newsletters accomplish this when including messages that are "anticipated, personal, and relevant." For example, an effective newsletter for a recording studio might share recording tips, perspectives on releasing an album, articles highlighting recent clients, and a short plug for the business.

How much communication is the right amount? Inundation runs the risk of diminished interest or even irritation, while disappearing acts cause connections to forget about you. Depending on what you do, aim for at least one relevant e-interaction each six-month period. Because not everybody will open (or even notice) every email, it may take multiple correspondences to make an impact. The key is setting expectations upfront and sticking to that plan, with rare exceptions.

> **Internet Connections**
>
> Jazzfuel, a PR/music business firm run by British saxophonist–turned–booking agent Matt Fripp, maintains two mailing lists. The first, distributed to 4,000 musicians, focuses on career strategies. The second, reaching 9,000 enthusiasts, highlights the genre's history and recordings. Weekly communications incorporate three to four quick-read stories, evocative images, prominent quotes, and website links for further exploration. His average open rate is 45%, with 4% clicking through. New subscribers are enticed with lead magnets like a checklist on getting gigs or a guide listing the 50 greatest albums of all time.
>
> Why does he do it? In part, this content is enjoyable to create. But it is also central to building trust. About 90% of product sales result from newsletters. "Email communication is perhaps the most underrated tool for musicians. In my experience, it is significantly more effective than social media."

There are many methods for increasing your level of permission. One involves a *lead magnet*. The idea is to offer something of value for free, enticing future potential clients to opt into your newsletter. Possible giveaways include PDFs or premier access to locked online resources. An effective gift earns the right to begin a dialogue, which in turn leads to increased trust and future purchases. But this comes at a cost—the recipient must disclose name and contact information.

The goal over time is to draw people deeper down a "funnel." As trust builds, commitment increases as they shift from newcomer to tester to repeat customer to superfan. Suppose you run a film-scoring education business. In exchange for an email address, individuals receive a free, beautifully designed PDF addressing gear recommendations. If this and your newsletters are helpful, some recipients may order an ebook you've published for $10. A fraction of those folks will love it so much they enroll in your eCourse, costing $150. By this time they are hooked, eager to learn about additional products and trumpet positive experiences.

Chapter 8
Music Business Is People Business

The music business is first and foremost about people. Not music. Not business. Not money. Not talent. *People.* Interpersonal skills can make or break careers and organizations. Professional satisfaction is often more about collegiality between coworkers than the content of tasks completed. Ensembles succeed or fail largely due to member interaction. More opportunities are offered to friends than unknown "wildcards." Savvy musicians understand that people skills are every bit as important as musical craft.

This industry is competitive. However, individuals have a better chance when joining forces, collaborating, and supporting one another. View colleague successes as triumphs rather than threats to self-preservation. Be good to those who help you. Look for win-win encounters.

SAVVY RULES OF ENGAGEMENT

Rule #1: Be NICE—to Everyone
Your talent doesn't really matter if you're a jerk. Some musicians charm people they think will help their career and are dismissive to everyone else. Not only does that create bad karma, but also it closes doors that may not be immediately obvious. People see through transparent insincerity. Be good to everyone, whether interacting with the president of Sony, hired stagehands, or complete strangers. The payoff will be considerable.

Rule #2: Be POSITIVE
Smiles and laughter are free, powerful, and contagious. Optimists are more likely than complainers to win the favor of others. Of course, everyone has bad days, and sharing difficult moments with close friends is necessary at times. But when existence gets stressful, take a step back to gain perspective. Remind yourself how lucky you are to be pursuing a field you love. Cheerful behavior has an additional benefit: You will be happier and healthier.

A Savvy Secret?

When writing this book, one striking feature was how positive the majority of interviewees were. Despite often sobering challenges, they overwhelmingly maintained humor and optimism. Many declared that there has never been a better time to be a musician than today.

Rule #3: Be RELIABLE

Dependability is as important as likeability. Arrive early, prepared, and sober; finish projects before the deadline; follow through responsibly. Many musicians have blown great opportunities simply because it took too long to return an email.

Rule #4: Be LOYAL

Reciprocity unleashes rich rewards. Demonstrate benevolence to those who have helped you.

Rule #5: Involve the COMMUNITY

Consider how your music can create synergies while enhancing quality of life. Embrace projects that immerse others. People become more excited about your success when they play a role in getting you there.

Rule #6: Allow Others to Feel IMPORTANT

A primary motivator for every human being is proving our existence has meaning, to the world and ourselves. To that end, we seek family, friends, fame, fortune, and fanfare. Without resorting to superficial flattery, endeavor to make others feel valued and valuable. Let them know their actions are seen and appreciated.

Rule #7: Ask QUESTIONS and Listen Actively

People who refrain from asking questions don't care, or give that impression. The act of inquiry demonstrates sincere interest. Similarly, nothing is more flattering than the feeling of being listened to attentively, without distraction. Look people in the eye, focusing completely on your conversation partner.

Rule #8: Clearly Articulate EXPECTATIONS Upfront

Don't beat around the bush. Whether working with a collaborator, employee, or client, let people know the full ask early on. It is better to have someone walk away than to con them and come to regret it. Changing requirements are frustrating and can harm relationships.

Rule #9: ARGUE SMART

Most musicians are passionate, but savvy ones pick their battles. While high-level debates about the nuances of a phrase may be important, be clear that opinions are purely musical, not personal. Never lose your temper—you are much more likely to advance goals under conditions of goodwill. Chewing someone out usually sets back your cause, as regrettable statements slip out during heated moments. *It is better to be friends than to be right.*

Rule #10: NEVER SPEAK BADLY... about Anyone

Beyond spreading negativity, this practice *always* comes back to haunt you, especially in a community as small as the music world.

Rule #11: Think LONG TERM

Make choices that allow relationships to thrive over time. Capitalize on ways to increase the longevity and vibrancy of each connection. Be wary of burning bridges behind you.

Rule #12: THANK People
Proudly give credit where it is due. Everyone, even those who contribute in small ways, enjoys feeling appreciated. Thanking too much is better than not enough.

> ### A Special Touch
>
> To make an impression, send an old-fashioned thank you note. While emails or texts suffice, they require little effort and are quickly forgotten. A card, however, is a collector's item.

ONE HANDSHAKE AT A TIME

Practice, practice, practice → excellence → dream gigs appear. Aspiring musicians may assume this formula, but it almost always works differently. More likely: practice, practice, practice → schmooze → solidify contacts → someone who likes you sends work your way. People hire their friends. The bigger and stronger your network, the more opportunities find you.

Everyone you meet has the potential to benefit your cause, though the ways may not immediately be apparent. Please don't interpret this as sinister or manipulative. Relationships are two-way streets—you have value to share with others as well. Here are a few ways in which individuals might advance your professional/artistic aspirations:

Knowing a thousand people won't help if you have no good way to communicate. Use spreadsheets to systematically record, find, and sort connections. In addition to contact information (phone, email, social media, website, company), it is a good idea to collect personal information (birthday, anniversary, names of spouse and children) or even stories and memories. When re-establishing contact five years down the road, wouldn't it be nice to say, "How is your daughter Julie? She must be 8 by now!" or "Do you remember when that juggler's ball flew into your saxophone bell?" Several databases should be maintained, helping you keep track of it all.

LIST	INCLUDES
Industry	Performers, composers, educators, contractors, producers, presenters, engineers, etc. Keep notes on expertise and project types preferred.
Media	Print, broadcast, and internet media contacts. Record organization name, interests/biases, and policies/deadlines. When promoting a project, use this list to track down connections who have been helpful in the past.
Fans/clients	Use this database to communicate news, events, and helpful information.

BUILDING YOUR NETWORK

Some musicians become so obsessed with the rich and famous that they forget about the "little guy." Sure, it would be great if an international influencer championed your cause. But chances are slim, even if you did manage to exchange a few sentences in the Hilton bathroom six short months ago. Most superstars are solicited far too often to give much thought to José Newcomer.

"Ordinary folk"—familiar faces, nonmusicians, those in comparable or lesser stages of their career—are more likely to invest energy and resources into your professional development. The people you already know may be infinitely more helpful than you realize. Brainstorm members of your current network. This list probably spans easily into the hundreds.

The first layer of your network is family and friends. Do not take these individuals for granted. They will be your biggest advocates time and time again. Then consider all the people with whom you currently interact: fellow musicians, work colleagues, teachers, students, doctors, beauticians, advisors, neighbors. Also recall folks who played these roles at earlier points in your life. Even if you've lost touch, reactivating their membership into your support fraternity may be simple. Most people are thrilled to hear from voices of the past. In fact, reacquainting may result in stronger bonds than were originally held.

Another group that can be activated is fans and clients. Failing to grow relationships with these constituents is a squandered opportunity. Already impressed with your value, they may be delighted to become better acquainted or even enthusiastic foot soldiers. A number of actions further expand your reach, placing you shoulder to shoulder with fresh personalities, including:

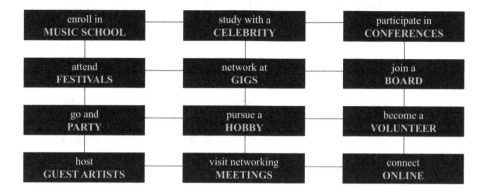

> **Facilitating Opportunity**
>
> "Forget about asking people you don't know for favors. Instead, provide value to others." When working for a church music series, hornist Seth Hanes contacted interesting musicians he wanted to meet. Strangers were invited to connect at chamber music reading cocktail parties hosted on his outdoor rooftop. Rather than asking influencers to promote his book *Break into the Scene*, Hanes interviewed them for his own blog, to be shared with a robust email list. Each gesture opened doors. New friends hired him or returned the favor in other ways. "My job is to facilitate opportunities. Do that, and the rewards boomerang back."

The Schmooze Factor

Ironically, the most intimating place to initiate conversation can be a room packed to capacity. If this resonates, keep in mind that most everyone else is just as "mingle-phobic." *Schmoozing*, or informal conversing, is an art form that pays off when mastered. In social situations, set goals about how many exchanges you hope to instigate, and don't chicken out.

Most people are delighted to chat when invited. All it takes to unlock conversation is a simple question or comment. Handshakes should be firm but reasonable—soggy or bone-crushing clasps do not create a good first impression! Make eye contact and utilize body language showing you are engaged. Relax! Ignore the impulse to impress. Instead, be your normal, lovely, authentic self and drop the agenda. Folks can tell if your primary motivation is self-serving. Project positivity and optimism. Individuals you just met don't want to hear about your recent divorce, nightmare gigs, or the depression that accompanies male pattern baldness. Keep conversations appropriate, avoiding controversial subjects such as sex, politics, or clowns.

After a great exchange, follow up. Within 48 hours, send a message to affirm how much you enjoyed the encounter. Take steps to keep the relationship alive.

> ### The Second Most Important Skill
>
> "Next to playing well, networking is the most important thing for freelancers," explains bassist David White. After moving to New York City with no connections, he began cold calling established theater players. Careful never to hit them up for gigs, he began communications with "I know your sub list is full. However, I haven't done Broadway before. Might I watch your book[1] and take you out for a beer after?" He also made a point of attending their "crappy Tuesday bar gigs," characterized by tiny audiences and plenty of hang time. Within six months, White had lots of friends and a contract with a touring production. His calendar has been full ever since. "Contractors think a lot about who they want to sit by on a bus for months at a time."

IGNITING SUPPORT

Every once in a while an opportunity falls into your lap. More often, however, it works differently. Getting results requires self-initiation, a relevant cause, perseverance, and the ability to interest others in your vision. But making an "ask" can be difficult. While many musicians feel embarrassed or guilty, this fear is irrational. We all need support. You may be amazed how much simply requesting referrals, donations, advice, or work can accomplish. Soliciting assistance is often the only way to bring dreams to fruition.

How much should be reasonably requested from any single connection? Even committed enthusiasts have limited bandwidth. Be sure to prioritize requests, reaching out for only the most important issues. Never take others' generosity for granted.

Sometimes it makes sense to cast the net wide. Distribute a newsletter or social media post and see who steps forward. Recognize that assistance is more likely to come from historically engaged colleagues than those who show up only when help is needed.

Individual communications often yield superior results. In this case, craft highly personalized notes, particularly if you haven't been in touch for a while. Address each contact by name, opening with a friendly paragraph to catch up, followed by a compelling, concise ask. Be direct about appeals; don't beat around the bush. If the issue is complex, request a call, video chat, or in-person meeting "over coffee, on me!" rather than cramming everything into an electronic communication. Be

---

[1] Sit in the pit during a performance and observe.

prepared to act quickly if supporting information is requested (webpage, project description, budget, electronic press kit, etc.).

Make it easy for people to help. If seeking a newspaper feature, send a well-written article that can be used verbatim if desired, along with links to downloadable photographs. When courting presenters, include a plan explaining how *you* will promote the event. Demonstrate that this proposal is not only a smart move but also a stress-free one.

Even if you get a "no," request permission to stay in touch. Though things didn't work out this time, the relationship is not necessarily dead. In fact, since you already have an established association, the odds of success are higher in the future.

Professional Communication

How you choose to interact with friends is entirely up to you. But professional digital communication should be...professional. Whether emailing, texting, or direct messaging, this is particularly important when connecting with new contacts. Individuals failing to employ at least basic etiquette are likely to see messages ignored or worse—a reputational stain branding them as unserious. Common pet peeves include:

- Messages to the wrong person
- Messages addressed to nobody in particular (reads like spam)
- Misspelled names
- Irrelevant gibberish
- Weak or super informal writing, man
- Emojis and other cutesy images 😈
- Missing, unclear, or hard-to-find action steps
- Run-on sentences with many twists and turns, requiring the recipient to read and reread several times, in order to understand, because it is easy to get lost, typically I recommend sticking to three or fewer clauses per sentence, though some experts disagree, you get the point, right?
- Excruciatingly extensive, "novel-length" paragraphs
- Wordiness
- ALL CAPS, WHICH FEEL LIKE YOU ARE SCREAMING
- all lower case and no punctuation making it hard to navigate
- Overly casual/unknown "text speak," even if it is SSDD, IMHO, though IFYP
- Speling and grammatical errors at
- Uninvited attachments, clogging up an inbox
- *Reply all* responses despite being relevant to just one person

To be taken seriously, craft concise, easy-to-comprehend notes. Grab attention immediately with a relevant subject header (when applicable) and opening sentence. Quickly get to the point. If content must be extensive, use **bold**, *italics*, and formatting techniques to aid the comprehension of even a skimmer. Clarify your singular "ask" and make compliance simple. Busy recipients are unlikely to welcome a multifaceted project being dropped in their lap, particularly by a stranger.

> **Signature Performance**
>
> Professional messages should conclude with a *signature*, typically three to five lines consisting of your name, website, and position/company. Better yet, emphasize a benefit: "For 23 revolutionary practice tips that *will* transform your music, visit www.mywebsite.com."

Cold Calling

One of the most dreaded phrases in the English language must surely be *cold calling* (besides *The check's in the mail!*). This entails contacting someone you've never met and asking for assistance. Perhaps you just moved to a new city and need work, or are hoping to convince presenters to book your show. Despite the possibility of rejection, this is one practice savvy musicians cannot avoid, at least occasionally.

A good start is making the contact less arctic. If you share a mutual acquaintance, drop their name. Better yet, have that person make an initial introduction. Another possibility involves finding congruence between your backgrounds (e.g., "You and I attended the same university!"). Personal associations shift your contact from the pesky-telemarketer to actual-human-being category. Your message should quickly:

1. Introduce yourself and develop rapport.
2. Clarify the reason for your communication.
3. Generate interest.
4. Suggest a next step (schedule a follow-up, submit materials, etc.).

You typically have two to three paragraphs in a digital communication, or one to two minutes on a call, to accomplish all four goals. This underscores the necessity of attention-grabbing, effectively delivered, succinct scripts. When phoning, use notes to stay focused, but avoid reading word for word. Without rambling, answer all questions, and maintain a friendly tone. Articulate next steps and always end with gratitude regardless of outcome.

> **Is it Chilly in Here?**
>
> Pianist Rhonda Rizzo gained confidence cold calling when working in the tech industry. "If I can sell pagers, I can sell anything!" For the corporate world, a 3% to 5% response rate is considered strong. Impressively, her track record reaching out to music presenters exceeds 30%. "It's all about knowing how to write a decent business letter."

> Step one involves research. Identifying series with a history of acts like hers, Rizzo asks, *What's in it for them?* She then crafts a carefully worded message. Paragraph one grabs attention and provides sizzle. Paragraph two argues why she is uniquely qualified. The conclusion includes gratitude and a call to action.
>
> Rizzo also receives unsolicited communications daily from folks hoping to be featured on her *No Dead Guys* blog. The majority fail to impress. Generic cut-and-paste notes, without personalization, are "horrifying." She is also turned off by spelling errors, cutesy emojis, profanity, and a lack of follow-through. Successful examples concisely articulate, *This is who I am. I know about your great blog. Might you consider interviewing me?*

Persistence versus Peskiness

In a perfect world, every sent message receives a prompt response. In reality, people are notoriously unreliable. They get busy. Despite the best of intentions, your proposal slides down the priority list. As each day passes, it becomes less likely any reply will come. Did they simply get distracted, or is silence an indication of disinterest? Should you follow through yet again? When do you cross the line from being responsibly persistent to an irritating pest?

Most musicians give up way too easily, throwing in the towel after one or two communication attempts. *It often requires several interactions to get noticed by a new contact.* Perseverance pays! Unless noninterest is explicitly stated, follow-ups are appropriate. Allow time for a reasonable turnaround, but waiting too long causes the proposal to escape memory. Consider alternative contact methods (i.e., phone following an email) and always remain pleasant. If no sign of life is made after five to seven reasonably spaced efforts, move on.

Just Say No!

There will undoubtedly be occasions placing you on the other side of this equation. Someone makes a request and you aren't interested. Rather than ghosting, take five seconds to reply. "Thanks for thinking of me, but I am unable to help at this time. Good luck with your project!" Beyond clarity, this presents you as a responsible professional. Silence does the opposite.

Staying Current

In the music industry, "out of sight, out of mind" is particularly applicable. When seeking a cellist, for example, the opportunity will likely be offered to a qualified player who was recently in touch. For this reason, it is essential to stay at the top of your connections' mental Rolodex.

As a rule, make contact with each valued member of your network at least once a year. Remind people you are still alive. Emails, texts, or direct messages may be easiest, but in-person visits, cards, letters, and phone chats make a stronger impact. It can be nice to check in with no agenda other than, "Hello, I've been thinking about you." Avoid coming across as a pest or stalker, or approaching only when you want something after having faded into oblivion.

You're Not Talking to the Right People!

A composer wants to secure more performances. So she attends a comp seminar. Problem is, most attendees (other composers) seek the same thing. Wouldn't it be better to visit a gathering where noncomposing performers are in great supply? She's not talking to the right people.

A rock band needs a better business model. So they meet with similar groups to see what can be learned. Problem is, DIY musicians aren't known for business savvy. Wouldn't it be better to meet with successful entrepreneurs outside music? They're not talking to the right people.

A local orchestra needs to raise capital. So they approach known arts donors. Problem is, financial resources from these patrons are already stretched thin. Wouldn't it be better to cultivate new relationships with wealthy citizens who don't currently have their fingers in the arts? They're not talking to the right people.

Jazz musicians are disappointed by low turnout at their gigs. So they go to a bar and complain how nobody appreciates great music anymore. Problem is, you can't solve a problem by groaning. Wouldn't it be better to meet with actual neighbors to learn what motivates them? They're not talking to the right people.

When there's a challenge, we often approach others who are kind of like us. It feels comfortable to be in the presence of familiarity. By networking with clones, we confirm assumptions and continue further down the same path with blind confidence. If you hope to discover a better way, however, those with different perspectives may be better equipped to help.

You hope to advance your vision. Are you talking to the right people?

Chapter 9
Winning the Money Game

I often ask musicians: "You are so engaged, smart, dynamic. You could have pursued anything! Why on Earth did you choose music?" The response is unanimous. *Because it's something I love!* Interestingly, I've had conversations with folks from the business sector following a similar setup. "Why on Earth did you choose business?" Just as predictably: *for the money!* Both groups have much to learn from one another.

Of all life's major challenges, money is perhaps the easiest to solve. This doesn't mean the road will be simple. But if you need more capital, there are often plenty of paths. If, on the other hand, you want more time, health, humanity... those are bigger lifts.

Winning the money game does not require becoming an accountant. However, a degree of literacy is necessary. This chapter explores a variety of personal and business finance issues, as both overlap seamlessly in the life of savvy musicians. Actual numbers are proposed. Apologies in advance for readers who cower at the thought of basic math. Calculators welcome!

> **Once Again, Conventional Wisdom Misses the Mark**
>
> Conventional wisdom argues that musicians (aka "starving artists") are bad with money. I respectfully disagree. In my experience, musicians are AMAZING with money. This group stretches a dollar further than just about anyone. The problem is they just don't have enough of it!

MONEY IN

FIVE WAYS TO GENERATE CASH

While some musicians generate 100% of their income from a single source, most draw from multiple streams.

1. Active income
Do the work, get paid. Whether hourly, salaried, or project based, this is how most musicians make most of their money. A challenge is that there are only so many hours in a day, and generated revenue may not be enough to reach your goals. Because you can't clone yourself, any energy on a given project comes at the

expense of many others. If you are unable to complete the work for any reason, payment stops.

2. Passive income
Earn money while you sleep! Passive income typically requires extensive work on the front end but can pay dividends over time. For example, it takes significant time and energy to write a book or record an eCourse, but once completed, in-demand products generate revenue for years. With performance or mechanical royalties, creators and recording artists are paid when works are shared publicly well into the future. Another example involves the stock market when funds grow over time. Of course, you must first earn dollars to invest (wisely).

3. Award income
Congrats on your accolade! Whether a grant or competition, awards are an honor. Designed to support specific objectives, some opportunities are restricted to nonprofits, while others are open to anyone. Spectacularly, they need not be repaid. However, most are cutthroat and far from guaranteed. Unlike active income—where you reliably get paid for the work—it is possible to spend untold hours preparing a proposal only to emerge empty-handed.

4. Contributed income
Individuals and businesses make financial gifts to support great causes and receive benefits (tax write-off, program acknowledgment, name on a building, etc.). Raising money also aids other goals, such as marketing. Recognize that contributed income does not come free. Generating support costs time, money, and energy that could have otherwise been spent elsewhere. Suppose you need $25,000. Does it make more sense to generate this through earned income or to build and market a fundraiser?

5. Loaned income
In a pinch, borrowing can save the day. Whether through bank loans or credit cards, these quick cash infusions support various expenses. Without enough money on hand, loans may be your only option. The problem, of course, is that they must be repaid. In addition to principal, interest quickly accrues. Borrowing is sometimes necessary to unlock future returns, but proceed with caution. Can you truly afford it? Are there other ways to reach your goals?

Filling Your Portfolio

Multiple income stream *portfolio careers* incorporate jobs, freelancing, and entrepreneurial ventures. Similarly, most music businesses sell a portfolio of products. When designing or analyzing your business model, begin by identifying all potential revenue types. Distribute ACTIVITIES into logical CATEGORIES. A map of one musician's portfolio career follows.

TEACHING	PERFORMANCE	EXPERTISE
1. Private lessons 2. Registration fees 3. Group classes 4. Adjunct college teaching	5. Orchestra services 6. Headline concerts 7. Background music 8. Dance class accompanying	9. Keynotes 10. Workshops 11. Master classes
COMPOSING	PRODUCT SALES	FUNDRAISING
12. Commissions 13. Score sales (your site) 14. Score sales (other sites) 15. Royalties	16. Branded T-shirts 17. Method book series	18. Crowdfunding campaign 19. Corporate sponsorship 20. Individual donors

How many streams are ideal? Without enough, it is difficult to reach earning goals. Too many means time, money, and energy get spread thin. For example, selling 100 physical products requires hefty financial investment when purchasing inventory that must be stored until sold. Similarly, an ensemble offering 20 programs is confronted by the arduous task of maintaining excellence across an extensive repertoire. Simplify your business model by offering just the right amount.

What's in Your Portfolio (Career)?

Over the years, the portfolio career of pianist Ashley Danyew has included a variety of income streams, such as (1) accompanying individuals, (2) accompanying middle/high school choirs, (3) various church music work, (4) freelance performance (weddings, funerals, etc.), (5) directing a chamber music festival, (6) studio teaching, (7) music business workshops, (8) online course sales,* (9) one-on-one consulting, (10) writing children's music curriculum, (11) retailing self-published works,* (12) earning performance royalties,* (13) logo design, (14) running an Etsy shop* (with original paintings and art prints), (15) digital product sales* (e.g., contract templates), and (16) affiliate income* (earning a commission on referrals).

All this variety inspires Danyew, though she has gotten more strategic over time. "One of the best things I discovered was how to generate income independently from ongoing time commitment. This helped me break out of the *freelance/employee mindset* (always exchanging time for money) and start thinking of my career as a business (often building something once that generates passive income for years)."

Generates passive income.

Setting a Price

Some musicians with great poise onstage quiver awkwardly when asked how much they charge. There is no reason to feel guilty. You are a pro. Present this number with confidence.

Before establishing a price, do your homework. Familiarize yourself with competitor fees as well as necessary direct expenses (supplies, subcontractors, transportation, etc.). Additional factors include the level of demand and your product's differentiation.

Early career musicians often undercut their value by depreciating rates. If what you offer is equivalent to the competition, this may be the best option. However, there are alternatives to undercharging. Many consumers begin searching for the lowest price but ultimately pay more for products with higher perceived value. Consider charging a slightly elevated rate while offering "more for the money."

> **Business Etiquette**
> - There are no "take-backs." After quoting a price, you may not change your mind even if the original ask was too low.
> - Be upfront about the entire amount. People hate "hidden fees."
> - Use clearly written contracts/invoices to avoid uncertainties.

In my own portfolio, I offer a variety of price points: *average, above average, slightly below average, really expensive,* and *free*. One amount I refuse to charge is *cheap*—my work has value and cheap feels insulting. "Free" is included because there are times the mission of a project resonates so deeply that donating time and talents is a worthwhile investment. A savvy musician can only do this, however, if the rest of their career/financial model allows for such inclusions. If accepting occasional unpaid work, be sure it offers some career/networking/purpose-driven perk. Promises of "exposure" are typically exploitative, to be politely but immediately declined.

To make the money work, offer at least one *high-ticket item* that pays handsomely. How much varies based on your profile and offerings (maybe four, five, or six digits?). Without such options, reaching your annual earning goal may be tricky. Of course, it only helps if sales are made, so be strategic. Who will pay these fees?

Here is a radical proposition: When earning more is important, *don't look where the money isn't. Instead, go where the money is.* Most musicians are intimately familiar with thinly resourced environments: regional orchestras, educational communities, arts nonprofits. At the same time, wealthy industries like health care, energy, technology, real estate, and other corporate strongholds are flush with cash. Design relevant products and reap the rewards.

That Piano Girl Who Talks

While a piano performance major, Jade Simmons discovered her gift for public speaking through an unexpected detour: competing in the Miss America pageant. Advocating for youth suicide prevention, she inspired audiences and even testified in front of Congress. Those experiences inspired her to combine music and storytelling, an unusual combination at the time. "Presenters started pursuing me, seeking *that piano girl who talks*."

Simmons thought she'd made it when gigs paid $1,200 to $1,500 per show. And then, after being offered a corporate musical keynote, she threw out a ridiculous number. "My rate is $12,000." Without blinking an eye, the company sent a contract. Since then, talks incorporating piano have addressed topics like leadership, innovation, and diversity. She was nicknamed "classical music's #1 maverick," and her reputation grew as rates increased.

"Some conferences pay $40,000 for bagels and coffee alone. I know my value is more than that!" The year she charged $50,000 per 45-minute speech was the busiest yet, with almost 50 bookings. Since then, her rate has doubled. "In music circles, strong verbal communication makes me a unicorn. Among corporate speakers, it is musical ability that distinguishes my voice from the others."

What's the ideal price? Some people argue it depends on the product, but that misses the point. Asking for too much scares clients. Requesting too little leaves you underpaid and establishes a precedent that devalues work. *The best price for anything is when the buyer and seller both believe they got a great deal.*

Projecting Revenues

How much money are you likely to generate over a year (or other period), and what will it take to get there? Though there is no way to predict with absolute certainty, advance a series of educated assumptions. Be realistic, but ambitious.

Set up a spreadsheet to experiment with various earning models. For each activity, identify the price of a single unit ($) as well as one or two additional variables (A and B). These can indicate the number of units sold, time periods tabulated (days, weeks, months), or other relevant considerations. Multiply for TOTAL projected revenue. When possible, calculate automatically within spreadsheets, inserting a mathematical formula.[1]

---

[1] On spreadsheets, use *formulas* to accurately and automatically calculate math. How to write these varies between platforms, but they include the cell number(s) in question. On Google sheets, formulas start with an "=" sign. The TOTAL amount in cell F2 in the following chart is processed with the formula: =C2*D2*E2.

For example, when teaching private lessons, considerations might be:

- $ = Cost of a one-hour lesson.
- A = Average lesson hours taught per week. (In this example, while the teacher has 30 students, a combination of half- and full-hour lessons results in 20 hours taught.)
- B = Average active weeks per year. (Though there are 52 weeks in a year, most students take time off during summer and holidays.) NOTE: If only the unit cost and one variable are needed, include a "1" for variable "B."

In the chart below, the meaning of variables A and B are clarified in the rightmost columns.

	A	B	C	D	E	F	G	H
1	CATEGORY	ACTIVITY	$	A	B	TOTAL	A=	B=
2	Teaching	Private lessons—school year	$70	20	34	$47,600	Hours/week	Weeks/year
3	Teaching	Reg fee (admin and recitals)	$50	30	2	$3,000	# of students	Terms/year
4	Teaching	Summer tuition (5 lessons + project)	$320	15	1	$4,800	# of students	
5	Performance	Gigs	$150	5	12	$9,000	Average gigs/month	Months/year
6	Performance	Church services	$75	2	30	$4,500	Services/week	Active weeks/year
7	Merch	Branded music T-shirts	$24	5	40	$4,800	Average sales/week	Active weeks
8	TOTAL					$73,700		

Tweaking the Formula

What does it take to reach an earning goal? Compare various models to see what makes most sense. For example, suppose a performer aspires to generate $5,000 over a 3-month summer period (around 12 weeks) through gigs/concerts.

Avg. $	# of Gigs	Total	Notes on $ Rate
$100	50 (4–5/week)	**$5,000**	Realistic rate for many per-service and freelance opportunities. This means you need gigs almost every day.
$200	25 (~2/week)	**$5,000**	Typical compensation for weddings/private parties.
$500	10 (3–4/month)	**$5,000**	You contract the wedding gigs, charging enough to pay musicians (including yourself) $200 apiece, in addition to collecting a $300 booking fee.
$1,000	5 (1–2/month)	**$5,000**	Focus on chamber series that pay midtier ensembles $1,000 per person.
$5,000	1 (just 1 in 3 months!)	**$5,000**	Designing and marketing this self-produced event may require significant time commitment. But might it happen with less energy than the fifty $100 engagements?

Let's ponder the final example further. How might a single show generate $5,000? Should it involve many tickets at a low price or just a few exclusive donors paying more?

Ticket $	# Sold	Total	Proposed Strategy
$5	1,000	**$5,000**	Convince many people to pay a little for a streaming event.
$20	250	**$5,000**	Design a compelling program that fills a small concert hall.
$25	200	**$5,000**	Raising the price slightly reduces the number of tickets required. People may not perceive a price difference between $20 and $25.
3 tiers: $25 $50 $100	130 total 100 30 10	**$5,000** $2,500 $1,500 $1,000	Offer different price points with additional benefits for folks at higher levels. Perhaps $100 patrons eat dinner with performers beforehand, a real treat! Just keep in mind that this increases your expenses.
$100	50	**$5,000**	Instead of tickets, solicit *donations* that support an exciting project.
$250	20	**$5,000**	VIP tickets are sold to wealthier fans, arts supporters, and businesspeople to attend an intimate house concert.
$5,000	1	**$5,000**	A single superfan donor sponsors the event, allowing everyone else to attend for free.

The point: There are many ways to reach a financial goal. Think through contrasting models and project what each path will take. *Embrace math.*

Generating More

If anticipated revenues aren't enough, how might you earn more? There are almost always creative solutions. For example, Viola Fidler is an independent music teacher whose primary income involves private lessons. She hopes to surpass the $50,000 mark but is coming up a little short. What strategies might she embrace? She currently charges $60 per hour. Her studio of 42, who take either 30- or 60-minute lessons, results in 25 teaching hours per week. The average student meets 32 times over the course of the school year.

CATEGORY	ACTIVITY	$	A	B	TOTAL	A=	B=
Teaching	Private lessons	$60	25	32	**$48,000**	Hours/week	Weeks/year

Strategy 1: Raise Price

Raising Viola's hourly rate by $3 brings in an extra $2,400. A $5 hike adds $4,000. This might discourage some students from continuing. But her teaching is outstanding and rates haven't changed in years.

CATEGORY	ACTIVITY	$	A	B	TOTAL	A=	B=
Teaching	Private lessons	$63	25	32	**$50,400**	Hours/week	Weeks/year
Teaching	Private lessons	$65	25	32	**$52,000**	Hours/week	Weeks/year

Strategy 2: Augment Sales

Viola could increase the number of lesson hours per week by accepting more students. However, 25 is already a hefty lift. Doing so will likely lead to burnout. A better option might be adding more total lessons per student. Currently, she teaches only 32 weeks per year, all during the academic year. What if students were enticed to continue in the summer?

CATEGORY	ACTIVITY	$	A	B	TOTAL	A=	B=
Teaching	Private lessons	$60	25	34	**$51,000**	Hours/week	Weeks/year
Teaching	Private lessons	$60	25	36	**$54,000**	Hours/week	Weeks/year
Teaching	Private lessons	$60	25	40	**$60,000**	Hours/week	Weeks/year

Strategy 3: Add Streams

Though 25 lesson hours per week is significant, Viola still has time. How might new income streams augment earnings by adding value to existing clients? For example, might she increase the number of recitals per year from two to four and start charging a recital fee? How about offering monthly workshops to interested studio members?

CATEGORY	ACTIVITY	$	A	B	TOTAL	A=	B=
Teaching	Private lessons	$60	25	32	$48,000	Hours/week	Weeks/year
Teaching	Annual recital fee	$50	42	1	$2,100	# of students	Payments/year
Teaching	Monthly workshops	$25	10	9	$2,250	Students/class	# of workshops
TOTAL					$52,350		

Strategy 4: Increase Efficiency

Though Viola is outstanding, she cannot tell students, "I am so good, my hour-long lessons are completed in just 45 minutes!" There is another way to think about efficiency, however. Despite obvious benefits, pairing one teacher with one student is highly inefficient. What if, instead, Viola moves to a group lesson format? Working with trios for an hour (42 students/3 per lesson = 14/hour lessons per week) offers numerous advantages: peer learning, social engagement, friendly competition, chamber music opportunities, etc. From a time and financial perspective, several important things happen:

1. Students are charged a third less ($40/ vs. $60/hour).
2. Viola's hourly rate doubles ($120/ vs. $60/hour).
3. Viola's teaching commitment drops over 40% (14 vs. 25 hours weekly).
4. Viola's annual lesson income increases by more than 10% ($48,000 to $53,760).

CATEGORY	ACTIVITY	$	A	B	TOTAL	A=	B=
Teaching	Group lessons (trios)	$120	14	32	$53,760	Hours/week	Weeks/year

This is a powerful example of simultaneously amplifying impact and income.

Strategy 5: Get passive

Viola considers filming and distributing an eCourse. While producing this takes time, it has potential to generate passive income for years to come (if demand exists). Consider various price points and sales projections for this income stream alone.

CATEGORY	ACTIVITY	$	A	B	TOTAL	A=	B=
Teaching	eCourse	$50	2	12	$1,200	Sales/month	Months/year
Teaching	eCourse	$100	10	11	$11,000	Sales/month	Months/year*
Teaching	eCourse	$25	6	48	$7,200	Sales/week	Weeks/year
Teaching	eCourse	$150	15	320	$48,000	Sales/day	Days/year

* Deciding to not promote each July, reducing months to 11 provides a buffer. (Use variable that match your model.).

Protecting Yourself

Every professional musician seems to have one story about a time they got stiffed. It always ends the same: "There was no contract, so I let it go." Most clients are honest brokers who follow through on obligations. But without a contract, you have no clout when someone refuses to pay up. A written agreement provides proof in the unfortunate case that you must go to (usually small claims) court. Whether hired to perform, compose, teach, or fulfill other tasks, contracts are essential. They clarify details for both the employer and employee, minimizing unexpected surprises.

Contracts typically include contact information (name, phone, address, email of employee and employer), gig details (date, time, deadline, location), and fee specifics (total payment, deposit info, due dates, rules around selling merch, acceptable payment forms). Also clarify special requirements (Piano tuned? Hotel? Arrival time?) and your cancellation policy.

Contracts only become legally binding after being signed by representatives from both parties. If responsible for drafting the agreement, have your client sign, date, and return it, along with the deposit (if necessary). It is important that you provide the final signature in case details are added or altered. If completing someone else's document, read the fine print and consult an attorney about unclear passages. There are numerous instances of musicians losing big money because of a clause that seemed "insignificant at the time."

MONEY OUT

It's not what you earn but what you keep that counts. To understand the financial health of a music career or venture, it is necessary to consider three types of expenses: (1) cost of goods sold (COGS), (2) overhead, and (3) taxes.

COGS

COGS are direct expenses associated with bringing something to market. If you didn't sell the product, you wouldn't have the expense.

Suppose your business manufactures guitars. Consumers can buy an instrument through your website for $1,000 (*revenue*). Each costs you $450 to manufacture (*COGS*), meaning you generate $550 after direct expenses (*gross profit*). In this example, you have a healthy *profit margin* of 55%. Very nice!

Gross Profit ÷ Revenues = Profit Margin %

The financial model changes substantially when instruments are sold through third parties such as music stores or Amazon. These vendors purchase items at a discount of 10% to 40%+ below *list price* and make money by reselling them to consumers for a higher amount. If a store purchases your $1,000 guitar for $700 ($300 less than list price) and you already paid $450 to make it, that leaves you just a $250 profit, or 25% margin. While products may be easier for customers to find through highly trafficked sellers, working with them comes at a significant cost.

Manufacturing large quantities of a physical item reduces its unit price. For example, printing a 150-page book might run $250 for 10 copies ($25 each), $850 for 100 ($8.50 each), $1,800 for 500 ($3.60 each), or $6,000 for 3,000 ($2 each). While more units reduces COGS/unit, weak sales mean you are stuck with unclaimed inventory and a higher out-of-pocket expense.

Not all products require COGS. An independent music teacher offering instruction from home may capture a 100% profit margin. However, if lessons require hiring a babysitter or renting a studio by the hour, these COGS reduce gross profit.

Sample Product	Sale Price	COGS	Gross Profit/Margin
Oboe reed (business model A)	$15	Supplies ($3.70), shipping to customer included in price ($3.50)	$7.80/52%
Oboe reed (business model B)	$15	Supplies ($3.70), 45% commission to distributor ($6.75), shipping to distributor ($2.50)	$2.05/14%

| Private hour lesson tuition—15 weeks | $900 | Weekly studio rental ($8/hour × 15 weeks = $120), sheet music for student ($55) | $725/~80.5% |
| Mainstage concert (self-produced) | $6,500 | Performer pay (4 players × $1,000/each = $4,000), equipment rental for gig ($500), travel to/from ($800) | $1,200/~18.5% |

Overhead

Unlike COGS, *overhead* (also known as *operating*) expenses are NOT directly tied to sales. These costs are unchanged whether peddling 1 unit or 1,000.

For example, the cost of a laptop or rented office space has no direct correlation to the quantity of products sold. Overhead includes items like rent, utilities, administrative salaries, employee benefits, travel, business and instrument insurance, marketing, office supplies, and equipment. A computer, work phone, company car, and holiday party all fall under this category. Some overhead is *fixed*, requiring a consistent, predictable monthly expenditure. *Variable* expenses fluctuate.

When projecting expenses on a spreadsheet, employ the same variable system used for revenues. Since these numbers must be subtracted, precede them with a minus sign (e.g. –$150) or place in parentheses (called *accounting style*). The example below showcases some overhead for a medium-sized music business.

CATEGORY	ACTIVITY	$	A	B	TOTAL	A=	B=
Facilities	Office rental	($1,500)	12	1	($18,000)	Months/year	Bills/month
Facilities	Utilities	($600)	12	1	($7,200)	Months/year	Bills/month
Salaries	Full-time admin	($4,000)	12	2	($96,000)	Months/year	# employees
Salaries	Hourly employees	($15)	50	60	($45,000)	Weeks/year	Avg. hrs/wk (3 employees)
Equipment	Electronics, office supplies	($400)	12	1	($4,800)	Months/year	
TOTAL					($171,000)		

Taxes

Unless you are running a nonprofit, one expense you won't be able to avoid is income tax. Around a quarter of every dollar earned in the United States will happily be claimed by Uncle Sam.

For-profit businesses must pay taxes on the money they earn. Various legal structures like sole proprietorship, corporation, limited liability company (LLC), or partnership each have unique tax implications. Most musicians begin by running a *sole proprietorship*, or nonincorporated business run by a single person. This is the easiest and cheapest kind of enterprise to operate—essentially just go about your business. Consult an accountant about which format is most advantageous for your venture.

Employed individuals receive a W2 from their employer(s) listing pertinent tax information. If there is no self-employed income to report, filing taxes is straightforward. A 1040EZ (short form) report can be submitted. Things become more arduous with self-employed income. Contractors who have paid more than $600 over the fiscal year must mail you and the government 1099-MISC forms, stating the amount earned and that taxes were not withheld. (If your business hires employees or contractors, keep excellent records so you can send documentation and avoid paying taxes on their stipends.) To maximize deductions, file a 1040 (long form) including a Schedule C for each business. Returns must be reported by April 15 unless an extension is requested. Self-employed individuals are often required to make quarterly estimated tax payments.

Resist the temptation to underreport earnings, which can come back to haunt you if audited by the Internal Revenue Service (IRS). The good news is that business expenses can drastically reduce the amount owed in taxes. Each *deduction* must be "ordinary and necessary" for your line of business, at least as far as the IRS is concerned. Maintain clear records proving the costs claimed, and only write off legitimate business—as opposed to personal—expenses. "Proof" can be in the form of clear record keeping, receipts, credit card statements, or check stubs. Research rules for each deduction category.

If expenses are greater than profits, sole proprietors may actually claim a loss on their taxes. To be considered a business, however, you must show a profit at least three out of every five years. If not, your music is only considered a hobby, and the benefit of deductions is lost.

Tax code is confusing and often illogical. Computer software like TurboTax makes filing more user-friendly, but if you're nervous about what to do or missing deductions, hire an accountant. A good CPA can save you significant money.

The Bottom Line

After all is said and done, how much will you have left over to spend or save? On the front end, project what you think will happen using educated, research-informed guesses. Later, compare forecasts with what actually transpired. Analyze results to determine next steps.

Revenue and Expense Worksheet[2]		
	PROJECTED	ACTUAL
Revenues	$_____	$_____
COGS	($_____)	($_____)
Gross Profit	$_____	$_____
Overhead	($_____)	($_____)
Operating Profit	$_____	$_____
Taxes	($_____)	($_____)
Net Profit	$_____	$_____

[2] Businesses use this structure to document financial performance over a period of time, typically a quarter or year. Known as an *income statement* (or profit and loss statement), it is one of three critical financial documents. The others are a *balance sheet* (showing net worth) and *cash flow statement* (clarifying available cash).

Spending Habits

When people and businesses struggle financially, they often act like revenue is the sole culprit. All of life's tribulations would be solved by bringing in an extra $10K (or whatever). Yet in a world where high-salaried individuals regularly find themselves in debt, earnings tell just one part of the story. *Spending habits often prohibit people from achieving financial dreams.*

Where does the money go? Many people and organizations have little idea. To truly understand your habits, track every penny over several months. Be precise, breaking down large categories into specifics so you can accurately analyze how dollars are spent. With creativity, there are often ways to curb expenses. Consider which line items can be shaved and what is essential. Even small expenses add up quickly.

How important are the things you buy? Be careful not to confuse "needs" with "wants." In fact, people often acquire things they don't even truly want! Have you ever made a purchase—exercise equipment, jewelry, clothing, computer software—only for it to lie around untouched? These squandered, costly acquisitions often result from impulse buying. If you earn $30 per hour after taxes and something costs $300, is this purchase truly worth 10 life hours? If so, forking over hard-earned cash may be worthwhile. Otherwise, save the money. Buying less may even make you happier.

Things often cost more than anticipated. Always factor in a 10% to 30% emergency cushion, just in case. It would be a shame to complete the majority of a project and then be forced to freeze because funding runs dry. Worse yet is plunging into unforeseen debt. If money is left over, on the other hand, the surplus can be applied to future ventures.

Health Care

Medical insurance in the United States is expensive. As a result, many self-employed musicians forego this expense. While the desire to save is understandable, skimping here is not recommended. More than half of all personal bankruptcies result from unpaid medical bills. Unless you live in a sterilized bubble, gambling against an accident or medical problem is extremely risky. A single incident can set you back tens or even hundreds of thousands of dollars.

If you or your partner have a job offering health care benefits, take advantage. In fact, some musicians maintain employment primarily for this reason. Associations such as Chamber Music America, the American Federation of Musicians, and the Music Teachers National Association offer group insurance rates to members. If running a company with at least two employees, you can create your own group plan. Universities offer coverage to current or recent students. "Starving artists" may qualify for public assistance, especially for their kids.

The best scenario is to stay healthy! As musicians, our intensive work can distract from basic human needs like exercising, eating well, and mental wellness. Without health, few things in this book are possible. Take care of yourself!

> ### A Healthy Organization
>
> SMASH is a Seattle-based nonprofit with the mission of keeping musicians healthy. "While we don't provide insurance, we fill in the gaps," explains electric bassist and executive director Denise Burnside. Addressing medical, dental, and mental health concerns, the organization has a network of providers who offer musicians free or very low-cost services. SMASH also helps musicians navigate our complicated health system and utilize insurance or services available through government and other organizations.
>
> A dentist recently donated their clinic for a day, providing free x-rays, exams, cleanings, and even a couple surgeries to a group of 29 musicians. Impacted by another initiative, one member reflected, "The opportunity for free mental health care through SMASH has helped me personally, and made me a better musician. I now have useful tools to calm anxiety without relying on booze or cigarettes." Joining is free, open to all working musicians within covered areas who earn less than certain income thresholds.

THERE'S NO PLACE LIKE HOME (OR IS THERE?)

Where you reside is significant on many levels. It influences neighborhood conditions, commute times, weather, proximity to family, opportunities available, and other variables. Financially, this factor contributes not only to cost of living but also earning capacity.

How important is it to live/work in Manhattan (or another major metropolis)? New York City is one of the world's artistic capitals. Inspiration is never far away. Lined with performance venues, there is considerable musical work, along with communities that value art making. Networking opportunities are abundant. On the flip side, New York provides significant challenges. Expect to pay more for just about everything. Forget about becoming a homeowner. Some jobs compensate with higher wages, but these rarely negate the cost-of-living differential. In fact, thanks to oversupply, payment for work is sometimes less in actual dollars than elsewhere. The end result: Getting ahead financially is difficult.

There are many other places to live: small cities, college towns, suburbs, rural communities. Each locale has unique appeals and drawbacks. No solution is ideal for all. While smaller communities may have a dearth of musical work, savvy musicians might find opportunity creation easier with less competition. They may even become revered as a local superhero. And who knows—with manageable living costs, perhaps you'll have enough spare change to vacation in New York!

> ### Rural Masterpiece
>
> After receiving a *rural residency grant*, DaPonte String Quartet (DSQ) spent four summers in rural Maine. The arts scene was nonexistent at the time, though

it has grown since then. "We probably had something to do with that," reflects violinist Ferdinand Liva. Falling in love with this community, the quartet ultimately made it their permanent home, relocating from Philadelphia.

Each season, DSQ presents three distinct concert programs in five to six locations within a 100-mile radius. When performing at a *meeting house* built in 1780, they showcased works composed that same year. A favorite venue involves a "gem of a hilltop church" in a tiny fishing village. "We've had audience members in the rafters, sitting outside, even cramming during a lightning storm power outage. I guess you could call them *superfans*."

Liva misses having a larger musical ecosystem and notes the hassle of traveling hours for quality instrumental repair. But he loves his hometown of less than 9,000 residents, where it's possible to own a home, have pets, and see the stars. "A second grocery store opens later this year (!). And unlike big cities, my neighborhood doesn't smell bad!"

A Word of Caution About Debt

America—land of the free, baseball, apple pie, country music . . . and debt. Mortgages, business/student loans, and credit card bills infiltrate the fabric of society. Our national motto: "Buy now, pay later." Our philosophy: "You deserve..." Though borrowing may enable purchases not possible any other way, beware the costs. Interest is charged in addition to principal at often alarming rates. While payments are spread instead of stinging all at once, the overall price tag skyrockets.

All debts accrue interest. Rates vary dramatically. Student loans and mortgages usually carry an APR (annual percentage rate) of 3% to 10%, whereas credit card and business loan rates can be staggering, from 8% to 30%+. A $10,000 loan with an interest rate of 20% paid over 36 monthly installments winds up costing $13,378, adding over 30% to the sticker price. The same loan repaid over 5 years skyrockets to a whopping $15,896. Before accepting any loan, consider the likely sum total you will be compelled to pay, including interest. Can you afford it? Is financing truly worth the cost?

Digging Out

Violinist and Suzuki educator Brecklyn Ferrin graduated college with outstanding technique, pedagogical expertise, and $30,000 in student loans. "When starting school, I was just a baby, with little idea how this liability would impact my future."

After getting married, the stifling weight of this debt became apparent. Ferrin made an aggressive, written budget. To boost income, she took on any student at any time for any reason. To diminish spending, all nonessentials were cut—no restaurants or movies! Coupons became a way of life. A long-term house-sitting gig for a traveling neighbor required next to nothing in rent and utilities.

> "I am not a marathoner. Feeling really uneasy for a few years trumped moderate uncomfort over a decade."
>
> Ferrin paid off her debt within 24 months. Then she and her husband threw a party. "People celebrate weddings and babies. This financial achievement also affects the rest of our lives." Within the next few years, the couple purchased a home, followed by a second that generates rental income.

MONEY FORWARD

Planning for the Future

To win the money game, you must save for the future. Suppose four musicians invest in the stock market for retirement. Wolfgang saves $5 a day, beginning at age 25. Claire-Annette waits until 35 but religiously socks away $10 daily. Johann delays until 45 and then invests $20 each 24-hour period. Unfortunately, Amanda-Lynn saves nothing until age 55. To make up for time lost, she shells out a monstrous $50/day. Assuming they all earn an average annual return of 10%, compounded annually, let's compare where things land at age 65.

AGE	WOLFGANG $5 per day $150 per month Amount Invested	Ending Balance	CLAIRE-ANNETTE $10 per day $300 per month Amount Invested	Ending Balance	JOHANN $20 per day $600 per month Amount Invested	Ending Balance	AMANDA-LYNN $50 per day $1,500 per month Amount Invested	Ending Balance
25	1,800	1,896						
26	3,600	3,982						
27	5,400	6,276						
30	9,000	11,576						
35	18,000	30,219	3,600	3,792				
40	27,000	60,243	18,000	23,152				
45	36,000	108,598	36,000	60,437	7,200	7,584		
50	45,000	186,474	54,000	120,486	36,000	46,303		
55	54,000	311,894	72,000	217,196	72,000	120,875	18,000	18,967
60	63,000	513,884	90,000	372,948	108,000	240,974	90,000	115,758
65	72,000	**839,191**	108,000	**623,788**	144,000	**434,392**	180,000	**302,186**

Wolfgang is the big winner. Though he invested the least ($72,000), his nest egg stayed in the market over the longest period, growing to $839,191 by age 65. Amanda-Lynn contributed the most, shelling out 250% more than Wolfgang ($180,000). Yet her ultimate retirement savings was less than half as large ($302,186), with funds growing only during a 10-year window.

These numbers illustrate a few points. First, it demonstrates one of the great principles of economics: *compound interest.* Investments increase exponentially over time, since growth is applied to total holdings (including previously earned interest). The bottom line: Start early, allowing for the snowball effect of compound interest.

This brings us to the second point: *It does not require great fortunes to make investing worthwhile, especially if you are young.* Small, regular savings quickly add up. Musicians "without enough to invest" often spend more than $5 a day on superfluous expenses like coffee, subscription services, or eating out. Can you find ways to consistently save a few bucks? Hopefully this chart provides the inspiration you need!

How Quickly Will Investments Grow?

The cardinal rule is that there is no free lunch: The greater the potential return, the larger the risk. Safe investments, like certificates of deposit (CDs) and bonds, have guaranteed predetermined rates of return. However, their *yield* is low. Stocks, mutual funds, and real estate may earn higher percentages but are precarious. They can also lose money.

Our retirement chart assumes money grows at an annual rate of 10%. That is far from guaranteed. However, if the possibility of losing money through the stock market makes you nervous, consider this: from 1926 to 2024, the average annual return was 10.32%. From 1990 to 1999, it exceeded 18%. On the other hand, in March 2020, the market plummeted 26% in four days. But chances are high that sagging markets eventually recover. While past performance cannot predict the future, the stock market has a long history of growth despite short-term recessions.

Since there is no crystal ball, it is important to evaluate your tolerance for risk, diversify your portfolio, and invest wisely. Stock investing is not an adrenaline rush or spectator sport but a means to achieving a less stressful, financially independent future. Do not obsess about daily fluctuations of the market. Investing for the long haul is a better strategy than micromanaging. The younger you are, the more risk you can afford (but don't be a fool!). As retirement approaches, conventional wisdom suggests shifting into more conservative funds with less potential of a large swing in either direction.

It can be difficult to put aside money when juggling a career, student loans, and living expenses. Many musicians in their 20s and 30s do not even begin thinking about retirement investment, either because they lack financial literacy or believe there isn't enough money to make saving worthwhile. They usually come to regret this oversight. Are you sure you can afford to wait until age 30, 40, or 50? Many experts recommend that, regardless of salary, 10% to 20% be directed toward saving. If that is too much, commit a smaller amount. The important thing is to start early and contribute consistently.

What to Do with Savings

While every individual has unique financial goals, here are basic saving guidelines:

1. **Build a "rainy day" fund.** Maintain a *liquid* (money easily withdrawn without penalty) emergency fund with three to six months of living expenses. This safety net is critical when unexpected expenses arise, a job is lost, or earned income falls short.
2. **Pay down debt.** Get interest-bearing debts under control ASAP. Pay off the highest rates first, then the next highest percentage, and so forth.
3. **Invest.** Many types of retirement, education, and other funds are worthy of consideration. Educate yourself about the pros and cons of various options.

Saving for Retirement

Though money from any source can be used during your golden years, special retirement accounts offer compelling benefits. The catch is that once dollars are stored, they may not be withdrawn without penalty before age 59½.

Roth IRAs (individual retirement accounts) allow income that has already been taxed to grow tax-free. In other words, you are not charged additional tolls on earned interest when money is withdrawn. *Traditional IRAs* and *SEP-IRAs* (for sole proprietors) are the opposite. Invested income is NOT taxed upfront. Instead, taxes are charged only when money is withdrawn during retirement.

If you work as a company employee, see if a *401(k)* or *403(b)* is available. These accounts function like traditional IRAs (invest pretax dollars now, pay taxes upon withdrawal), but with an additional benefit. Employers often make additional contributions, even matching the amount you put in. Take advantage of this free money!

Investing in Your Career

Musicians must determine how much personal capital to invest in their career. Should you self-finance recordings? Buy a $100,000 violin? Pay to enter competitions? Shell out cash for web design? Do your homework and make sound decisions. Good assets eventually produce positive return. Be careful not to get seduced by extravagant projects that suffocate your financial future, however.

"I believe musicians should invest in learning skills that turn their situation around, even when that requires debt," contends pianist and business strategist Fabiana Claure. "I'm an advocate for building businesses and financial self-reliance in ways that create value for others. While this strategy entails risk, successful ventures can eventually be delegated and/or sold as founders earn many multiples of the initial investment while gaining time freedom and making a lasting impact."

Consider directing a percentage of income into a "career fund," just as other currency is filtered into retirement savings. A separate account minimizes the temptation to splurge on indulgences, while providing a clear picture of how much is available. And always remember that while money is important, it isn't everything. Build your plan accordingly.

Chapter 10
Funding Your Dreams

Most musicians have no problem dreaming up inspired undertakings: launching a business, buying equipment, recording an album, hosting a series, studying abroad, commissioning new works. Bringing them to life, however, is another story. These projects require capital. To that end, *philanthropy* offers promise.

Phi·lan·thro·py

Noun: When donors, foundations, corporations, government, or others provide project/program support to impact positive change.

Gifted/granted money does not come free. Writing proposals, cultivating relationships, and "making the ask" are time-consuming endeavors. Once support has been secured, strings are often attached. What happens if just half the necessary resources are secured? Do you take on debt or abort and refund contributions?

Philanthropy is among the most competitive marketplaces. Your proposal battles against hundreds of causes, including those far outside music. Savvy musicians build a solid "case for support" that generates enthusiasm.

PHILANTHROPIC FRAMEWORK

What Will Be Funded?

Every fundraising campaign must have a clearly defined focus, be it to support the entire organization or a specific initiative. Most donors prefer bringing something tangible to life such as an album, commission, video, performance, tour, building, educational initiative, scholarship, social justice programing, or something else concrete.

Restricted dollars can only be spent on predetermined expenditures, specified in the agreement. While *unrestricted* gifts typically generate less enthusiasm, their flexibility makes them highly desirable. In addition to project support, they can be used to subsidize operating costs such rent, utilities, health care, or administrative salaries, as needed.

How Much Do You Need?

A specific, quantifiable fundraising goal must be clarified. "As much as possible" is never acceptable. Some musicians identify the absolute minimum necessary for an initiative to fly. Others cite a high number but are satisfied when lower thresholds are met. It can be helpful to articulate a *stretch goal*. If the initial target were exceeded, what would more funding achieve?

Your fundraising goal may differ depending on whether it is raised for a for-profit or nonprofit. Recall that nonprofits are not required to pay income taxes, meaning 100% of raised funds can directly support the project. For-profit entities are required to pay taxes on this "income."

When Is It Scheduled?

Solidify an official start and end date. Most campaigns span weeks or months, though major drives can last for years. Short bursts of a day or less are also possible. For example, many nonprofits participate in Giving Tuesday, a global celebration of "radical generosity" scheduled each November.[1]

Throughout the duration, prepare to devote hours daily to reaching out, promoting via social media, offering updates, and thanking donors. Also, realize that launch date is not when the hard work begins. Weeks or months of preparation are required to write copy, build alliances, intrigue influencers, identify prospects, secure major gifts, film videos, and prepromote. Schedule campaigns when you (and your team) have ample capacity.

Which Campaign Type?

Many fundraising mechanisms exist, each with pros and cons. When selecting an approach, consider audience, time frame, project needs, and what will be approved/supported by your organization's leadership. Be creative and strategic. Initiatives are rarely funded by a single source. A combination of earned and contributed income is typically in play.

APPROACH	OVERVIEW
Membership drive	Increase the number of subscribers to an organization who receive benefits (e.g., season tickets) in exchange for support.
Annual giving drive	Money raised through these recurring campaigns can be spent as desired, including overhead/operational expenses.
Crowdfunding	Capture support for small- or medium-scale projects from fans and other primarily low-dollar contributors.

---

[1] For more information, visit www.givingtuesday.org/.

In-kind donations	Noncash contributions such as loaned items or gifted food and space. Services like event support may also be donated.
Special events	Planned activities, such as a benefit concert, designed to generate enthusiasm and financial support for an organization or project.
Corporate sponsorships	Financial contribution from a company in exchange for public acknowledgment.
Grants	Competitive awards to support various outcomes or project types, offered by foundations, corporations, trusts, and government agencies. Need not be repaid.
Major gifts	Large contributions given at once or over years. Significant donors often have a project or program named after them.
Planned/legacy giving	Secured future contribution, often after the benefactor passes away. Can include assets like money, real estate, or life insurance.
Equity investment	Raise capital from venture capitalists or angel investors in exchange for a percentage of a for-profit business.
Endowment building	Gifts directed to a large investment fund, where generated interest provides long-term support.
Capital campaign	Often spanning months or years, solicit a large sum of money to fund a major project or initiative.

WHO WILL GIVE?

Corporate foundations, along with ultra-wealthy philanthropists, are an important target for fundraising efforts. Jill Timmons, author of *The Musician's Journey*, claims only half-jokingly: "We are here to drain the 1%, in the name of making the world a better place!" Of course, most such funders and donors are already inundated with requests. To strengthen your proposal or direct "ask," take the time necessary to cultivate a relationship. There is no shortcut.

Also crucial are people you already know. Most individuals have discretionary income, and those who already like you are most prone to help. You may be surprised at how much family, friends, and committed fans will contribute. Don't forget existing customers, aligned organizations, and enthusiastic influencers.

Build a robust database with the names and contact info of potential leads. Organize this by population, since messaging will vary. Create a *VIP list* with the 25 to 100+ people most likely to support your cause. Contact them well in advance, explaining their importance while requesting an early boost.

12 Fundraising Missteps

Beware of common mistakes.

1. **Making it all about the money.** Philanthropy is first and foremost about relationships. *Fundraising is friendraising.*
2. **Assuming a good cause is enough.** Compelling rationales are essential, yet more is necessary. To attract support, you must earn it.
3. **Not asking.** Donors won't give magically, even if they love the vision. When you need support, make the request unapologetically.
4. **Appearing desperate.** Avoid dire messages like "Please help, we are in trouble!" People want to support winners. Fundraise with bold ambition, projecting vision for the long run.
5. **No deadlines.** Urgency motivates. Too long means people wait and forget.
6. **Not cultivating connection.** Avoid solicitation during an initial encounter, just as you wouldn't propose marriage on a first date. Building relationships takes time.
7. **Failure to secure large gifts first.** Supporters of any level favor campaigns with momentum. Before launching, secure some major donations, to be posted early on.
8. **Requesting the wrong amount.** Asking for too much scares. Soliciting too little—$100 from someone who might give $10,000—squanders. Know your audience and propose appropriately. When suggesting a range, optimize low and high numbers.
9. **Telling the wrong story.** There are many ways to frame any initiative. Not all are equally effective. Find a buzzworthy angle that connects emotionally.
10. **Using the wrong platform.** Grants, crowdsourcing, annual giving, and membership drives make sense for different projects/audiences. Be strategic.
11. **Lacking gratitude.** Nobody owes you anything. Thank people through direct communication and public acknowledgment.
12. **Disappearing until you need more.** Perhaps the worst move is accepting support, going into seeming hibernation, and showing up only with the next fundraiser. Keep supporters engaged and updated, growing bonds over time.

DONOR CAMPAIGNS

Musicians often experience wobbly knees around the notion of donor fundraising. Requesting support somehow feels selfish, even terrifying. Is "begging" truly necessary? The short answer is probably yes. Earned income alone is not enough to facilitate many worthwhile endeavors. Remember that you are effecting positive change through art and philanthropy. Furthermore, the best initiatives offer a win-win-win, providing value to beneficiaries, you/your organization, and the donor. What drives people to offer support? In a sense, the psychology behind philanthropy is similar to any nonessential "purchase"—contributors feel their existence will somehow be enhanced. While gifts to nonprofits are tax deductible, there are many other rationales for charitable giving.

Solicitations for general support can be shared via direct mail, email, or social media. Personalized communications yield significantly better results than mass distribution (e.g., "Dear Toby" vs. "Dear Friend"). Regardless of platform, provide a brief project pitch. Convey enthusiasm and proudly request support. Always point to a webpage or resource with more information. Make giving easy.

The most effective way to solicit large gifts is in person. Phone/video calls also activate friends and geographically distant colleagues. Use initial conversations to plant seeds rather than making an "ask." Establish a relationship, build rapport, and consider how to best align their passions with your needs. By the time a major request is made, patrons should be hooked and anticipate the move. Another technique involves foregoing the donation inquiry altogether. Instead, see if contacts have suggestions. *Asking for advice often triggers contributions, and vice versa.* People want to feel like they're part of the solution.

Politely accept contributions of any amount. Even small donations make a world of difference. Never haggle, and expect rejection. Thank contributors for their generosity, and stay in touch. Give people unwilling or unable to donate an out, without resorting to high-pressure tactics. Don't take rejection personally. Instead, express appreciation for the time spent. In fact, "no" today often becomes "yes" tomorrow.

> ### Smart Stewardship
>
> In just three years, pianist and executive director John Holloway nearly tripled the budget of the Seattle Chamber Music Society (SCMS). Remarkably, none of his 10 employees have fundraising backgrounds. "Large organizations traditionally employ a development team. But without their hand in the product, folks are driven by dollar amounts rather than first-hand visioning."
>
> In great contrast, every SCMS team member—including the administrative assistant—is responsible for building relationships with a portfolio of around 20 prospects. Ten soft touches (text, email, phone call) and one hard touch (lunch, meeting) are expected annually with each contact. Employees and donors are matched largely on extramusical interests. For example, the branding director is often paired with those sharing his passion for golf. At staff meetings focused on initiatives such as building a 40-foot violin to top Seattle's Space Needle (a real project), they consider which contacts might be good candidates to champion the cause.
>
> Though donor cultivation is essential, it is only the beginning. "The most important thing is to stay connected AFTER a gift is made."

Annual Giving

Typically scheduled the same period each year, annual giving campaigns are cornerstones for many organizations. Generating consistent, predictable funding with few restrictions, contributions may be directed as needed: maintaining traditions, expanding programming, even supporting general operations. Additionally, this activity plays a role in strengthening donor relationships as you move further down the path toward larger/major gifts.

When crafting a giving letter, integrate masterful storytelling. Determine angles likely to intrigue. Without falling into the weeds, introduce the problem you solve, your BIG idea, WOWables, and quantifiable evidence demonstrating success. Clarify the fundraising goal, what this money will achieve, the size (or range) of each ask, and giving instructions. Communications may benefit from a *but wait there's more* add-on (P.S.) following the signature.

Shorter is usually better. A paragraph to a page is plenty. For video and spoken communications, one to two minutes suffices. Use friendly, personable language and make every word count. If a paragraph, clause, or expression doesn't strengthen your case, take it out.

Supporters want assurance that fundraising targets are attainable. If progress has been made, highlight this momentum. *We've already reached 30% of our goal!* Showing the impact of giving also motivates: *Every $50 provides a guitar for underprivileged youth!* Some donors prefer choosing where dollars are directed, rather than adding to a generic pot.

> **Help Us Transform and Uplift**
>
> Play On Philly (POP), a tuition-free after-school program offering daily music instruction to underserved students, aims to uplift participants by cultivating musical excellence, confidence, and life skills. To support this meaningful work, trumpeter and founder Stanford Thompson raised $23 million over a 13-year period. His annual giving campaigns focus on positive storytelling: "Though our students may not have much money, we consider them rich with so much high-quality music education in their lives."
>
> One letter, written by "A Proud Parent," featured attractive graphic design and several photos of her daughter. An excerpted passage includes:
>
> *"When Zakyya was a little girl, she was quiet, shy, and rarely interacted outside the family. I enrolled her in Play On Philly knowing that children exposed to music fare better in other areas of life, including mentally and emotionally.... Because of POP's support, she has a quality instrument, experiences master classes, meets incredible performers, and has flown across the country to music festivals. My daughter now wants to travel the world as the first African American woman to become principal clarinetist of a major orchestra."*

CROWDFUNDING

No longer is it necessary to win the grant lottery or secure ultrarich patrons. *Crowdfunding* invites fans who already care about your vision/cause/success to offer financial assistance. Interestingly, some people eagerly support the creation of art even if they would never pay for the thing itself.

Crowdfunding offers numerous advantages. You control everything: dates, costs, vision. No ownership is relinquished. The process helps gauge demand, test ideas, and market/presell products. Better yet, backers become active members of your "tribe." If not enough gets raised, nothing is lost but time and pride. On the flip side, crowdfunding can be stressful. You must constantly self-promote, drumming up interest for days on end, and there is no guarantee it will work. According to Kickstarter, the largest crowdfunding platform for creative projects, over 60% of campaigns fall short of their stated goal. Ten percent fail to attract a single pledge.

Though it is possible to crowdfund from your own website, musicians typically opt for trusted, dedicated platforms that make projects discoverable. Each site maintains unique rules and costs (typically 4% to 12% of contributions, plus transaction fees around 3%). Websites like Kickstarter are *all or nothing*—pledges get refunded unless the stated goal is reached. Minimizing risk, "this ensures creators have enough money to do what they promised.... This also assures backers they're only funding creative ideas set to succeed."[2] Other sites, like GoFundMe, bank

---

[2] https://updates.kickstarter.com/why-is-funding-all-or-nothing/#:~:text=By%20not%20releasing%20funds%20unless,that%20are%20set%20to%20succeed.

donations regardless of outcome. Conduct careful research when determining which approach makes sense for you.

Crowdfunding pages include:

1. **Title/overview/image.** Displayed alongside competing projects, the title, one-sentence overview, and primary image should immediately grab attention.
2. **Time frame.** Campaigns of 30 days or less tend to be most successful, thanks to their urgency. Two months is a typical maximum.
3. **Funding goal.** The minimum amount to be raised, though more is possible. Most sites do not permit this number to change once a campaign launches.
4. **Pitch.** Can be one paragraph or go into depth. Be compelling!
5. **Video.** As a rule, projects spotlighting a short, relevant video (typically 30 seconds to 3 minutes) do better than those without one.
6. **Rewards.** Most platforms allow incentive packages for different support levels. Be sure to include low, medium, and high options (e.g., $20, $35, $50, $100, $250, $500, $1,000, and $3,000), ideally five to eight tiers. While digital rewards like exclusive online content or prerelease recordings don't require additional spending on your part, physical gifts reduce the ultimate amount netted. (Think of them as COGS.) Reward items are limited only by your imagination: autographed paraphernalia, VIP tickets, private house concerts, books, handwritten postcards, flash drives filled with playlists, composition dedications, etc.

The website Patreon offers a different crowdfunding model. Backers pledge a certain amount per month or "thing" (recording, video, song, etc.). Attracting support here can secure predictable income over time.

Our Fans Did This!

Hoping to make an album featuring Great American Songbook classics, trumpeter/vocalist Joe Gransden and his 16-piece big band decided to crowdfund. Their Kickstarter was so successful—generating $40,000 from 173 backers—that there was enough to record *two* albums and hire a string section!

"I thought investing a little money upfront would give us an advantage over other projects." Creating a professional-looking video was a priority, complete with script, makeup, and an experienced film team. They also shot short endorsements from band members and fans, to be circulated via social media. These aspects, along with carefully crafted text, helped earn the distinction of a Kickstarter Project We Love, which in turn increased visibility.

Thirteen pledge levels, from $20 to $10,000, included rewards like digital downloads, signed CDs, backstage passes, album credits, recording session attendance, or even choosing a tune that would be arranged and recorded (one supporter did this for $5,000). "Shipping out the right sized t-shirt with each package was insane. But having so many people support this art convinced me that big band music is alive and well!"

SPECIAL EVENTS

What better way to raise money for a music venture than a black-tie benefit, cabaret night, house concert, or other captivating experience? In-person events strengthen bonds with current/prospective donors/sponsors while sharing your art and vision in carefully curated ways. Use the engagement to mobilize board members, expand reach, and generate media coverage.

This fundraising category is more expensive than others, often significantly. It requires a great deal of marketing and logistical planning. There may be little left over after paying for venue rental, food, drinks, decorations, and entertainment, even when charging a hefty fee. To make it worthwhile, at least 50% of revenues should be banked. Beyond ticket sales, live/silent auctions, raffles, and donation boxes increase the amount generated.

An Amazing Benefit

Intonation Music (IM) provides a collection of instruments and engaging rock band training to schools, parks, and community centers lacking music programs. "I was subjected to the traditional, boring way of instrument learning, and quit," reflects executive director Tonya Howell. "In this program, our students play songs they love, by ear, regularly rotating instruments. And they stick with it!" The cost to run each program is $18,000 annually, but partners can typically only afford $3,000. Fundraising must make up the difference.

Each spring, IM throws a gala featuring a youth band (grades 3 to 8), teen band (high school), instructor band, and DJ. The 250 attendees also enjoy food, open bar, and silent/paddle auctions for unique donated items (autographed guitar, Airbnb by a music museum, etc.). Guests may purchase tables for $3,000 to $10,000 (depending on perks) or individual tickets at $250 apiece. Last year, hosting the celebration cost $75,000 (COGS). They raised $320,000.

Smaller fundraising affairs also help. Music trivia nights generate a few thousand dollars. December Student Showcase pays for itself with suggested-donation tickets. A Halloween tradition features musician board members who choose a favorite band, dress in costume, and play cover tunes for an evening. "Folks look forward to that all year."

Sponsorships

Corporations support musical artists and products in exchange for public acknowledgment. Doing so amplifies their brand awareness and positively impacts customer perceptions. Generally charged to a company's marketing budget, sponsorships may account for 1% to 5%+ of net profits. Musical instrument, accessory, and technology companies often lend or gift products to artists with followings in exchange for public shoutouts.

> ### Reciprocity
>
> Clarinetist Nick Brown discovered a gap. The local orchestra scene is robust nine months each year but shuts down during summers, leaving musicians/audiences with less work/culture. Viewing this as an opportunity, he founded the Boston Festival Orchestra.
>
> To fund programming, an expensive proposition, Brown sought sponsorships in exchange for reciprocal benefits. One event, underwritten by a children's hospital, was live-streamed to thousands of patients through an internal TV network. A museum provided financial support and their beautiful venue (in kind) as a means to expand their own subscription base, since both organizations target families and young professionals. Additional support came from businesses like an assisted living facility and a university.
>
> Individuals can also sponsor section players ($1,000), principals ($2,500), soloists ($5,000), or the conductor ($10,000). This is more than transactional, as musicians and their benefactors are encouraged to build relationships.

In-Kind Donations

Noncash, *in-kind* contributions include free housing, rehearsal space, transportation, frequent flyer miles, reception catering, instrument usage, or services such as printing, marketing, legal, and accounting. Volunteer hours also fall into this category.[3] Graciously accept these expense-alleviating gifts. Beyond the great feeling that accompanies helping others, contributors to nonprofits are entitled to a tax write-off. When drafting your budget, include the equivalent amount for in-kind donations.

Grants

It is no wonder so many artists and organizations pursue grants. Beyond providing capital that mustn't be repaid, some sources give repeatedly to appealing projects

---

[3] According to Points of Light, an international nonprofit, one volunteer hour in 2024 equates to an in-kind contribution of $31.80.

(though many require a specific period to pass before reapplication is permitted). Unlike competitions that select a single winner, most grants are awarded to multiple recipients. The downsides are that it requires time-consuming, advanced planning (sometimes a year or more), and funding is by no means guaranteed. Most grants limit what may be supported, disallowing organizational overhead or work outside regions served by the funder.

Navigating the Maze

Grants are awarded by universities, foundations, religious institutions, musical societies, arts councils, corporations, private endowments, and government agencies. They range from a few hundred dollars to $100,000+. Organizations engage in this philanthropic tradition to fulfill some aspect of their mission. The goal can be fostering art for art's sake, but there are often more specific agendas. Some awards are open to anyone, while others back only members of a particular region, race, ethnicity, religion, age, profession, etc. There are grants that support:

1. Career fellowships
2. Collaboration (often interdisciplinary)
3. Commissioning
4. Community engagement programs
5. Copy work
6. Educational programs
7. Finishing a project
8. Hosting a concert series/festival
9. Physical spaces
10. Recording
11. Research
12. Residencies
13. Social causes
14. Studying domestically/abroad
15. Touring
16. Unique projects
17. Video production
18. Working abroad
19. Writing about music

The majority of grants are earmarked for nonprofits. If you don't carry this designation, however, there may still be ways to qualify. One possibility involves joining forces. For example, a composer may apply in conjunction with a nonprofit ensemble. Another is working with a *fiscal sponsor* such as Fractured Atlas. These umbrella nonprofits collaborate with musicians in exchange for a percentage of acquired funds, typically 2% to 7%.

Some awards are available to individual applicants, though amounts tend to be lower, typically $500 to $10,000. *Internal grants* are open only to an organization's employees/members (universities, churches, etc.). *External grants* support those without prior relationship to the funding institution, preventing bias and ensuring fairness.

The neighborhood library is a great starting point for researching opportunities. Several annual directories detail grant programs, requirements, amounts, deadlines, and contact info. Local, regional, and state arts councils often maintain funding lists, as do artist organizations such as the American Composers Forum. Read musician bios to learn what colleagues have secured.

Apply for multiple grants when possible, since winning a particular award is rarely assured and few are intended to single-handedly finance a project. Consider various ways to position your project, targeting even programs that haven't previously supported music. For example, a touring program of Latin American sacred music might prove compelling for grants geared toward music, arts, touring, Latin American culture, education, and religious causes. It is sometimes advantageous to alter a project's design to align with grant requirements. However, never make a "false sale" by fudging the facts. Dishonesty burns bridges with the granting institution and word has a way of traveling.

And the Winner Is . . .

- Native American composer Elisa Harkins won an Interchange grant for the Teach Me a Song project, allowing her to travel to Canada and record Indigenous performers, to be interpreted through video, sculpture, photography, and sheet music.
- The Aaron Copland Fund helped subsidize a recording of *Zero Grasses: Ritual for the Losses*, an extended theatrical work composed by and featuring Jen Shyu, who sings, dances, and plays violin, piano, Chinese erhu, Japanese biwa, Korean gayageum, Taiwanese moon lute, and percussion.
- Periapsis Music and Dance received grants from New Music USA and the O'Donnell-Green Music and Dance Foundation to support *Unbeknownst*, a 16-minute work for four dancers, viola, and piano.
- The National Endowment for the Arts awarded a grant to Music for All Seasons, supporting a therapeutic music program that impacts at-risk children living in shelters for victims of domestic violence, focused on education and healing.
- Lakeland Cultural Arts Center received a multiyear, matching grant from Levitt Foundation, intended to foster economic growth and inclusivity through a concert series held in a rural, once-segregated high school.

COMPILING SUBMISSIONS

When applying for grants, follow instructions verbatim. Commonly requested items include a submission form, abstract (short summary), project proposal, resume/CV, work samples, budget, agreement letter from collaborators, and references. While all are important, none hold as much weight as the proposal, which describes a project's structure and its applicant's qualifications. Address *every* requested point. Place important information early on to ensure it gets noticed. Focus on an initiative's value—rather than simply how you will be benefited—clearly articulating evidence-based *outcomes*. For example, you might propose that

80% of participants will demonstrate increased music proficiency before the grant period concludes.

Recognize that grant committees often include members who are not specialists in your field. In fact, many have just one music representative, or zero. Assume nothing. Avoid technical jargon. Explain the significance of each claim, supporting arguments with specifics. Having won the planet's most prestigious harmonica accolade may be mind-blowing to those in the know, but simply naming this achievement has little resonance with an architect or lawyer.

Another crucial element is the budget, clarifying why money is needed and how it will be spent. Build spreadsheets with well-constructed, realistic projections. Include line items for all important expense categories, noting equivalent values for in-kind contributions. Revenues may combine earned income, donations, grants, and in-kind gifts. Clarify which additional funding is confirmed or likely. *Note that expenses and revenues must be equal.* Suppose you want to offer afternoon group lessons to an underserved middle school.

EXPENSES	JUSTIFICATION	AMOUNT	
Staff	$80/class × 5 classes/week × 24 weeks/year	$9,600	
Materials	Music, books, snacks, games	$1,000	
Space	Classroom usage: $20/hour × 5 hours/week × 24 weeks	$2,400	
Travel	Instructor travel support	$750	
TOTAL PROGRAM EXPENSES		**$13,750**	
REVENUES	FUNDING SOURCE	AMOUNT	SECURED?
Contributed	XYZ school (classroom usage, in kind)	$2,400	Y
Contributed	XYZ school parents (snacks, in kind)	$500	Y
Contributed	Band boosters donation	$2,000	Y
Fundraiser	Bake sale (run by students)	$1,000	N
Grant	Local arts council	$2,500	Y
Grant	ABC Foundation	$5,350	N
TOTAL REVENUE		**$13,750**	($6,350) still needed

Accurate financial projections are as important to the applicant as the evaluator. An all-too-common scenario involves entities being awarded, say, $10,000 to complete a vision requiring twice that amount. Do you claim the capital and assume debt or jump ship and decline the honor?

Before submitting, proorfead (see what I did there?). Run proposals by trusted colleagues or past winners. Someone within the organization may be willing to answer questions or provide feedback. Most do all they can to ensure strong proposals. If suggestions are offered, follow them! Make the decision easy for jurors.

Granting Advice

Grants are paramount to Musaics of the Bay, an arts series that facilitates "radically inclusive" experiences involving composers, performers, and visual artists. City, county, state, federal, and foundation awards ranging from $2,000 to $30,000 help support 20 projects per year, from standalone showcases to week-long residencies. "Being relatively young, our first task is convincing jurors we are serious, high impact, and here to stay," explains artistic director Audrey Vardanega.

Crafting proposals takes time. Large grants may have 15 to 20 "meaty" questions, each requiring 500 words. While language can be recycled from other proposals, it is important to customize and align with each granting body's mission. "It is challenging to translate artistic interactions into words alone. I work slowly in short bursts, allowing ideas to marinate." Drafts are run by board members, who look for grammatical errors and missing elements.

Rejection is a familiar character. Just 20% to 25% of proposals are greenlighted. Some take three cycles to lock in, or are never funded. But Vardanega doesn't get discouraged. "There are also pleasant surprises. Some seemingly out-of-our-league awards have come through. What a morale boost!"

Selection Process

Adjudicating panels—made up of past award winners, experts in the field, and employees of the grant-giving institution—want to identify outstanding projects aligned with their program's goals. While there may not be enough money to aid every worthwhile proposal, assume judges are looking for those most likely to make a difference. Each juror reviews every application. With large pools, projects may be divided among "lead readers" responsible for taking a deeper dive and guiding discussion. The process involves several rounds, each narrowing the field.

Review committees do not begin by looking for winners. Rather, they search for red flags justifying elimination. One misstep gets a file purged. Late or incomplete proposals are disqualified, as are those that are ineligible (e.g., submitted from the wrong region or age group). Judges do not look favorably at documents with poor writing or sloppy presentation, assuming that messy proposals suggest poor workmanship. Jurors then rank remaining files in order of merit, with rubrics that consider:

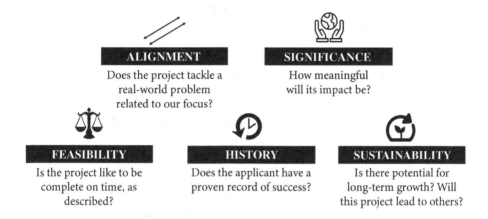

ALIGNMENT
Does the project tackle a real-world problem related to our focus?

SIGNIFICANCE
How meaningful will its impact be?

FEASIBILITY
Is the project like to be complete on time, as described?

HISTORY
Does the applicant have a proven record of success?

SUSTAINABILITY
Is there potential for long-term growth? Will this project lead to others?

Many grants do NOT go to the most qualified applicant. Instead, those with clear, well-crafted materials are favored. However, if you receive many denials, it may indicate fundamental problems. Either the project is a weak fit for available sources or documents are poorly framed. Solicit feedback and apply lessons to future projects.

After receiving a grant, follow through with requirements. If not, the organization will blacklist you from future awards and may circulate your lack of compliance to others. Many programs require a report after the initiative has been completed. Be sure your account is high quality and submitted on time.

Judging Points

Maurine Knighton, chief program officer at the Doris Duke Foundation, has served on countless grant panels. Regularly devoting two to three hours to evaluate a single application, she takes this role seriously. Beyond clarity around each project's *raison d'être*—why it matters—the evaluation process weighs initiative details, track record of success, program alignment, and feasibility. (Are referenced gigs/supplemental funding streams secured, or at least likely?) "Preparation matters. Typically, a small set of submissions far exceed the minimum requirements, introducing meaningful, innovative solutions. That gets me excited!"

Sensitive to an applicant's background, Knighton is careful not to penalize nonnative English speakers for minor grammatical errors or independent

> artists without a professional grant-writing team. That said, inconsistencies or numbers that don't add up are warning signs.
>
> Knighton advocates for granting agencies to loosen restrictions by offering more *unrestricted* support (to be spent on anything, as needed). "Many programs only cover public-facing activities, a narrow slice of what's required. Rather than dragging artists down with hidden costs, funders should pave the path for getting ahead."

Raising Money in Difficult Times

The challenge of fundraising becomes more acute during troublesome financial times. Yet even then, there is potential for projects offering true value. In fact, economic downturns provide a unique opportunity. As society reexamines its priorities, music offers unique potential to build hope, community, and joy.

Consider the question from another perspective. "Vanity projects" that fail to solve compelling real-world problems will have a tricky time securing funding during even moments of prosperity. And despite economic downturns, funding for highly relevant projects is almost always attainable.

Chapter 11
A Life in Music

Some people thrive when it comes to imagination. As ideation wizards, they work with seeming magic, inventing opportunities out of thin air. Starting is a cinch—both motivating and pleasurable—and early momentum comes naturally. But for any host of reasons, things ultimately break down. Thanks to procrastination, inefficiency, boredom, distraction, team dysfunction, strategic blunders, or other disorders, these folks struggle to deliver.

In my experience, there are two types of people and organizations. Which describes you?

1. Those who get things done
2. Those who don't

What's the key to productivity? We've talked a lot about entrepreneurship, but this puzzle demands something else. Savvy musicians require discipline, strategy, and careful management.

TIME MANAGEMENT

Practice those scales. Work on sight reading. Draft a grant proposal. Ignite a passion project. Be a good friend. Go to concerts. Take kids to the ballgame. Leave a legacy. Build a brand. Develop a website. Improve tone. Read blogs. Rewrite bio. Pay bills. Meet spouse. Market. Teach. Study. Network. Sleep. Think. Eat. Compose. Gig.

AAAAAARRRRRGGGGGGHHHHH!!!!!!!!!!!!!! Who has time for all this stuff? By their very nature, musicians regularly have too much on their plates, with a steady eruption of projects in the pipeline. Finding enough time can be tough. As a result, some people make little forward progress day after day, year after year, despite what feels like habitually frantic busyness.

I am an innovator to the core, yet cannot figure out how to pack more than 24 hours into a day. Each week contains just 168 hours. After subtracting 6 to 8 per night for sleep, just 112 to 126 remain. That is the time we have to work, eat, play, and experience life's glorious adventures.

Time is paradoxical: *There is never enough, but there is always enough to do what is most important.* Don't waste precious minutes complaining about how overworked you are. Instead, make a plan, focus, and take action. There is a path to completing life's essential work. Time management can be improved with commitment and strategy. Reaching personal, professional, financial, and artistic goals may not even require longer hours. It does, however, demand working smarter. Time is life's most precious resource. Use it wisely!

Write It Down

Study after study shows that people who keep written to-do lists have exponentially greater chances of getting things done than those who simply store items in their head. Whether using paper, a smartphone, or a tablet, keep this checklist accessible, ensuring items aren't forgotten or ignored. Rather than compiling an endless list of competing activities, prioritize. Use numbers to show what must be addressed first, second, and so on. Cross off entries as they are completed. A great sense of accomplishment accompanies this ritual.

Urgent versus Important

One of my favorite tools is Stephen Covey's "time management matrix," first introduced in his classic book *The 7 Habits of Highly Effective People*. To take advantage, compare the meaning behind two terms.

IMPORTANT
Activities helping achieve meaningful life goals

URGENT
Items demanding immediate attention

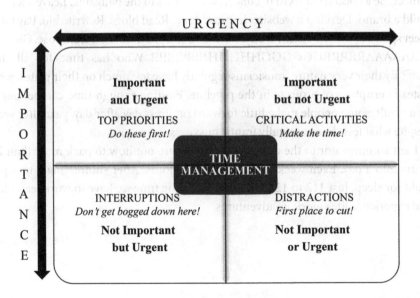

Important and urgent TOP PRIORITIES such as scheduled lessons, gigs, or editing a recording project under label contract are likely to get done because you care about these things and the clock is ticking.

In the opposite quadrant are *not important or urgent* DISTRACTIONS like social media addictions, video games, long coffee breaks, British mini-series, or conversations about the weather. Though everybody needs mindless breaks on occasion, these items squander valuable minutes while providing little in return.

Recall a frantic day of errands when, despite constant activity, nothing significant is accomplished. The pressing nature of *not important but urgent* INTERRUPTIONS—irrelevant homework, laundry, knocks at the door, day jobs, working on taxes, unforeseen "emergencies"—convinces you to drop all else. Though they do not unlock life's dreams, there are often negative consequences for failing to complete such tasks on time.

Often sacrificed are *important but not urgent* CRITICAL ACTIVITIES: passion projects, life aspirations, health concerns, marketing, networking, entrepreneurial visioning, finally completing your method book that will change the world. Despite their role in advancing long-term success, a lack of pressing deadlines results with inaction.

So what's the secret to success? Almost everyone completes TOP PRIORITIES. Eliminate DISTRACTIONS when you're in a crunch. The real trick comes with balancing the remaining two fields. Folks overwhelmed with INTERRUPTIONS find little time for important, nonurgent projects. Highly effective people, on the other hand, are intentional about reserving time every day for CRITICAL ACTIVITIES, tackling these before the urgent takes over. In fact, by assigning deadlines to these items, they can be transformed into TOP PRIORITIES.

Work Forward

How long does it take to get something done? is a question I've posed to many groups. The most common response: "Depends what you have to do!" In the vast majority of cases, however, my experience has shown otherwise. For most people, it takes exactly the same amount of time to complete just about any task: *as long as you've got*. If it's due next Monday, the final touches are added the night before. The same holds true whether deadlines are a week, month, quarter, or year in the future. The possible exception to this rule is when something has, say, a three- or five-year target date. This project is unlikely to ever get done. *Not enough urgency.*

Most people work backward. Procrastination is the ritual, evading even the hint of a "start" until impending deadlines rear their ugly, impatient faces. By that point, stress runs high as you shoot for an 11th-hour finish. It may require an all-nighter. When last-minute emergencies arise, the assignment must be late.

Try another approach. Work forward. Begin as soon as time permits. When you have a spare moment, bank progress or cross something off your list rather than pitching it down the road. Consider submission dates as adversaries, doing all in your power to beat them mercilessly with time to spare. Heck, make it into a game.

Schedule Your Schedule

The best time managers meticulously reserve time for important activities: product design, marketing, logistics, planning, practicing, eating, errands, family, socializing, to-do list items, even downtime. Investing a half hour at the beginning of each week to strategize a detailed calendar clarifies priorities and increases the likelihood that important, nonurgent tasks aren't lost in the shuffle. If you want to get more done, determine how and when.

This approach only works when matched with commitment. Don't allow yourself to procrastinate or get distracted—start and end on time. Working within constraints, rather than drowning in a single activity for hours, boosts productivity. If an emergency demands attention, rework your calendar, ensuring that important projects aren't shortchanged.

Human beings respond well to routines. When possible, slate comparable tasks at consistent times. Whether your best practicing is done before sunrise or after midnight, block out congruent windows. Conversely, negative habits wreak havoc. Throwing an hour away on video games or hyperbolic tabloids one Thursday afternoon won't cause much harm. But as that phenomenon becomes ritualized, wasted time is etched into your existence.

PROJECT MANAGEMENT

Though disciplined time management matters, *project management* may be more important. Which projects should you tackle in the first place? What does it take to see things through?

Projecting and Reflecting

The world is full of opportunity. Just about any puzzle can be solved with enough creativity and grit. If a vision is truly meaningful, there are often multiple solutions for getting it done. Successful entrepreneurs begin with a destination in mind. Setting the compass helps plot the course even if journeying involves radically unexpected turns. Block off one day each year to identify three to five priorities in the following categories, mixing grand fantasies with a sense of realism. Over time, your list is likely to expand and transform. That's OK, even encouraged!

1. **Short-term goals.** Within 12 months.
2. **Medium-term goals.** 1 to 3 years.
3. **Long-term goals.** 3 to 10+ years.

> **Mapping the Future**
>
> At age 25, bassist and aspiring orchestral musician Jason Heath mapped his short-, medium-, and long-term goals on a yellow legal pad:
>
> - **6 Months:** Apply for all openings; Make binder; Plan preparation schedule and do it.
> - **1 Year (by age 26):** Salaried orchestral position.
> - **3 Years (by age 28):** Have a good salaried position ($40,000+).
> - **5 Years (by age 30):** Member of top 5 orchestra; Teach at local university.
> - **10 Years (by age 35):** Principal bass, Chicago Symphony; Teach at Northwestern University; Own a house in Evanston.
>
> Unfortunately, life had other plans. Ten years later, zero of these goals had materialized. (OK, he did make several binders.) Audition after audition ended in rejection, a story depicted in his autobiographical account *Road Warrior without an Expense Account*. Realizing that just three options existed—(1) continue failing, (2) drop out of music, (3) redefine "success"—he opted for the latter.
>
> Following another decade, Heath has built a prosperous career. About a third of his income comes from entrepreneurial bass-related pursuits: podcasting (3.4 million downloads to date), online courses, sponsorships, a digital product store. "It turns out, the double bass is a really good niche." Another third is part-time salaried work as an orchestral strings product specialist. Interestingly, the final third involves subbing with the San Francisco Symphony, an unexpected surprise his 25-year-old self would have coveted. "It only happened after I gave up the dream!"
>
> Today, Heath's goal list is less specific and quite ambitious. His top "big, hairy goal" involves designing a life model that is fun and fulfilling. A few other items on the list:
>
> - **6 Months:** Grow YouTube subscribers to 25,000 (currently 18,000, a stretch goal).
> - **1 Year:** Increase workout abilities by 20% (health is critical to all else).
> - **5 Years:** Present at least two solo recitals per year, featuring newly learned rep.
> - **10 Years:** Amplify bass-related enterprises by 10× in size, scope, and profit.

In addition to futurecasting, take a look in the rearview mirror. What were your most meaningful past achievements over the short, medium, and long term? Recall the extraordinary road already taken. Celebrate victories along the way.

Choosing the Right Puzzle

Savvy musicians often find themselves drowning in an ocean of opportunity. Far too many projects vie for attention. You can't do them all. Which should win the day?

In theory, it seems obvious. If Project A would benefit you/the world 50 notches (whatever that means), and Project B offers just 20, the former should be prioritized. But people regularly make the opposite choice. College students obsess over class grades yet never build an entrepreneurial venture to propel their career. Independent teachers schedule 30 lessons per week at the expense of filming an eCourse that could enroll 1,000 eager learners, generating passive income for decades. Scholars write esoteric articles read by few rather than hyperrelevant books to launch in-demand public speaking careers.

On the flip side, squeeze maximum benefit out of each project pursued. Many performers spend months perfecting a program, only to share it once and start over. What if instead 20 repetitions were booked? Or you turn it into an album? Or write and sell related curriculum? With imagination, there are plenty of ways to amplify impact.

One common challenge within portfolio careers is that projects don't align. Each gig, initiative, or pursuit competes for attention. It may be necessary to play, compose, teach, record, and write. But are there ways each activity might propel others, rather than diluting the composite effect?

Pivot or Persevere?

At some point, you will hit a wall. Your partner bails. The venue gets flooded. A dream gig turns you down. The question at that moment is whether to *pivot or persevere*. Do you pursue a new direction or double down on the current strategy?

When encountering obstacles, lean into your entrepreneurial spirit. Innovate solutions even better than the original. Take COVID-19, which caused music opportunities worldwide to evaporate overnight. Most practitioners faltered or even suffered paralysis. But a small percentage leaned into the moment, including many featured in this book. They tried something new, developed fresh skills, changed the business model. It took an international pandemic to help identify big, new success! *Let no crisis go to waste.*

Savvy musicians are nice, generous people with a sincere desire to support others. Unfortunately, there are not enough hours in the day to pursue every worthwhile endeavor. Without becoming a Scrooge, learn the difficult but crucial art of saying "no" to distractions. Just as importantly, be open to "yes" when confronting treasure. Too many people get these scenarios backward.

Mapping the Process

Beginning an ambitious project feels like hiking Mount Everest. You are standing at base camp as this awesome natural spectacle towers over you. The distance ahead is great. So many things can go wrong. Success feels impossible. It is no wonder so many head home before taking the first step.

While it is impossible to accurately predict the ins and outs of any journey, it would be foolish to launch without a strategy. One fundamental trick to productivity involves breaking down large goals into smaller ones. Here is a process that can help. Identify up to three major buckets of activity where attention must be focused. (Larger amounts are possible, though it quickly overwhelms when too many top-level objectives compete.) Write each on a different-colored sticky note. When launching a venture, perhaps your priorities are:

Divide each top-level point into smaller second-level "bullets." *Indicate just one standalone task per Post-it*, and stick with the corresponding color for each category. More bite-sized goals are preferable to fewer overwhelming ones. Perhaps erecting a WEBSITE requires:

Next, break out a calendar to schedule deadlines. One visual approach utilizes a poster board, flip chart, or white board. Divide into months, then weeks, and days if desired. Clearly mark off-limit periods (going out of town, holidays, etc.). Then adhere Post-its to indicate self-imposed due dates. The flexibility of stickies allows you to experiment with various arrangements. Always front-load deadlines and leave buffers since emergencies inevitably arise, causing things to take longer than anticipated.

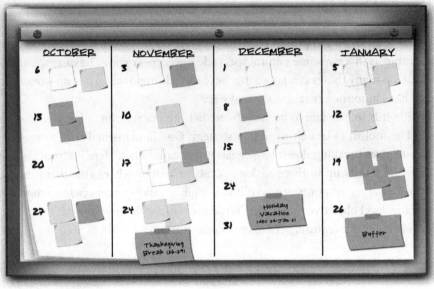

How will you know when tasks are successfully completed? Fuzzy goals such as "make more money" or "grow the business" are difficult to assess. After all, you can always earn more or get bigger. The best objectives are clearly defined. Said another way, they are SMART: Specific, Measurable, Achievable, Relevant, and Time bound. As a final step, define the rubric for key tasks by adding a corresponding SMART goal.

SMART goal	MEANING	EXAMPLE
Specific	Describes a concrete action.	Launch my new eCourse.
Measurable	Includes a number.	Secure at least 100 subscribers at $75 each.
Achievable	Is realistic to complete.	My email list is strong, and several people have already indicated an interest.
Relevant	Helps advance large-scale dreams.	This product emphasizes my unique identity and will propel my reputation.
Time bound	Specifies a deadline.	Complete campaign by March 15.

While success means reaching a stated goal, challenge yourself to beat it. If a stated metric indicates 400 customers, shoot for 401. If you hope to drive down costs by 20%, aim for 20.1%.

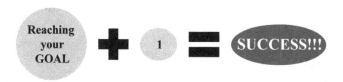

TEAM MANAGEMENT

You can't do this alone. Success requires a village. For starters, each of us has limited capacity. And certain tasks are exponentially more productive when engaging fresh perspectives. For example, we are often too close to our own circumstances to objectively analyze weaknesses or discover bold innovation.

AILMENTS AND REMEDIES

When it works, collaboration is extraordinary. Multiple team members, unified by a common sense of purpose, share the burden. Responsibilities are delegated. Creativity amplifies as multiple minds intersect. Individuals motivate one another while holding colleagues accountable. As basketball player and businessman Michael Jordan explained, "Talent wins games, but teamwork and intelligence win championships."

Unfortunately, teamwork does not always go so swimmingly. Horror stories describing dysfunctional teams abound. Some experiences are so bruising that participants shy away from future collaboration. That's a shame. Fortunately, most challenges are solvable.

You Do All the Work

AILMENT: Have you ever single-handedly rescued a flailing project while others fail to pull their weight? If so, you aren't alone. All this responsibility falling on one person's shoulders is stressful and unfair, cultivating resentment. But what choice was there? Without proactivity, the work simply would not get done. If this phenomenon tortured you once, I am sorry. If it occurs regularly, look within. Might your approach be at least part of the problem?

REMEDY: This challenge is not always as one-sided as it first seems. The person bearing the brunt of responsibilities sometimes comes across as bossy and overly eager, quickly disapproving output contributed by others. Pretty soon, a learned set of behaviors emerges. One type-A person takes charge while colleagues watch from the sidelines.

Ensuring this does not occur requires direct communication about expectations and responsibilities. When someone fails to follow through, empathize and explore root causes of the problem. Determine if positive motivators might encourage buy-in or if responsibilities can better align with that contributor's strengths and interests. While some people simply don't have what it takes, most can become productive collaborators under the right circumstances.

Leadership Void
AILMENT: Is there truly a need for formalized leadership? Why not operate as a democracy? A "flat" structure ensures every voice gets heard. While this sounds lovely in principle, the fantasy is inherently flawed. Who is responsible for making assignments or ensuring results? Who sets the agenda? When challenges arise, who steps up to the plate?

REMEDY: Leadership is crucial. For every project, someone should top the org chart. This person bears ultimate responsibility for the team's success or lack thereof (though they must not single-handedly do all the work!). Also consider secondary leadership roles for various capacities. In fact, on small teams, members may need to assume multiple positions. Perhaps the CEO reports to the marketing director for promotion-related activities, yet the marketing director then details progress to the CEO. Develop a clear leadership hierarchy, and stick to it.

Temporarily suspend the pecking order for certain activities. While brainstorming, for example, each idea should be evaluated on its own merit rather than the title of its proposer.

Founder's Syndrome
AILMENT: Leadership often falls to the person who dreamt up the concept. It's their baby, after all; they should guide the carriage. The problem is that these folks are often too close to the issue, unable or unwilling to consider new possibilities, even brilliant ones. After a few failed attempts to transform the vision, teammates give up.

REMEDY: Consider assigning leadership to someone who isn't the originator. This way, the founder is still permitted to advocate for the original vision. But a neutral figurehead oversees the action, ensuring new directions receive ample consideration.

Tasks Aren't Finished on Time
AILMENT: Because complex projects require interlocking assignments to be completed in a particular order, dropping one ball may trigger a chain reaction. The failure to deliver on time also takes a psychological toll, slowing momentum and enthusiasm.

REMEDY: Create a shared calendar or spreadsheet that articulates what must be completed, who is responsible, and the deadline. Eliminate ambiguities.

> **Break Down**
>
> Seraph Brass, an all-women quintet, performs 50 to 70 shows annually. Pulling off such complex logistics requires sophisticated coordination. "In the past, I had a habit of staying up all night doing everything myself," confesses founder and trumpeter Mary Elizabeth Bowden. "That's unsustainable. I had to learn to delegate and trust my colleagues."
>
> In addition to musical activities, everyone has weekly administrative responsibilities. Bowden oversees financial matters, programming, and communication with management. Others handle tour itineraries, social media, merch, and contracts.
>
> To keep track, Bowden's Google spreadsheet system includes a color-coded to-do list describing tasks, priority level, person in charge, and instructions. Tour and rep notes are meticulously broken down, "invaluable when you're on the road for a month." They even track the color dresses owned by each player, for easy coordination. "We live by these sheets!"

Communication Falters
AILMENT: Groups that communicate poorly lose the game, every time. A failure to convey developments leads to waning trust, missed deadlines, and frustration.

REMEDY: Agree upon communication platforms and protocols. Will you text, email, call, ping, or something else? Is an acceptable response time 60 minutes, half a day, or 24 hours? Does that expectation change at night or during weekends/holidays? Be respectful of everyone's time. Few things are more off-putting than an "urgent" email with 1,000 words lumped into a single paragraph. If several points must be addressed, find the clearest way to convey each item. Avoid negative or inappropriate content in any written format. These messages will come back to haunt you and can be easily misconstrued.

Meetings are Lame
AILMENT: Suppose your team of eight schedules a 60-minute meeting. One person arrives late, the conversation veers off course, updates are irrelevant, and little gets achieved. How much time did that interaction eat up? The common answer is "one hour," but I respectfully disagree. Eight hours were squandered, one per participant.

Too many meetings get it backward. They incorporate activities better addressed individually, while neglecting what groups do best. Many are dominated by information-sharing lectures that could just as easily have been distributed electronically. Some content is relevant to just a portion of the room. Collaboration involving the full group involves tasks that are more efficient solo (i.e., wordsmithing a passage).

REMEDY: Have a leader prepare the agenda upfront. Consider which issues will be tackled, in what order, for how long. Balance flexibility with respect for colleagues' time. When people gather, take advantage of their potential. Meaningful group activities include analyzing data, brainstorming solutions, providing feedback, making decisions, building prototypes, etc. Such tasks also provide the opportunity to bond as a community in ways passive engagement cannot.

People are Prickly
AILMENT: Just about everyone brings a quirk or two (or 10!). This is particularly true when collaborating alongside strong-minded musicians. Some folks ramble, get off topic, exhibit narcissism, hate everything, contribute too little, fight progress, or are perpetually glued to smartphones. Such personalities complicate progress and team dynamics.

REMEDY: *Your people are the right people!* If the team has been predetermined, don't waste a moment wishing fate had dealt you a different hand. Instead, find ways to boost community spirit despite individual idiosyncrasies. When recurring issues emerge, decide whether to address them head on or embrace the weirdness. Avoid triggering defensiveness by putting someone on the spot. Instead, have a leader or neutral figure meet privately with the offender to discuss the dysfunction and seek a win-win. Another option involves protocols. If a few folks constantly dominate the conversation, implement a policy requiring comments to be capped at 90 seconds (measured by a sand timer). Or draw names out of a hat, mandating equitable participation from all.

TEAM MAKEUP

If you have the opportunity to build a team from scratch, make choices intentionally. Identify the collection of people most likely to gel, blossom, and solve the problem at hand.

Most of us surround ourselves with others who look and think a lot like we do. A saxophonist might naturally collaborate with other reed players. This seems to make sense. When others share our core assumptions, experiences, and beliefs, there is less learning curve and more agreement. However, such homogeneity may not be ideal, particularly when approaching complex or creative challenges.

The most insightful teams meld contrasting perspectives. When someone has a weakness, it helps if other collaborators excel in that area. Imagine the benefits of combining dreamers with pragmatists, writers with designers, arts-first with business-first types. Diversity is invaluable to creativity, since innovation most often occurs when taking an idea from one place and applying it elsewhere. A powerhouse team charged with launching an arts venue might include a musician, dancer, arts administrator, sports stadium CEO, influencer for the target audience, and nonarts *imagineer* accustomed to designing unique solutions.

CAREER PARTNERS

Being a savvy musician does *not* mean you have to do everything yourself! On the contrary, build a team of outstanding collaborators who understand your vision and help bring it to fruition. Employing specialists in various areas allows you to benefit from their strengths, expertise, and network of contacts while saving a great deal of your own time. Of course, professionals cost money, whether an upfront fee or ongoing commission. Weigh what work to contract out and which to self-produce.

Friends or family may help, but proceed with caution—when something goes wrong, it can be taxing or even detrimental to a relationship. Considering engaging "interns" at reduced rates (or even gratis) in exchange for experience. Skilled individuals serving on your board may be willing to donate services. In fact, I'm an advocate of appointing a *personal board of directors*, available to offer you personalized career-related feedback upon request. Seek smart people with relevant perspectives that contrast your own.

Build a Board, One Ukulele At a Time

Ukulele Kids Club (UKC) is a global music therapy nonprofit that supports hospitalized and medically fragile children. They have donated 15,000 ukuleles to youth who learn to use them therapeutically and continue after discharge. "These kids come to understand the power of music for life—its capacity to help them cope and heal during difficult times," asserts Mexico-based Marlén Rodriguez-Wolfe, board chairwoman and former CEO.

When recruiting their national board of directors, UKC's top priority is identifying mission-aligned individuals willing to contribute time, talent, or treasure. "The ideal candidate brings all three." Collectively, they encompass a range of expertise: legal, marketing, industry, finance, fundraising. Early on, before the organization could afford staff, a *working board* contributed services for free. Today, their role is primarily fiduciary and strategic. Members must "give or get" at least a minimum contribution. The entire group meets quarterly, and ad hoc on subcommittees. A separate advisory board is consulted as needed, and a music therapy advisory board assembles every three months to provide purely programmatic insights.

In addition to artistic collaborators, key individuals in the life of a musician often include:

1. Accountant
2. Administrative assistant
3. Artist manager
4. Attorney
5. Booking agent
6. Concert producer
7. Contractor
8. Copywriter
9. Financial manager
10. Grant writer
11. Graphic designer
12. Personal assistant
13. Photographer
14. Publicist
15. Publisher
16. Record label
17. Record producer
18. Recording engineer
19. Travel agent
20. Web designer

LIFE MANAGEMENT

As important as music and your career may be, they aren't everything. A healthy lifestyle also involves quality time with family and friends, hobbies, lifelong learning, and—well—tending to your health. Musicians often ask about *work-life balance*. In reality, there is no such thing. There will never be a period when these aspects are in perfect counterpoint, neatly divided 50/50. Nor does there need to be. Existence is always lopsided, demanding more attention on one side or the other at a given moment. The key is not to find balance, but rather a model that works for you.

Is it possible to have kids AND a vibrant career? The answer is categorically yes. If this is important to you, a family must not be forsaken in the name of professional success. I am living proof, as are so many others. Having children can be incredibly meaningful (shoutout to Ashton and Alaina). They do require a great deal of time, money, and energy, however.

Time is like money. The sooner it is invested well, the better off you will be in the long run. Build your life with intention, like a composer carefully mapping an extended work. *Either you design your life or your life will design you.* Enjoy the journey!

Chapter 12
Leaving a Legacy

What kind of legacy will you leave? As a musician, it's easy to become overwhelmed with "just getting by." Committing to a foundational sense of purpose may seem like icing on the cake, an extra goal worthy of consideration, but one that must be postponed until more pressing issues are solved. Of course, our ever-increasing list of responsibilities grows as we age: marriage, kids, mortgage, making a living, saving for retirement. Sure, leaving a mark would be fantastic. But that will have to wait or happen by accident.

Why not change your thinking? What if legacy IS the cake, and everything else qualifies largely as icing? The mission we pursue—our life's meaning—can influence everything: how we spend time, choose projects, build relationships. Savvy musicians are driven by a sense of higher purpose, which in turn focuses priorities and gives strength during difficult times.

> **Legacy through Education**
>
> Orchestrating Diversity, a tuition-free music education program in one of the poorest Saint Louis neighborhoods, was founded by composer Mark Sarich to create equity and inclusion "before they were buzzwords." It is run out of what used to be a drugstore owned by his grandfather, and students learn more than musical excellence. By playing in orchestra, studying keyboard, and exploring theory, they cultivate self-empowerment, mental health, socioeconomic mobility, and a sense of hope.
>
> Some examples of impact: (1) When the daughter of a mentally disabled father and hoarding mother joined, the only word she spoke was "meep." Violin training gave her a voice. She graduated as valedictorian and went on to study computer science. (2) An ultra-poor immigrant child from El Salvador missing two fingers desperately wanted to play piano. Using his hands proved transformative, leading to a career in carpentry. (3) The gay son of an abusive mother who had thrown him down a flight of stairs is now an active freelance performer in Paris.
>
> The legacy of Orchestrating Diversity expands to its community. In part, it put the brakes on gentrification. "Seeing Black folks playing music on the corner suggests that maybe we can all live together. In fact, some people now move here precisely for that promise."

A sense of unwavering mission has the potential to affect everything.

FOCUS
A "legacy dream" favors certain activities over others.

BRANDING
Distinguishing your work helps you get known for something.

OPPORTUNITY
A strong calling will almost certainly unlock doors.

VALUE
Potent projects shape the lives of others.

COMMUNITY
Ecosystems benefit when members contribute value.

FULFILLMENT
Purpose generates personal happiness and motivation.

Few people have the luxury of directing 100% of professional efforts toward their life's primary motivation. Everyone must pay dues and bills. Sometimes that means tackling projects that aren't in perfect alignment. But with ingenuity, there are often ways to transform even these tasks from grunt labor into that which achieves a higher purpose.

> **Legacy through Commissioning**
>
> When PRISM Quartet was founded, the notion of a professional saxophone ensemble almost felt ludicrous. With precious little repertoire and a chamber music scene dominated by piano and strings, the path was uncharted. Some four decades later, "Our group has transformed this genre! And we're not done yet," explains Tim McAllister. Over the years, they have commissioned and premiered 300 compositions, the majority of which are documented through studio recordings. Spanning an eclectic range of styles, these works collectively demonstrate the beauty, versatility, and virtuosity of their instrumentation.
>
> Sax quartets are no longer a fringe oddity. Pro, college, and even high school groups are increasingly common. Most perform pieces from the PRISM catalog or, better yet, pursue their tradition of commissioning new ones. "We've inspired a lot of competition," chuckles McAllister. "There are also loads of converts who view this ensemble as a serious, premier medium for contemporary music. Our legacy involves opening the chamber music landscape."

Legacies come in all shapes and sizes. Some emerge as the result of a simple interaction, while others require a lifetime of dedication. Ambitions often evolve over time as various communities and causes touch our lives.

Legacy is not simply doing your job well. Some people work compulsively yet fail to leave much impression. Take, for example, teaching. Most educators effectively impart information. But only some are remembered forever. And the primary lessons that live on do not always stem from core content. Even if you are the world's best theory professor, some alumni may recall little about voice leading—they might not even care (sorry). Instead, your name may trigger memories about a quirky sense of humor, sincere interest in student success, or the way you pushed them to dream big. *That* is the legacy.

It's never too early to begin thinking about legacy, nor is it too late. If you're still in school, consider ways to evolve and elevate your institution. Start a club. Begin a tradition. Mentor younger students. Similar thinking can be applied to musicians or organizations in any area or phase of their career. Let's play a game of Mad Libs. How would people who know you, or have seen you in action, complete the following?

"_____ (Your name) is the most _____ (characteristic) person I've ever known!"
"More than anything, _____ (your product) makes me _____ (action)!"
"_____ (Your name) revolutionized the way I think about _____ (subject)!"
"My life changed after _____ (initiative you initiated)!"
"_____ (Your name) is responsible for _____ (important accomplishment)!"

What would you like the response to be? Consider various legacy categories.

CATEGORY	OVERVIEW
Inspiration	Catalyzing others to live a better life.
Cause	Advocating and fighting for a meaningful purpose.
Niche	Bolstering an important area where there is a shortage of resources.
Uniqueness	Challenging conventional wisdom in ways that alter the status quo.
Project	Organizing an initiative that makes a lasting impression.
Tradition	Founding a ritual that takes hold and lives on.
Education	Teaching particularly consequential (life) lessons.
Personality	Being the nicest, sweetest, funniest, quirkiest, etc.
Compassion	Being supportive during a time of need.
Community	Creating or strengthening a sense of solidarity.
Support	Donating time, talent, money, or attention to a worthy cause.

Another powerful exercise sounds morbid but helps you focus on what matters most. Write the obituary you'd like to be shared following your life's closing chapter. In 200 to 400 words, how do you hope to be remembered? Which contributions will be cited? This activity forces you to look beyond short- and medium-term urgencies. Consider professional and personal priorities.

The impact of powerful legacies is felt long after the initiator has been forgotten. If you found an organization that changes lives 20 years after your retirement, the gift continues to give even if no name is footnoted on its website. Similarly, when you positively touch someone's life who then pays it forward, your influence lives on. Legacy is not just self-preservation and glorification—it is making a true, palpable difference.

Legacy through Advocacy

"Larger than life" would be an apt description of trumpeter Ryan Anthony, who loved the spotlight and bringing joy to any stage. Being diagnosed at age 42 with multiple myeloma (a bone marrow and blood cancer) brought everything to a screeching halt. While recovering from a brutal stem cell transplant, a BIG idea gave him strength and a sense of purpose. *What if a blowout concert featuring all my trumpet-playing friends raised money to help discover a cure?*

His community rallied in support. Twenty luminary brass players agreed to fly in, on their own dime. The Dallas Symphony volunteered, as did the top big band from the University of North Texas. "Cancer Blows" quickly sold out a hall of 1,900 seats, generating over $1 million. To learn more, view the award-winning documentary *Song for Hope: The Ryan Anthony Story*.

Anthony lived six more years until the disease tragically claimed his life. His wife, Niki, the executive director of Cancer Blows, continues to organize benefit concerts big and small. To date, they have raised around $4 million. Just as importantly, their events bring hope to countless patients and families afflicted by cancer. That is the power of music. Talk about a legacy larger than life.

PART II
ART THAT MATTERS

Live performance. Audio recording. Video. These are the primary mediums through which music is shared today. Fantastically, there are more accessible platforms for affordably creating and disseminating these products than ever. Problematically, everyone else has comparable opportunities, oversaturating the marketplace. Getting noticed, demand, and paid requires strategic positioning (and a bit of luck).

Part II: Art That Matters considers:

- How can various artistic statements advance professional/organizational goals?
- Which innovations might help my art stand out?
- What considerations should be prioritized?

Chapter 13
Outstanding Performance, Plus...

Music has played a vital role in every culture since the inception of humanity. For most of that time, there were just two ways to engage this mystical phenomenon: witness others playing or create the sounds yourself. In stark contrast, music now bombards us from every direction: streaming services, radio, television, film, social media, elevators, strip malls. This prominence is exciting, but what are the implications for live performance?

To the tried and true, there is no substitute for experiencing a presentation in real time. More often, however, people view concerts as one of many options vying for attention.

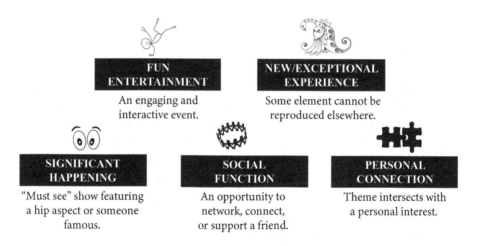

To take time out of a busy schedule, drive downtown, and pay for tickets/parking, the experience better be—well—extraordinary. At the least, it should provide *something* beyond the digitally edited, flawlessly mixed recordings that can be enjoyed from the comfort of home. Savvy musicians breathe life, credibility, and relevance into live performance.

PROGRAMMATIC CONSIDERATIONS

By and large, audiences and presenters today prefer "shows" over "recitals." *Concerts are visual. Music is theater.* Every aspect matters, from the moment people enter to the time they depart. Many considerations are described in the pages that follow. Obviously, not all are appropriate for every occasion. The inclusion of even a single innovation may be transformative, like a stroke of red paint on a black-and-white canvas.

Setlist

How many times have you attended a concert featuring wonderful individual selections that somehow didn't make sense together? Think of each event as a throughout-composed "play" made up of several "acts" (compositions/songs). Beginning with a title or theme can serve as a muse. Evaluate the role of each work, deliberating the threads, narratives, and recurrent motives that unify a show. Is there enough variety? Continuity? Connection?

> **Storytelling Concerts**
>
> For the Vienna-based pianist Chanda VanderHart, concert programming is an art form. Repertoire/sequence choices have nothing to do with keys and everything to do with storytelling. Each work plays an important role in the overall arc. Some selections cross-fade. Standalone snippets may be programmed.
>
> VanderHart's monthly series *Mosaïque* combines art song with elements such as jazz, dance, visual art, and fashion. Each show is built around a theme. "Morgenland" introduced folk songs that multiple countries claim as their own. "Nuns and Monk" (referencing Thelonious Monk) explored eternity and immediacy. "A Day at the Zoo" combined animal-referencing literature, costumed performers, a zookeeper narrator, a burlesque dancer, and a colorful jungle-like set design. "Programming a concert is like imagining a landscape. A lake makes no sense if there are many hills. Following a peak, there must be time to recover. It is sometimes clear that nothing can follow a particular piece, or *only this* makes sense."

Duration

Musicians are often shocked to discover that performances lasted longer than anticipated. This demonstrates poor planning. It is better to leave an audience wanting more than fidgeting, wishing the show ended 20 minutes ago. Rarely should an event extend beyond two hours. Shorter is better. Carefully time all pieces, and overestimate. Calculate for applause, talking, beginning late, set changes, and intermission.

Also consider the duration of individual works. Under the right circumstances, extended compositions are effective. Short pieces also provide effective contrasts. A 45-second interlude can be refreshing, especially in the midst of half-hour masterworks. On a related note, it is *not* a criminal act to excerpt individual movements or to space them throughout. For popular and jazz music, not everyone must solo on every tune.

> ### Make It Quick
>
> Hoping to advocate for as many composers as possible, Rob Voisey arrived at a novel concept. Called *60x60*, this intermissionless, hour-long electronic music mashup integrated 60 pieces "starting at the top of each minute." To date, 60 (ironically) unique collections have been presented in 50 countries at 350 events. Some iterations add video, sculpture, fine art, or dance (imagine 60 choreographers leading 180 dancers!).
>
> *Fifteen Minutes of Fame*, Voisey's acoustic twist on the concept, has explored one-minute works for traditional chamber groups, wind ensemble, unique combinations (e.g., flute and trombone), even instruments like chromatic harmonica, oud (Middle Eastern lute), and hichiriki (double-reed Japanese flute). "This is a great way for composers to explore new timbres, get performed, and network."
>
> Brief pieces are central to Voisey's own compositional identity. He has a 10-minute opera, fifty 50-second works named after US states, and an orchestral *tour de force* lasting 6 (!) seconds. "Music should be as long as it needs to be, not a microsecond more. Short works resonate in our immediate gratification culture where people want to quickly try a lot."

VENUE

Performances can be held anywhere. Some people love fancy, downtown, sprawling music centers. Others resist dealing with traffic or parking, preferring events in their own community. When choosing a venue, consider acoustic properties, stage dimensions, general décor, and price. What is the audience capacity? (Two hundred people packed in a 180-seat auditorium feels vastly different from the same amount sprawling across a stadium.) Will the piano be tuned? Are there lighting capabilities? The site's ambiance can be integrally linked to an event's concept. For example, a modern art museum might be ideal for projecting graphic notation. Park concerts can explore nature themes.

> ### Music Everywhere
>
> - The English Multi-Story Orchestra hosts musical events in car parks and other unexpected locations.
> - Flutist Emlyn Johnson and cellist Daniel Ketter cofounded American Wild Ensemble, which organizes concerts in national parks, connecting music to placid lakes, ancient forests, and lava fields.

- Each summer, a working farm in Washington state hosts chamber music in their Concerts in the Barn series.
- The Caverns, equipped with state-of-the-art sound and lighting, presents touring shows to crowds of up to 1,200 from an underground Tennessee cave.
- AquaSonic, an avant-garde Danish band, features five musicians playing and singing while fully submerged in underwater aquariums.
- Italian pianist/composer Ludovico Einaudi highlighted environmental threats when performing "Elegy for the Arctic" from a floating platform within 100 meters of a decaying Norwegian glacier.

Attire

Clothing frames an event's tone and performer's image. Traditional dress may look nice but quickly fades into the background. Challenging the norm immediately makes an impression (for better or worse). Period outfits, ethnic clothing, full-blown costumes, and accessories such as shoes, hats, jewelry, or scarves add a distinctive touch. Consider the impact of various options. Would you like to establish a formal or casual tone? What colors are emphasized? Should performers dress alike or contrast one another? Will there be an intermission metamorphosis?

Dressing the Part

"Every musical performance involves costuming, set design, lighting, and choreography," explains Andy Meyerson, half of the percussion-guitar duo The Living Earth Show. "Simply adopting default settings is a choice with its own political and cultural baggage." To produce projects with intention, this group builds collaborative, interdisciplinary teams that push the limits of what chamber music can be and do.

During *Tremble Staves*, an evening-length statement about public land and water, Meyerson is dressed in a birdlike costume as he guides a submerged cello through a pond. In *Commando*, produced with a rap-metal collective of queer and trans artists, provocative outfits suggest what "super hero" means to each performer. Throughout *Lordship & Bondage: The Birth of the Negro Superman*, duo members are disturbingly hooded and chained, painting an aesthetic world on Black consciousness and transcendence.

Speaking

Talking does more than convey information. It is a tactic for building rapport. Good stage presence, combined with a likable demeanor, can win over the toughest of crowds. Consider the audience's background and experience. Avoid technical jargon. Rather than regurgitating historical facts, hook listeners. One effective technique is to demonstrate excerpts in combination with verbal explanations. When the full version follows, listeners experience deeper connection. Another possibility involves personal anecdotes. Why did you choose this work? What crazy thing happened during rehearsal? Public speaking tips:

- **Prepare.** Predetermine a basic outline of what will be said, and practice!
- **Connect.** Wear an appropriate facial expression. Make direct eye contact. Do not play with hair, fidget with hands, or pace aimlessly.
- **Communicate naturally.** Do not read. A lack of spontaneity comes across as stilted, robotic, and disingenuous, no matter how meaningful the content.
- **Laugh.** Audiences appreciate humor!
- **Respect.** Thoughtful commentary places audiences in the palm of your hand. Condescending remarks turn them against you.
- **Project confidence.** Speak loudly, with enthusiasm. Don't drop the end of sentences.
- **Pause.** Consider pacing, framing important concepts with white space. Give listeners time to absorb what has been said.
- **Be brief.** Never ramble. Too much verbosity is as irritating as audience ignoring. Two minutes is plenty.

> **Becoming the Composer**
>
> Growing up, pianist Hershey Felder had two passions: classical music and classical theater. The "experts" argued he had to choose. But in his early 20s, he worked up the courage to combine these expressions, weaving together a solo act where he *became* George Gershwin. Eighteen distinct shows (plays and films) and thousands of sold-out performances later, a cottage industry is booming.
>
> When developing each production, which takes "two years plus the rest of my life," Felder asks three questions: (1) Who are you? (2) Who are you talking to? (3) Why are you there? Assuming the role of a composer (Tchaikovsky, Beethoven, Irving Berlin, etc.), his costumed characters speak in the first person. The audience also plays important, organic roles. For example, in *Monsieur Chopin*, a Polish-accented music teacher gives lessons to his students. Though 90% of the script is set, improvised dialogue occurs when attendees pose even surreal questions like: *What happened when you died?* "I always have to be on my feet."

Persona

Players who physically interact with music are more likely to engage than those who hide stiffly behind music stands. Though each instrument has physical limitations, any performer can communicate passion. What message do you convey? To find out, study a performance video with the volume down. Are mistakes broadcast with sour faces? What happens during multimeasure rests? Do bows communicate warmth? Audiences pick up on these cues. Whether disconnected or joyous, viewers will follow your lead.

More deliberate choreography is possible. Something as simple as standing while playing makes a difference. Another possibility involves changing locations periodically. For example, why not reposition quintet members for each movement? In addition to visual impact, this highlights new musical relationships. Extensive staging can be effective, as show choirs and marching bands demonstrate.

> ### Flying to Success
>
> Listening to violinist/pianist/singer Janice Martin play music ranging from Copland to Zeppelin is a treat. Understanding how she does these things while suspended high in the air, simultaneously performing aerial tricks, boggles the mind. Her unique talent combination has attracted headline status on orchestra concerts, variety shows, cruise ships, even TV shows like *America's Got Talent*.
>
> How does a classically trained musician come to embrace such nontraditional feats? "Overcoming challenges is a great motivator!" Tendonitis forced her to take physical health seriously. Studying dance, working out, and joining the army got her thinking about how music might *look*. "I still feel pain while playing. Interestingly, some of that tension fades away when I'm on silks, upside down."

SCENERY

Even simple set design can transform an event. It needn't be expensive to make an impact. Backdrops can be created by dispersing instruments across the stage (be careful where you step!) or incorporating platforms of various heights. Unusual music stands or chairs add pizzazz. Lamps, tables, sofas, or other living room props allow audiences to feel right at home.

Typically, performances occur centerstage. With more than one ensemble, the area is reset so the next group is also centered. This awkward tradition interrupts continuity and often looks unprofessional. View logistical challenges as a creative departure point. Set changes are ideal for dialoguing, film projections, poetry recitation, or incidental music. Performers can play from the pit, balcony, aisles, behind the curtain, different sections of the stage, or even audience seating. Beyond eliminating downtime, such formations introduce fresh relationships. At the least, minimize pauses through careful planning.

Prism concerts (aka "collage concerts"), featuring nonstop cross-fading acts placed in different locations, offer an exciting way for audiences to experience music in surround sound. Some events have a unifying theme, while others aim for extreme variety. This model can also incorporate dance, acting, or film.

> ### Setting the Stage
>
> Every percussionist must consider stage setup and choreography when moving between multiple instruments. But for French-Canadian Krystina Marcoux, these elements are an integral part of the music itself. For *Mélange à trois*, a violin/cello/percussion trio, performers moved through a stage with four zones: (1) bench where cellist and percussionist simultaneously play cello; (2) "forest" with percussion

> instruments strewn about; (3) dining room table with cutlery, dishes, and wine glasses; and (4) duel area where crisscrossing bows suggest sword fighting.
>
> An electroacoustic piece, premiered in Europe's largest climbing gym, began with Marcoux playing marimba hanging from above. Various drums/metals were struck while moving vertically and horizontally around walls and the ceiling. A rope-holding assistant aided with positioning and security.
>
> In another work, she and a dancer appear trapped in a tiny apartment, driving one another to insanity. To do anything, something has to move, be it the marimba, coffee maker, clothing, computer (which gets destroyed during the performance), or even their baby (doll). To shrink the stage area, blackboards serve as walls, allowing "roommates" to pass the time drawing. "It is not enough to merely walk onstage. In my shows, everything matters."

INTERDISCIPLINARITY

Partnerships are possible with dancers, poets, actors, visual artists, cinematographers, aerialists, circus performers, pantomimes, magicians, balloon artists, hand/shadow puppeteers, comedians, and chefs (why not?). In addition to fresh and powerful artistic results, well-done collaborations attract diverse crowds.

> **Art with a Social Conscience**
>
> The new music Ensemble π (Pi) has a long history of producing interdisciplinary events with a social conscience. To highlight the travesty of mass incarceration, an actor and recently released convict (from a 17-year sentence) provided narration. To protest book banning, six world premieres accompanied by sign language and spoken word highlighted absurd rationales used to justify each act of censorship. To illuminate the depth of Israeli and Lebanese cultures, Ensemble π served their music and cuisine "on the same plate." Other events—championing themes like Black Lives Matter, posttraumatic stress disorder, and peace—have incorporated paintings, puppetry, animated charcoal drawings, dance, and video projection. "Marrying multiple art forms amplifies our music and message," explains founder and Israeli-born American pianist Idith Korman.

PARTICIPATION

Most audience members enjoy feeling like cherished contributors rather than dispensable onlookers. Here are a lucky 13 participatory frameworks: (1) humor, (2) questions requiring a response, (3) clapping, (4) conducting, (5) singing along, (6) call and response, (7) whistling, (8) requesting a volunteer, (9) audience roaming, (10) improvisations on audience-generated themes, (11) dancing, (12) choosing program order, and (13) smartphone voting.

> **Wonderbags**
>
> When Australian composer Cathy Milliken wrote the oratorio *Night Shift*, she wanted to do more than merely intrigue the audience. What if they became central to the art-making process? At every show, 500 to 1,500 attendees receive a *wonderbag*. Each includes some combination of stones, bells, egg shakers, paper, pencils, aluminum, and "whirlies," to be played by both audience members and onstage musicians. A 20-minute preperformance rehearsal gets everyone comfortable with their instruments and roles.
>
> Another participatory element includes a choir of around 35 locals. Rehearsing before the event, they learn three set pieces plus a fourth cocreated with the composer. "I am blown away by how deeply people can connect to contemporary music, including those new to it, when the roles of listener and participant merge in democratic musical exchange."

SURPRISES

Who doesn't love a surprise? Unexpected twists delight and keep people talking for months. Possibilities include instrumentalists performing a vocal number, vocalists performing an instrumental number, cameos by local celebrities, costumed ushers, bringing an animal or child onto the stage, introducing a musical genre out of character with the production.

PRE-/POST-/MIDCONCERT

Taking inspiration from circuses or live-audience TV, consider how a crescendo of preconcert happenings might generate excitement. Opening acts, talks, videos, or a comedian can generate energy before a show begins. A postconcert wrap-up or "Meet the Musicians and Their Instruments" allows attendees to ask questions and offer feedback. Online blogs take the pre-/postconcert experience further, allowing participants to ask questions and express beliefs.

There is no cardinal law requiring intermission. A break provides time for people to sneak away. However, some pauses are necessary. Singers and wind players need downtime to rest their "chops." Intermissions are used to sell concessions, recordings, raffle tickets, and swag. Additional activities include performer-guest interactions, instrument demos, or game playing.

> **Introducing ... The Crowd!**
>
> Intermission and pre/postevent are wonderful times to mingle with fans. Fight the temptation to hide out. Appreciation grows after learning you're a great performer AND a likable person.

A CLASSIC CONUNDRUM

The level of accomplishment among today's classically trained musicians is mind-blowing. Yet their experiences often fail to generate sufficient demand. This section provides ideas for reimagining classical music's value and relevance. Consider two competing performances.

CLASSICAL	POPULAR
The event, called "Chamber Music Recital," featured a variety of regionally known ensembles performing works written 100 to 250 years ago. Prior to the concert, audience members entered the brightly lit hall and took their seats. Music stands and folding chairs were placed in a neat semicircle on the stage. The lights dimmed as performers wearing tuxedos entered and bowed. The audience clapped politely as players assumed their positions without offering a word. Silence engulfed the hall, and attendees sat attentively. Each musician was a virtuoso. The ensemble was tightly rehearsed. The first movement lasted 12 minutes, received by silence. (Actually, a few people clapped, but others responded with looks of disapproval, so they aborted further enthusiasm.) The lyrical middle movement was 7 minutes, followed by a rousing 9-minute finale. The audience applauded as players bowed and exited. A crew took 5 minutes to reset the stage for the next group. This routine duplicated itself for other high-quality acts. To conclude, all musicians walked to center stage for a closing bow as the audience rewarded them with applause and a few hoots. When exiting the hall, someone said, "What extraordinary performances! But did you notice that not one player smiled?" Someone else declared, "I concentrated so hard, I'm exhausted!"	The event, titled provocatively, featured a regionally known rock group performing original music. Prior to the concert, audience members entered the dimly lit hall and took their seats. Instruments were displayed onstage along with an elaborate set. Smoke rose from the floor and recorded music pumped through speakers. The band entered, dressed in crazy costumes. They moved theatrically and energetically through various parts of the venue, accompanied by a light show. The audience went wild, screaming at the top of their lungs. Each musician was a showman. The choreography was tightly rehearsed. As the loud music pierced, spectators danced while singing (shouting) at full blast. The first song ended three minutes later and the crowd went nuts. The lead singer then welcomed the audience with questions requiring a group response. The next song began. Such a routine duplicated itself throughout the event. Players constantly moved about the stage, even charging through the audience at one point. To conclude, all musicians ran to center stage for a closing bow as the audience rewarded them with applause, whistles, and screams. When exiting the hall, someone said, "What a crazy performance! Did you notice how much fun the players were having?" Someone else declared, "I danced so much, I'm exhausted!"

No value judgment is expressed for or against either archetype. There is plenty of room for both formats. However, these descriptions highlight fundamentally different approaches. To those familiar with classical models, the rock concert may appear superficial, with theatrical elements distracting from core musical content. Similarly, it partially explains the perspective of a public more familiar with pop antics. In their experience, highly interactive productions engulf the senses, combining visual and aural stimulation. Under this light, traditional classical recitals fall short, illustrating a core challenge facing this music's perceived relevance.

"Classical" Has an Image Problem

When asked to describe fun, exciting, engaging music, most people don't consider classical genres. Unflattering connotations may arise from ignorance, a single negative experience, damaging media portrayals, or a lack of linguistic comprehension. Comparing classical shows with pop-world counterparts unearths some clues.

- **Boring.** For audiences accustomed to "watching concerts," a lack of visual stimulus and spectacle may seem humdrum and uninspired.
- **Overly formal and stuffy.** Many classical events require formal attire. Entire shows may elapse without a spoken word.
- **Elitist.** Clapping between movements elicits the evil eye from those in the know.
- **Old fashioned.** Nonconnoisseurs often believe "classical" implies tunes by dead white guys and a concert model that hasn't changed much since the 19th century. Coincidentally, many classical performers play only music by dead white guys with a format that hasn't changed much for over 100 years.
- **For old people.** This perception is often mirrored by reality. Large percentages of many audiences fall into the senior demographic.
- **Relaxing.** Classical marketers reinforce this notion when radio stations favor inoffensive literature that can function as background dentist music. A recording series is called "The Most Relaxing Classical Music in the Universe." (Where can we purchase "The Most Vibrant/Controversial/Violent Classical Music" albums?)

Considering these explanations, it is no wonder that so many view classical as foreign, disconnected, and largely obsolete. No guardian angel is protecting this music. To thrive, savvy musicians must take steps to reimagine their art.

"Popular" Has a Musical Problem

When it comes to relevance, the popular music world does a lot right. Pop styles reach almost everyone in some capacity. They dominate streaming platforms and provide the soundtrack for much film and television. Many bands create spectacular presentations that attract huge audiences, even when charging significant ticketing fees. Promoters know how to market not just the music, but also the image of artists. Pop stars, for better or worse, are icons of our society.

While it's exciting to see music playing such a revered role, the industry comes with unfortunate downsides. My argument here focuses on a specific shortcoming: *Popular styles have a musical problem.* This is by no means an indictment of certain grooves, offensive lyric content, wailing guitars, or repetitive electronica. Rather, the desire to ensure maximum profitability often comes at the detriment of artistic integrity. Many record labels seek formulaic tunes that may become the flavor of the week, dismissing creative alternatives that push the envelope. By design, musical output is dumbed down, to be fully absorbed in a single hearing by the least sophisticated of listeners. This explains why so many people struggle with more intricate expressions. In fact, common classical critiques illustrate ways in which such pandering has dwarfed the public's aural literacy.

1. **"Too complex."** Many pop tunes include limited variety and excessive repetition. As a result, lay listeners are not used to following counterpoint, transforming melodies, harmonic and rhythmic sophistication.
2. **"Too long."** Most pop songs are capped at three minutes. Classical pieces are often much longer—consider a Mahler symphony!—requiring intense concentration. People are not accustomed to extended active listening.
3. **"No words; not good for dancing."** Popular tunes fulfill functions other than pure music: a vehicle for presenting lyrics, dancing, etc. Processing sound on its own merits may feel unfulfilling and daunting.

Complexity, development over time, pure music—such classical elements may actually be strengths. But the average pop listener struggles to push past such differences.

A Dysfunctional Relationship?

The relationship between musical choice and audience is analogous to marriage partners. Constant in-fighting is unhealthy and often leads to divorce. But placating one another, trying to never offend, is equally dysfunctional. Imagine what would occur if the average English speaker's vocabulary were drastically reduced. Communication would still be possible, but the range of nuance, sophistication, and expressive potential would be greatly restricted. It would negate centuries of linguistic and sociological evolution. Such is the case when it comes to music and our public majority. *Challenging listeners at times to think and listen in new ways is an important responsibility bestowed upon artists.*

Who's to Blame?

Who is to blame for challenges facing the classical music community? Some accuse the media. Others point to a lack of government funding or failed education system. Fault can be placed on capitalism, the nature of consumer-driven societies, corrupt managers, or musicians who "just don't get it." There are many legitimate places to point the finger.

But playing the blame game does little to help. The world simply changes. We must adapt or go the way of the dinosaurs. Why waste energy on negativity when you can embrace exciting new solutions? There is a lot we can do, as individuals and a community, to turn things around.

Is There a Middle Ground?

Many musicians are squarely positioned on one side or the other when it comes to music and audience. Are there just two extreme, polar-opposite options: (1) interactive user-friendly formats with shallow expressions or (2) intimidating academic presentations with depth? Whether musicians offer profound statements but fail to connect with their audience, or dumb down their product in order to attract one, they are making sophisticated music less relevant.

A third paradigm exists—one that seeks a happy medium between accessibility and exploration. The more foreign, complicated, or out of the comfort zone an experience is for observers, the more essential audience-engaging tactics become. On the other hand, when extramusical elements and accessible formats are embraced, programmers should not cower at the incorporation of adventurous offerings. Perhaps this hybrid can engage proponents of both sides, submitting a middle ground for both musical aristocrats and the masses.

There are plenty of individuals with no interest in being challenged—they watch only feel-good films and read cheesy romantic novels (OK, listen to audio books). But in today's immediate gratification world, many people feel unfulfilled by the superficiality and lack of depth that is too often prevalent. A sizable chunk of society craves the new, the exciting, the unfamiliar. They eagerly flock to the latest gadget, film, or internet trend. *Many people love the roller coaster ride, as long as they know they'll be safe.* Savvy musicians can become part of their solution, just as they can be part of ours.

Can Classical Be Popular?

Response #1: Absolutely, but packaging is crucial. Many American families reliably attend *The Nutcracker* year after year and celebrate every Fourth of July attending outdoor orchestral concerts. Movies like *Amadeus*, *Fantasia*, and *Tár* generate widespread enthusiasm. The Three Tenors, Renée Fleming, Bobby McFerrin, Yo-Yo Ma, Hillary Hahn, Joshua Bell, Wynton Marsalis, Marin Alsop, and Gustavo

Dudamel have inspired vast audiences. Countless smaller-scale success stories confirm classical can indeed be popular when framed effectively.

Response #2: Perhaps this is the wrong question. What if we ask instead: *Can classically trained artists be popular?* Expanding the potential of what we offer beyond a single "style," it unlocks additional genres, secondary talents/skills, new concert formats/venues, and daring initiatives. This perspective emboldens the savvy performer, composer, teacher, or administrator, allowing past models to be embraced when desirable, without enslavement.

Experience Design

When Andrew Goldstein cofounded the Seattle-based nonprofit Emerald City Music, his vision was to get millennials excited about classical chamber music. By season two, every show sold out. The 250 attendees, who worked predominantly for companies like Amazon, Facebook, Google, and Boeing, averaged 30 years of age.

Performances featuring diverse repertoire often combine classics with newer works. "But experience design is just as important." Rather than segregating artists and audience, musicians set up in the center of an urban-feeling space with high ceilings and concrete floors. Guests reclining in couches are seated inches away. Tickets include an open bar and all-you-can-eat snacks. Visitors are encouraged to roam. During *Insomnia*, which featured Bach variations, attendees brought sleeping bags. *In the Dark*, a Halloween show with the tagline "Are you scared of classical music?," showcased a string quartet in pitch blackness.

RETHINKING THE CANON

For decades, classical repertoire has been largely fixed and immovable. *The Tradition* revolved around masterworks composed by primarily white, male, European composers. A profound shift was prompted in part by outrage surrounding the brutal police murder of Black American George Floyd in 2020. Entire sectors suddenly woke up to recognize the embedded inequities that define our institutions. Many classical artists took a hard look in the mirror and did not like what they saw—a systemic lack of inclusivity. Seemingly overnight, the canon burst open. Performers made concerted efforts to showcase compositions of women, people of color, and other underrepresented populations. What a positive, liberating development!

Regardless of instrumentation or genre, the amount of available music is enormous, particularly for those open to transcriptions and recompositions. The literature you select makes a statement, intentional or not, about genre, aesthetics, representation, and more. Choose art that emphasizes your vision and values.

> **The Everything Orchestra**
>
> Following years with the Juilliard, New World, and Singapore Symphonies, trumpeter Sam Hyken wondered how orchestras might be updated for the 21st century. To that end, he cofounded the Miami-based Nu Deco Orchestra, which has grown to an annual budget of $3 million. Repertoire for this 28-member "hybrid ensemble" varies wildly, combining music by living composers, reimagined classical masterworks, and recreations of pop artists like Radiohead, Daft Punk, and the Beach Boys. Most concerts showcase a guest artist, including many who have not previously worked with classically trained musicians. Around 50% of Nu Deco's catalog highlights composers of color. "The orchestra is a great place to elevate all genres of music! We design surprising experiences that take audiences on a journey like never before."

CREATIVE PERFORMANCE PRACTICE

When most classical musicians perform, their goal is to achieve *authentic performance practice* (APP). This involves remaining faithful to the composer's intent. As an educator and performing artist, I've benefited immensely from spending literally thousands of hours pursuing this reconstructive approach, which emphasizes goals like artistic preservation, attention to detail, stylistic consistency, and the pursuit of excellence.

Authentic Performance Practice

*Honoring the intentions of a composer/printed music,
play the "right" notes, rhythms, dynamics, articulations, timbre, and form
in stylistically appropriate ways.*

I've asked many musicians, "Is there room for creativity in classical music?" The invariable response: *Of course!* Can you creatively add a crescendo, or make nonarticulated notes a bit more staccato? *Sure, why not?* If a repeat is written, is it possible to leave it out? *Absolutely!* How about the opposite? Suppose you love bar 9. Could you replay it four or five times to emphasize its coolness factor? *Hmm, probably not.* Can you switch the octave? Alter various notes? Reorder the measures? Play fortissimo where it says piano? Add extended techniques and razzle dazzle flourishes to make melodies more virtuosic? *No, no, no, no, NO!*

Who makes these rules? Does classical have to be a genre that always values the creative genius of composers exponentially more than the creative genius of performers? I coined the term *creative performance practice* (CPP) to describe an alternative approach.

Creative Performance Practice

*Using written music as a foundation,
alter notes, rhythms, dynamics, articulations, timbre, and/or form as desired
to build highly personalized statements.*

CPP empowers performers to make customized choices. Particularly for standard literature played thousands of times before, begin by asking, "How might I make this familiar expression uniquely my own? *What makes my version more interesting?*" Visioning becomes a collaboration of sorts between composer and performer(s). Sometimes the goal involves amplifying the original intent (e.g., make a scherzo funnier/rhapsody more passionate). Also possible is turning a piece's meaning on its head, transforming it into something quite different. How far might you go?

Of all ideas in *The Savvy Musician*, this may be the most controversial for some readers. APP is so deeply ingrained into the classical psyche that challenging it may feel blasphemous. Please understand, CPP is not for every performer or performance, nor should it be. That said, innovators often challenge the most conventional wisdoms held by a community or culture. Every great leader, including those we study in music history classes, has broken rules. Doing so always comes at a cost. It can also change the world, your career, and your legacy.

Reach for the Supernovas

"SuperNova," by multigenre pianist/composer David Cutler (and your humble author), is a reimagination of the most performed string collection in the world: *Suzuki Violin School, Volume 1*. While melodies from the 17 tunes remain untouched, rhythm section accompaniments are wild and virtuosic, inspired by genres from around the globe: boogie, funk, Spanish Baroque, tango, techno, you name it.

For the recording, violinist and Suzuki educator Rebecca Hunter was presented with an intriguing challenge. While notes and rhythms could not be changed, anything else was fair game. She was free to alter dynamics, timbre, articulation, ornamentation, bowing, octave placement, and more. Doing so transformed familiar melodic presentations into sophisticated, highly personalized statements. "This creative approach to classical music making is fun, difficult, and empowering. It opened my thinking about pieces I have taught literally hundreds of times."

Is All This Appropriate?

Much of society views classical music as a historic relic. Here's the kicker—many classical musicians agree! They fight passionately to preserve the integrity of The

Great Tradition, playing standard lit, wearing standard attire, following standard etiquette. In their minds, any twist to this model is a cheap trick that detracts. With history on their side, they stay true to authentic practices, longing for an earlier period when audiences were more sophisticated and great music alone reigned supreme.

In response: Time does not stand still. Traditions that cease to evolve render themselves obsolete. And what's the problem with inventing new performance practices? *Any argument that musicians must embrace conventional rituals is just as perilous as unilaterally rejecting them.* Furthermore, the basic premise is flawed. In Kenneth Hamilton's book *After the Golden Age*, he describes various recitals from the 19th century that, astonishingly, have little to do with the way we "remember" them. Isolated movements were often programmed. Applause during flashy numbers was desirable. Many presentations favored the variety-show, anything-goes model. Wagner coined the term *gesamtkunstwerk*, or total artwork, which combines music with theater and visual arts. Concerts were entertaining and interactive—even rowdy. Paradoxically, it seems that many of our practices today are based on faulty revisionist history.

As a savvy musician, you are in the driver's seat. No fines will be imposed upon those who experiment. Just remember that challenging the status quo *will* yield results, positive or negative. Make decisions carefully. Our job is not to keep Bach, Beethoven, Brahms, or Berlioz from rolling over in their graves. (They're too busy decomposing.) It is to contribute meaningfully. If your performance does that, there is no reason to apologize, whether it challenges every convention in the book or strictly adheres to them. Isn't the most important tradition the one of preserving vibrant live performance for generations to come?

Chapter 14
The New Recording Paradigm

If live performance is inherently human, think of audio recording as superhuman. These artifacts can be overdubbed by even geographically distant players (or simultaneous performances from the same artist), manipulated extensively, and edited to perfection. Whether shared with individual listeners or huge crowds, almost everyone everywhere encounters recorded music on a daily basis.

Recording plays a variety of roles in the career and artistic life of a savvy musician: artistic expression, marketing content, reference tracks, video scores, practice aids, self-evaluation, inspiration, archival memories preserved for all time. Whether you're a performer, composer, educator, therapist, or administrator, how will this tool define your impact?

THEN AND NOW

Over the past few decades, no aspect of the musical universe has transformed as dramatically as the recording industry. Disruptive technology, changes in listening habits, and additional developments have rewritten all of the rules. The biggest metamorphosis was the shift from recorded music as a physical product (vinyl, cassettes, compact discs [CDs]) to an invisible digital commodity that can be downloaded or streamed. As with any dramatic change, developments crowned new winners and losers. Contemporary recording artists confront an unprecedented set of challenges and opportunities.[1]

THEN...	NOW...
The late 20th century.	*The current period.*
An era of behemoth record labels, tabloid megastars, and fairly homogenized taste.	A time where music is invisible and everywhere, flowing like an endless waterfall.

[1] To learn more about current trends, view reports by the Recording Industry Association of America, issued twice a year.

Label Backing

LABEL BACKING THEN...

Throughout the latter part of the 20th century, the music industry was dominated by a handful of powerful record labels. As profit-minded businesses, they sought artists with potential to maximize earnings, often irrespective of musical merit or depth. Executives, sometimes without musical background, commonly dictated "artistic" choices with the goal of increasing the bottom line.

Record labels took on significant risk, investing heavily in their roster. In addition to the high price tag of recording, duplication, and distribution, they marketed intensively and organized tours in order to sell their products. With that level of backing, a majority of albums lost money. Beyond an advance, musicians only got paid after all related project expenses had been recouped, a rare occurrence. If one recording by an artist turned a profit but others did not, the surplus covered the remaining deficit before compensation was disbursed. The majority of recordings were not lucrative, and musicians who proved unprofitable were quickly dropped.

While popular music generated the lion's share of revenues, several major labels maintained nonpop wings. By the end of the century, classical and jazz recordings each accounted for only a small percentage of total sales—down significantly from the 1960s, when classical albums alone captured 30%+ of the market. More often than not, these recordings lost money, requiring companies to subsidize such efforts. Eventually, labels began shrinking these arms of their business. Independent, nonpop labels also emerged, tackling projects that required smaller investments (i.e., chamber as opposed to orchestral). Many "indie" labels failed to survive, but some eked by and a few did well.

LABEL BACKING NOW...

With the exception of megastars, gone are the days of labels investing heavily in artists they represent. Companies tend to be conservative when signing untested talent. For nonpop genres, most of the majors favor reissues and new recordings by established celebs, or eliminate this part of their business altogether. Not a single American orchestra holds a multialbum contract.

That said, getting a record deal today is easier than ever. Small, independent companies have proliferated, thanks to the diminishing cost of doing business. What's the catch? In many cases, *you have to be willing to pay them*. Think twice before agreeing to this kind of deal. Most such labels operate more like service centers than full-blown sponsors. "Signed" artists are frequently required to raise all funds necessary to cover recording expenses. Some labels charge additional fees. Given these realities, it often makes sense to eliminate the middleman and release music yourself.

Recording Costs

> **RECORDING COSTS THEN...**
>
> In the late 20th century, every phase of the process was expensive: recording, design, duplication, packaging, marketing, distribution. To create and promote an album, it typically required $25,000 to $100,000+ (with some climbing into the multimillions).

RECORDING COSTS NOW...

Today, it is possible to record and release music with a drastically reduced price tag. Suppose you plan to release a digital-only album:

1. **Recording.** This can still be pricey, particularly with a professional studio and union musicians. However, as equipment costs drop and quality improves, home recording has exploded. All you need is a laptop, quality mics, and (possibly free) digital audio software.
2. **Design.** It is still necessary to create "cover art," to be displayed online. However, artificial intelligence and user-friendly graphics programs can make this step affordable or free, particularly for those willing to self-design.
3. **Duplication.** While some artists continue to release physical products, those without one eliminate this expense category entirely.
4. **Packaging.** This cost is also avoided with digital products.
5. **Marketing.** Social media advertising is less expensive than traditional mass marketing and more easily micro-targets customers interested in your genre of music.
6. **Distribution.** With nothing to ship or store, once a company is set up with a particular online vendor or site, the cost of offering 10 or 10,000 products is negligible.

Affordability unlocks opportunity. It also creates challenges. Without prohibitive pricing, just about anybody can release a recording. This is the double-edged sword. Even a "little guy" can compete in previously unimaginable ways. Yet an oversaturated marketplace makes it difficult to break through for anyone without robust funding or uncommon savvy.

Financial Objectives

> **FINANCIAL OBJECTIVES THEN...**
>
> Historically, the goal was to get consumers to *buy* as many recordings as possible. Since each physical product or download generated direct revenue, more sales equaled more income. From a financial perspective, whatever happened

after the point of sale was immaterial. It did not matter if someone played a track just once or 1,000 times.

The primary aim of touring was often to boost album sales. The visibility of going on the road increased demand for physical products.

FINANCIAL OBJECTIVES NOW...

In a streaming environment, attention becomes the driving priority. The financial objective is to have consumers *listen* as much as possible. Because royalties are paid by the stream, habits are important. One person repeating a song 1,000 times is equivalent to 1,000 users listening once apiece.

The primary aim of recording is often to boost touring. Recordings are necessary for establishing credibility, growing a loyal fan base, and generating buzz. When that happens, presenters who rely on ticket and merchandise sales are more likely to "bite and book."

Musical Choice

MUSICAL CHOICE THEN...

The range of exposure the average Joe had to recorded music was limited. True, he *could* have purchased any item in the record store. But most people favor that which is familiar. Joe learned what was "cool" primarily through radio and music television (like MTV). His favorite stations—a subset of the 30 or so music options available in his area—replayed the same tunes repeatedly. Predictably, these became his preferences. Friends, who listened to similar channels, also influenced his taste. Not surprisingly, Joe's collection closely resembled most other folks' in town, and across the country for that matter.

Record companies essentially controlled public taste. They determined what was promoted and therefore purchased. Radio stations and music TV channels were paid large sums in exchange for prioritizing certain songs.[2] Music that caught on was played repeatedly. Under this system, some recordings sold through the roof, and labels made out like bandits. The megastar was born, propelling a relatively small percentage of artists to filthy rich status.

MUSICAL CHOICE NOW...

The average Jane has unprecedented access to a huge array of recorded music through streaming services, playlists, social media shares, mainstream/satellite/internet radio, podcasts, independent websites... and the list goes on. She

---

[2] The term *song* is now ubiquitous with a recorded piece of music, whether or not it is sung.

discusses musical taste not only with friends in her neighborhood but also with "friends" online from across the globe. On a fairly regular basis, she stumbles upon exciting unfamiliar sounds, broadening her taste. The tracks she explores, more eclectic than Joe's, are not necessarily a match with other folks in town.

This shift from scarcity to abundance has had a major impact on listening habits. With so many low-risk choices readily available, it seems logical that musical taste will decentralize and expand. While there continues to be superstars and dominating trends, more emerging/midlevel artists find niche audiences if they break through and attract attention. The "distribution of (listening) wealth" has been reproportioned. Great news for savvy musicians!

Product Psychology

PRODUCT PSYCHOLOGY THEN...

Shopping in a "record store" was a multisensory adventure. Flipping through racks of physical products (whether LPs, cassettes, or CDs) was tactile and visual. Once a purchase was made, the owner had access to more than just audio. Consumers proudly displayed acquisitions on prominently displayed shelves, even hanging packaging as artwork.

When music became invisible, its perceived value changed. In the early 2000s, piracy of illegal downloads was rampant through websites like Napster. While this act of theft was detrimental to the recording industry, many consumers didn't see the problem. *If I download your digital product for free*, the thinking went, *what does it cost you?* Not time. Not energy. Not a physical thing. Not money. My actions don't require you to make additional expenditures (beyond an initial investment already spent). True, you earn less, but there is no loss. I win; you are... unaffected. Consumers began feeling entitled to get what they wanted, when they wanted it.

PRODUCT PSYCHOLOGY NOW...

The vast majority of recordings are accessed through streaming services. Audiences pay subscription fees in exchange for an unlimited buffet or opt for *freemium* access subsidized by paid advertisements. Still as important as ever, music is viewed largely as a utility.

People still buy physical recordings, though in smaller quantities. This is sometimes motivated by a desire for superior audio quality, partially explaining the recent spike in vinyl. More often, however, physical artifacts rather than audio content motivate such a decision. Its artwork, an autograph, or other nostalgic benefit offers value. Some consumers prefer physical products because significantly more profit is directed to the artist.

GENERATING THE PRODUCT

Why to Record

Recording is a rite of passage. It provides a souvenir that can be shared with the world and will be around for all of time. Reflect on professional and artistic aspirations. Musicians who fail to articulate priorities upfront often pursue resource-intensive pet projects that provide little return on investment.

- **Credibility.** Recordings are modern-day business cards, baseline expectations for serious pros.
- **Documentation.** Add to the canon while preserving your voice.
- **Opportunities.** Demo reels showcasing breadth and talent help obtain gigs and more. Some employment requires recorded auditions.
- **Fan base.** Grow commitment from existing enthusiasts while generating new ones through social media and streaming sites. Being well known increases ticket sales, students, endorsements, and media buzz.
- **Income.** The majority of artists make little money selling recordings. (Much more likely is losing it.) Think strategically about what is most likely to create demand and sell. Recordings also drum up indirect income through royalties and other opportunities.
- **Function.** Recordings serve as soundtracks for films, podcasts, video games, commercials, books, and campaigns. They can help market sheet music. Customized songs make great gifts.
- **Community.** Collaborative projects with fellow artists develop relationships that in turn catalyze more work, connections, and friendship.
- **Fulfillment.** Some artists record for sheer joy alone. As long as you have ample resources, go for it. This is a hobby, however, rather than a career strategy.

A Thousand Sessions

Woodwind doubler Jimmy Bowland can be heard on hundreds of recordings, with a discography spanning film, TV, video games, pop artists, and his own band. Another category includes education and church music, where demo tracks allow conductors to preview arrangements or even "karaoke." Some sessions involve large ensembles. For others, he is the only player present, overdubbing saxophone, clarinet, and flute parts.

Since time is money, there are no rehearsals. Session players must be flawless sight readers with impeccable intonation. "The initial take is often superior, when hearing music for the first time. It still gives me goosebumps." Some of the best advice he received was to sound like an improviser when playing written music and to sound like he's reading when improvising. Also critical is being flexible, capable of immediately integrating feedback rather than taking it personally. "Ego-driven superstars don't last long here."

> Breaking into the local Nashville scene typically requires five years and "often short-notice sub gigs" as your reputation grows. After moving there, Bowland bought a good mic and digital audio workstation. "To hone skills, I practiced every day in my own studio."

WHAT TO RECORD

Repertoire should be directly linked to your goals. For example, wedding band demos and film composer reels must incorporate various styles showcasing strengths and breadth. If your hope is simply to collaborate or demonstrate excellence, musical choice is largely inconsequential.

For artists looking to generate significant demand (streams, downloads, sales, income, media attention), however, revisit lessons from Chapter 2. This marketplace is as competitive as they come. A streaming site like Spotify archives north of 100 million tracks, with around 60,000 added daily. Needless to say, even quality recordings struggle to gain traction. Breaking through is no small order unless you're already famous or have a bloated promotional budget.

Cover bands that record familiar music (whether popular, classical, jazz, or beyond) have an opportunity and a challenge. On one hand, listeners regularly look for music they already know and love. "I believe every musician should record at least one cover song," argues Rebecca Chappell, founder and director of Orangehaus Records. "It's a great strategy for expanding an audience. Cover songs also increase opportunities for licensing music, since music supervisors who can't afford to license original master recordings often opt for more affordable versions."

On the flip side, all standard literature/tunes have been archived extensively. Is there truly a need for yet one more version? Will listeners opt for a less-known artist over the array of existing options? A good strategy involves reimagination, providing a distinctive take on the familiar. A brass transcription of a standard string quartet may have more potential than an actual string quartet playing the same piece!

The alternative involves showcasing something new: an original, a commission, work by an underrepresented composer, etc. In this case, consider how your music might be discovered. One strategy is to fill a gap, highlighting niche, underexplored themes relevant to some audiences. For example, a song about someone called "Sienna" (or Bruce, or Leslie) may generate excitement from anybody with friends or family possessing that name. Tunes celebrating holidays (beyond the oversaturated Christmas market) face limited competition and generate seasonal appeal year after year. Songs in the Star Trek language Klingon or something commemorating World War II are likely to appear on playlists highlighting related themes.

Good concert programs do not necessarily make strong recorded products, and vice versa. For example, it's common for recordings to feature a compilation of works by a single composer or stylistic bias. This lack of variety might (*might*) make for a boring show but a compelling album. Albums should be unified, logical, and attractive.

> **Meditate on This**
>
> Tired of fighting to secure gigs week after week, Montana-based cellist Jesse Ahmann thought, "There's got to be something else." Then it hit him. For years, he had been accompanying yoga classes (in exchange for gym membership) and wellness retreats. "What if I record healing, meditative music?"
>
> Ahmann's first such project, *Ten Hours of Sad Cello*, involved endless looping of a 12-minute solo improvisation. Released on YouTube, it quickly attracted hundreds of thousands of views. Since then, he has layered cello, bass, violin, mandola, and guitar tracks on 10 self-produced solo albums. Available through every online service, the most streams—and thus thousands of royalty dollars each month—typically come through Amazon Prime.
>
> While few listeners know this recording artist's name, they are drawn to titles like *Sad Cello*, *Gregorian Cello*, and *Music to Fall Asleep To*. "I tell musicians that it's hard to be a cover band. First, you've got to do originals that are so different they spark interest, or incorporate compelling titles people are likely to search."

How Much to Record

CDs have a maximum capacity of 74 minutes, though most contain just 45 to 60 minutes of music. LPs are shorter, accommodating 22 minutes per side, or 44 minutes total. Albums might include an isolated extended work (e.g., Mahler symphony), scores of short tunes, or another formula.

Today, however, the constraint of producing only full-length albums is behind us. There is no shame in releasing a small collection of tracks, or even just a single. In fact, it sometimes makes more business sense to drop a fresh song each month over a full album all at once.

> **It Adds Up**
>
> Self-dubbed "the most prolific songwriter of all time," Matt Farley has released north of 450 albums and 25,000 songs. Early on, he noticed that silly, weird tracks about unusual topics got the most attention. "There are so many love songs out there, but few about office supplies." He got featured on *The Tonight Show* after its host discovered his ditty about Pizza Hut. Tunes with potty humor are released under the pseudonym Toilet Bowl Cleaners. In addition to themes about body parts, clothing, and common phrases, The Very Nice Interesting Singer Man (another of his 80 alter egos) released a biographical album about the sad, lonely, pathetic life of this fictional artist.
>
> While many songs get little to no attention, it all adds up. Last year, Farley's music generated 40 million streams and thus $200,000 of income. "More musicians should do this. People say it's tough for independent artists now, but unlike 200 years ago, careers are possible. You can get by on creative stuff, without approval from gatekeepers. Life is good."

Paying to Record

People listening to your tracks couldn't care less how much it cost to produce. If the music is glorious, nobody will notice if it was bootstrapped from home with free apps and donated equipment. And if it fails to connect, the no-expense-spared studio orchestra on a glitzy New York City stage feels irrelevant. Yawn.

While the price tag of production may not matter to listeners, it certainly does to you, the artist! Costs quickly balloon, particularly if utilizing a professional studio and hiring players by the hour. The ensemble size, project complexity, time required, and going rates impact musical collaborator fees. An engineer, producer, and other involved staff must be compensated for production (recording the session) and postproduction (editing, mixing, and mastering) efforts. Additional expenses include venue/studio rental, album design, physical production (if records or CDs are pressed), and marketing.[3]

Before committing, project a budget with room for surprises. There are several ways to defray expenses. A combination of funding sources is often necessary.

SOURCE	OVERVIEW
Labels	While smaller labels may require artists to cover recording expenses, larger ones often include a budget. The amount committed is related to your level of "fame" and how well the project is anticipated to do.
Self-funding	Personal savings, revenue from previous projects, or loans.
Donors	Crowdfunding and other types of solicitation generate support from fans, family, friends, and others intrigued by the proposal (see Chapter 10).
Grants	Some awards are designed to fund recording projects (see Chapter 10).
Collectives	Artist communities pool resources to support meaningful member efforts.
Investors	Money is contributed upfront in exchange for a percentage of profits.
Partnerships	A recording studio might reduce or defer fees in exchange for a portion of money generated.
Sponsorships	Companies may be willing to contribute to a recording project, particularly if content overlaps with their brand or purpose.

---

[3] Michael Jackson's 2001 album *Invincible* cost somewhere between $30 and $40 million!

THE BUSINESS OF RECORDING

Record Label Dilemma

How important is it for artists to secure the backing of a record label? Companies offer a variety of benefits, including assistance with:

In exchange for representation, labels claim a hefty percentage of generated revenue. Small independents often split royalties 50/50 with the artist. Midsized and major companies require more, up to 90%! There are even contracts stipulating that musicians earn nothing. Be sure you fully understand the terms of any agreement upfront. Do you retain rights? What expenses are required on your end? How is payment allocated? Can the contract be easily terminated? Will they promote your product? Overpromising and underdelivering are prevalent, so do your homework. Seek feedback from artists who have previously worked with the label. Consult an entertainment attorney before signing anything.

Major labels today commonly extend only *360 deals*. Beyond previously described stipulations, they claim 15% to 30% of dollars earned from all nonrecording income streams for the duration of the contract. This includes musical (performing, publishing, licensing, merchandising, teaching, television appearances) and nonmusical (public speaking, acting, secondary businesses) activities.[4] The argument is that creating and promoting a recording requires a substantial investment, often propelling many career aspects. In exchange, they are entitled to benefit from the full 360 circle of the artist. While a major deal is potentially life changing, the price tag is consequential. Carefully consider implications before signing.

When seeking a label, search for those specializing in genres you perform. Get referrals and do research online. Websites such as *All Record Labels* and *Musical America* catalog hundreds of companies. Each has unique submission policies. Most don't accept unsolicited materials,[5] while others consider just about anyone. Regardless of size or prestige, all labels have one predominant concern: Will your product sell? Do not approach them until you've formulated a cogent marketing strategy.

---

[4] Performance and songwriting royalties cannot be claimed, however.
[5] Beyond being overwhelmed with solicitations, labels often decline this practice for fear of copyright infringement accusation. If they open and play a song and later release something similar to it, litigants can prove they had access to the original source.

> **Follow the Data**
>
> With the goal of promoting talented musicians who are too often overlooked, violist and composer Sergey Bryukhno founded the Estonia-based, digital-only classical music label Oclassica. His small but efficient company analyzes marketplace data, licenses tracks from artists, earns income through streaming platforms, and pays royalties.
>
> *What will I do if Deutsche Grammophon calls?* is a common question Bryukhno hears from musicians worried they will miss a bigger professional opportunity. "Our sales data shows that even well-known classical musicians' solo albums get just 10 to 50 streams a day. This often happens when approaching recording with a *What do I want to play?* mindset. Our approach is to ask: *What do listeners want to hear?*" This shift in focus from artist to repertoire has led Oclassica to release compilation albums featuring "the right tracks with the right album titles." As an example, his own Sonnet in C Major—originally released as a single—has been included on 50+ compilations, growing a Spotify audience of up to 20,000 monthly listeners.

The entrepreneur in you may be perplexed. If artists are responsible for so many expenses, why not start your own label? Weigh each model carefully.

EXTERNAL LABEL	YOUR OWN LABEL
Less control	More control
Less time and energy	More time and energy
Less risk	More risk
Distribution already established	Distribution more difficult
Some $ investment usually required	More investment $ required
Less bookkeeping required	Organization/bookkeeping required
More potential sales	More $ earned per unit sold

Another possibility involves hiring a *pass-through*, which allows the use of an established company's distribution pipeline for a fee (typically 10% to the label plus 10% to their distributor). If your independent label has 15 to 20+ products and an established sales history, you may be able to hire a distributor directly for a 10% commission.

Each stage of a project—recording, design, marketing, distribution—takes time, energy, and resources. When you assume all the financial risk, you are entitled to the highest reward if products sell. Other parties who share that burden rightfully take a cut. Some labels today require you, the artist, to make the big investments while they retain the majority of profits. Think carefully before entering this type of agreement. Going it alone requires more work, but the potential payoff differential can make it worthwhile.

> **Release Yourself**
>
> Canadian singer-songwriter Joey Clarkson recorded two albums and five singles with external labels before going independent. "It wasn't a negative split, but I wanted more control." Self-releasing allows autonomy when determining what to record and the final mix. It permits her to move quickly rather than waiting on labels managing numerous artists, particularly important for songs related to today's world. Eliminating the producer required a learning curve but forced critical thinking about desired sound, a net positive.
>
> Beyond streaming, Clarkson's album *The Year That Never Happened* was released on cassette, CD, and vinyl. While the market for physical formats is relatively small, doing so opened professional doors. For example, a London-based primetime TV three-minute segment featured her discussing and holding the LP. "As a kid, I spent candy money building my music collection. These nostalgic products provide a unique way to connect with fans."

How Recording Artists Get Paid

Quantifying how much an artist makes from "record sales" is complicated. Many factors play a role: list price, where it is purchased, how profits are divided. For physical products and downloads, here is an oversimplified explanation.

STAKEHOLDER	EXPLANATION
Customer	Pays a set amount.
Vendor	Physical (e.g., Walmart) and online (Amazon) stores typically retain 30% to 50% of list price. (Items "on sale" diminish their profits.) Venues charge a 10% to 20% commission for products sold during concerts.
Record label	Typically the copyright holder, labels receive the remainder and must make further disbursements.
Cost of goods sold	Deduct the amount to manufacture a physical item (e.g., $1 per CD). For digital products like downloads, this number is $0.
Recording artist	Receive a percentage of the label's share, depending on what was negotiated. Some labels offer up to 50%; most pay just 10% to 25%.

Publisher	Paid *mechanical royalties*. In the United States, this is disbursed by copyright holders to the Harry Fox Agency and then distributed to publishers. Since 2024, that amount has been 12.4 cents for songs under five minutes and 2.39 cents/minute for longer works.
Songwriter/composer	Receives half the mechanicals in a 50/50 split with the publisher.

Consider a CD or LP with 10 tracks that sells for $15. An artist could theoretically claim most of that amount (minus COGS) if selling it through a personal website or event, self-releasing the album, and self-publishing original music. More often, however, the pie gets divided further. If the album is released with a label and sells through Amazon, revenues might break down as follows: Amazon takes 50% ($7.50); mechanical royalties (10 tracks × 9.1 cents/track = $.91) are split evenly between the publisher ($.45½) and composer(s)/songwriter(s) ($.45½); COGS to produce this item are deducted (perhaps $1.09); the remaining $5.50 is divided 85/15 between the record label ($4.67½) and performing artist ($.82½), as agreed upon in their contract.

For streaming platforms, digital service providers (DSPs) like Spotify and Apple Music charge consumers a set monthly fee in exchange for unlimited access to their library. One million subscribers paying an average of $10/month would generate $10,000,000 every 30 days. If the DSP keeps 20% of revenue (each platform has its own formula), the remaining $8,000,000 is then divided among the number of streams. Some platforms allocate equivalently for every stream; others negotiate different rates with each label. For *freemium* streaming sites, where listeners are not charged a fee, the same principles apply except revenue is collected from advertisers.

In real dollars, how much does the recording artist receive? Typically, sites offer copyright holders $3,500 to $5,000 per million streams, or $.0035 to $.005 for each individual stream (anytime someone presses play for more than 30 seconds). The label collects this money and allocates what was negotiated. For example, artists with a 10% share receive $350 to $500 for every million streams. If that money must then be divided among multiple people (e.g., a trio splits profits evenly)—well—you do the math.

The financial model is more complicated yet. Those working with a label must first recuperate all "advanced" funds before collecting royalties. This includes recording, marketing, touring, and other expenses supported by the company. Once the initial investment has been repaid, a host of additional factors shrink royalty amounts, including issues as ridiculous as "anticipated product damage."

Needless to say, few artists generate much or any capital from recordings. With the exception of blockbuster hits, projects typically lose money. However, in-demand products can attract gigs, grow your fan base, and propel ancillary professional goals.

Increasing Streams

Make your music available everywhere. Recordings get streamed when consumers:

1. Search for an artist, song, or keyword.
2. Discover something through ads, recommendations, or curated collections.

For the first option, listeners seek a specific destination. Scoring a stream comes from fan cultivation or releasing what people want to find. The attached title and description are extremely important. Optimize your profile on platforms like Spotify.

To amplify discoverability, promote your art and the buzzworthy story behind it.[6] Consider which influencers/platforms might highlight your release: playlists, social media, podcasts, AM/FM radio, satellite radio, digital jukeboxes, airline/cruise ship entertainment, hospitality/retail venues (background music), licensing sites, karaoke services. Also possible is flipping the process and becoming a tastemaker yourself. For example, build playlists that combine your tracks with in-demand statements from other artists.

> ### You've Been Playlisted
>
> The electronic rock, self-produced recordings of drummer Tom DuPree III have been streamed over 2 million times. After discovering submissions to third-party playlists were largely ineffective, his primary marketing strategy became paid social media advertising. Combining 15-second audio clips with animations of catchy cover art, "I make it obvious that ads lead to a streaming service, without being overbearing." Spending $10 to $25 per day typically catalyzes 2,500 to 10,000 monthly streams, enough to trigger Spotify algorithms.
>
> Radio, an ongoing shuffle playlist, recommends similar songs within a genre. Release Radar promotes new releases within the first four weeks to an artist's followers (DuPree has 12,000). Tracks that generate enough attention, typically 2,500+ plays in week one, get shared more widely. Discover Weekly, one of his favorites, features songs of any age that generate 10,000 streams within a 28-day window. "The hardest part is getting there. Once engagement is high, it is like a surfer swimming out to catch the next big wave."

Copyright Protection

Recordings are *intellectual property*. Someone cannot use an existing, copyrighted audio file for a film, TV show, video game, website, etc., without first paying for the right to use it. Theoretically, a musical creation is automatically protected under

---

[6] As you consider ways to market recordings, revisit lessons from Chapters 5 to 8.

copyright law the moment it is represented in tangible form, whether notated or recorded. However, if someone "steals your sounds," it may be difficult to prove you are the legal owner.

To protect yourself, submit a Sound Recording (SR) form for recordings and Performing Arts (PA) form for original compositions to the *United States Copyright Office*. A $45 application fee[7] (or $65 for multiple works) is required when submitted through their website. This domain also answers a host of copyright-related queries.

When including nonoriginal pieces on a commercial recording, you may need to obtain the rights. Compositions fall into the following categories:

1. **Premiere recording.** The first time a copyrighted composition is recorded, obtain written permission from the publisher, composer, or estate that owns it. A signed contract should outline agreement stipulations. You're off the hook when performing original music.
2. **Previously recorded, under copyright.** If a work under copyright has been previously recorded, you do not need special permission. Instead, obtain a *compulsory mechanical license* through the Harry Fox Agency. For each recorded work, you are required to pay a small fee multiplied by the number of recordings sold. The expense is minimal, and licenses are easy to obtain. However, they are crucial. Without one, you can get sued.
3. **Public domain (PD).** For works no longer protected by copyright, there are no restrictions or required payments. As of January 1, 2024, this included all music composed before 1928. Since then, the length of copyright has been expanded dramatically. For example, works written after 1977 are protected for the life of the composer plus 70 years. Please note: *It is possible to copyright a new arrangement of a PD work.*

---

[7] 2024 rate.

Chapter 15
Got Video???

Sophisticated, highly produced music videos became a worldwide phenomenon in the 1980s with the launch of Music Television, better known as MTV. Suddenly, recordings became something to watch rather than merely hear. Since then, the omnipotence of music video has exploded. Today, more than 150,000 clips are uploaded to YouTube *every minute*, a good chunk of which are music related. Site visitors consume more than 1 billion hours of video each day!

How important should video be to the identity of a savvy musician? That, of course, is up to you. But as you ponder, consider this: Unlike live performances or one-on-one lessons, videos can be viewed repeatedly by anyone. They are easy to share, with the potential to go viral. Videos make a statement, establish credibility, and promote your vision. In addition, these electronic artifacts will be around for all of time. Talk about a legacy!

VIDEO PRODUCTION

When compared to their audio-only counterparts, fewer resources exist on producing music videos. For that reason, I am including a basic tutorial to get you started.

Envisioning the Concept

There are many reasons musicians invest time, energy, and money into making videos: to learn a skill, capture a memory, demonstrate competence, attract customers, sell products, amplify impact, build buzz, go viral. Be strategic. Digitized performances showcasing standard repertoire abound, including those by renowned performers. Going viral requires something unique: uncommon virtuosity, over-the-top humor, heartwarming stories, current-event connections, helpful information, quirky unexpectedness, anything with cats.

What kind of video should you make? Here are a dozen options:

1. LIVE PERFORMANCE	2. PRODUCED MUSIC VIDEOS	3. MULTISCREEN VIDEOS	4. MASHUPS
Documenting a concert or other runthrough.	Combining A-roll and B-roll imagery.	Tracks recorded in isolation blended via a split screen.	Demo reels combining various excerpts.

5. OVERLAYS	6. USER-GENERATED	7. ANIMATIONS	8. INSTRUCTIONAL LESSONS
Superimposed scores, lyrics, analyses, or more.	Featuring footage submitted by fans.	Music plus cartoons!	From teaching demos to full-blown eCourses.

9. SOCIAL MEDIA ADS	10. MESSAGE STATEMENTS	11. INTERVIEWS	12. BEHIND-THE-SCENES
Paid promotions for various initiatives.	Project overviews, promotional statements, storytelling, artist profiles.	Answers to questions posed by an interviewer or typed captions.	Concert and rehearsal footage, interviews, bloopers, and more.

Great Music Videos

A few fantastic music videos, and some reasons they are so effective, include:

- **OK Go:** *This Too Shall Pass.* Continuous shot of a Rube Goldberg machine.
- **Childish Gambino:** *This Is America.* Simple but powerful choreography and storytelling about social justice.
- **Caroline Shaw & Sō Percussion:** *Other Song.* Beautiful A- and B-roll footage.
- **Claire Chase:** *Density 2036.* A varied, virtuosic, visual three-minute flute demo.
- **The White Stripes:** *Fell in Love with a Girl.* Stop-motion animation with Legos.
- **Salon Salut:** *Competitive Foursome.* The power of humor and talent.
- **Sandbox Percussion:** *Pillar VII by Andy Akiho.* Stage performance integrating close-ups and lighting.
- **Anderson and Roe:** *Der Erlkönig.* Filming amplifies this composition's sense of horror.
- **Zic Zazou:** *La Marche Nuptiale.* Mendelssohn's *Wedding March* absurdly performed on beer bottles, wine glasses, bong funnels, and pans (struck by hand blenders).

Mammoth budgets are not required to produce effective videos. Creativity, however, is critical. After choosing a general direction, consider the specifics. For music recordings, determine which piece, who plays, interpretive concerns. For spoken statements, draft a script or outline.

ELEMENT	DESCRIPTION
A-roll	What you see is what you hear. This *primary footage* features performers or speakers in real time. A-roll can come from one or multiple cameras.
B-roll	What you see is NOT what you hear. This *supplemental footage* may include photos, different videos, time lapse (slowed or accelerated video), and other enhancing imagery.
Overlay	Photos, videos, musical scores, or other images are superimposed on top of a portion of the screen's primary video.
Title slides	Introduces the title, subtitle, and primary characters or performers. Can be overlaid on top of main content or added as a standalone intro.
Captions	Typed words that are not spoken. Can be used to identify speakers or performers, questions to an interviewee, or other messaging.
Subtitles	Transcribed spoken words are most helpful if speaking is hard to decipher or in another language, or listeners are likely to view with volume down.
Voiceover	Scripted narration that isn't connected to an image of the speaker.
Soundtrack	A music video's soundtrack is obviously the main point. For spoken statements, scores emphasizing the appropriate mood amplify effectiveness and emotional impact.
Credits	Typically at the end, acknowledging those involved (musicians, speakers, composer, director, etc.). Credits can be rolling or still.

What is the ideal duration for a video? People have short attention spans, particularly online. Even with compelling content, it is unlikely many viewers will watch 10-minute statements from top to bottom. Typically, 1 to 5 minutes is best. Ads must be shorter (often 15 or 30 seconds). When sharing long compositions or presentations, consider whether to release a full run-through or highlights only.

Another consideration is emotional impact. Do you want smooth, gorgeous, colorful imagery or quick, edgy, black-and-white cuts? While nitty-gritty edit decisions can be accomplished in postproduction, upfront visioning influences the filming approach.

Filming the Shoot

Effective filming need not require state-of-the-art equipment. Chances are you already have all you need to get started. As video becomes more central to your identity, invest in equipment or see what you can borrow.

Location/set
Where you film impacts look and acoustics. Sometimes the choice is obvious, such as a concert hall or project-related site. If multiple venues are under consideration, weigh factors including appropriateness, aesthetic appeal, accessibility, traffic, noise level, and natural lighting. Too many mirrors or windows complicate efforts, requiring complex maneuvering to avoid reflections of a camera operator. Outside settings are weather dependent.

After arriving, build your "set." Keep the background simple. Clear away clutter, including unwanted cables. If the backdrop is ugly, hang a curtain. Add desirable props. Perhaps it makes sense to include a poster or other relevant item. Consider the color scheme.

> ### Cloning and Teleporting
>
> In his video "Aulos," the "enigmatic French producer with a passion for recorders" Vladimir Cauchemar is seen playing his ancient instrument along with an electronic loop. While dancing (somewhat awkwardly) by a statue, in a playground, and on a cobblestone road, numerous Cauchemars often appear simultaneously. How is that possible? The key to "cloning" is maintaining an exact camera shot. Multiple takes of the same person in various parts of the frame may be overlayed while editing, thanks to a process called *masking* that provides the illusion of a single episode.
>
> In "Here We Come A-Wassailing," Jazelle Green appears to play saxophone in the forest and sing with multiple clones of herself. It was filmed in front of a *green screen*, which she created by taping multiple sheets of green poster board together and attaching them to the wall. When filming in front of a solid backdrop (any single color works), editing software easily erases the background using an effect called *keying*. Foreground images may be "teleported" to appear on top of background photos or videos. Plugins allowing for similar effects without the green screen offer mixed results.

Costuming

Costuming contributes to the overall effect and image projected. What will your "actors"—performers and speakers—wear? Formal or casual? Unique costume elements? Special hairstyles? Makeup or natural? Different attire for various scenes?

Lighting

Good lighting is imperative. Any camera, no matter how modest or sophisticated, processes light. To capture sharp images that pop, be sure to *backlight*. In other words, the area behind your subject(s) should be brighter than what's in front.

Natural lighting is a free source available at certain hours each day. (Apologies to our Norwegian friends who experience 24-hour "polar nights.") This option is ideal for many shoots, particularly those on a budget or with crews with limited lighting expertise. Even with natural illumination, beware of shadows. *Artificial lighting* is necessary where sunshine isn't available, or to ensure a consistent look regardless of filming time. To optimize results, indoor and even outdoor locations may benefit from additional brightness. Available lighting products shine a variety of colors and luminosities. *Accent lighting* highlights props or areas of the set. When shooting indoors, it can dramatically enhance the appearance of images captured by a camera.

Audio

Great audio is as important as the imagery, especially for music videos. While many cameras have built-in microphones, capabilities are limited. When possible, integrate external sources. Use the best microphones available, whether room mics, individual pickups for each instrument, or a combination. Capturing microphones in a visual shot is preferable to confronting poor-quality audio without them. One common technique involves making a studio recording first and capturing video later while "lip syncing." For spoken passages, capture nice crisp audio. Handheld, lapel, or shotgun (overhead) mics are ideal, particularly in noisy settings. Place these as close to the orator as possible.

Headphones are indispensable. While recording, listen back to optimize the sound. Check the audio meter (if available) to ensure that input is set as high as possible without distorting. Listen for unwanted echoes and intrusive ambient noises prior to hitting "record." It is almost cliche for musicians to spend hours capturing audio, only to learn that an air conditioner, tapping, or other annoyance wreaks havoc.

Video

Compelling aesthetics have as much to do with shot composition as subject matter. Varied framings, sizes, and angles make for visually stimulating content and invested audiences. Though it is possible to fix shooting shortcomings while editing, getting things right on the front end is preferable.

Video cameras on many smartphones and tablets today are stunning. Using these devices may be all you need to shoot high-impact videos. Professional-grade video cameras, however, offer superior features. How many should be incorporated? While just one may suffice, this option lacks variety. Using multiple devices opens a world of opportunity. For example, when recording a duo, perhaps camera A focuses on player 1, camera B captures player 2, and camera C is a wide shot of both. With a little planning, most people can make this happen, perhaps scrounging two smartphones and a tablet. Consistently set *resolution* (number of pixels), *frame rate* (images per second) *exposure* (amount of light reaching camera's sensor), and white balance (color temperature) so the look is similar across devices.

Capture ample content, both A- and B-roll. Multiple takes enable you to pick and choose. Possessing more footage than needed is preferable to discovering desirable shots are missing. When filming, it is possible to zoom in/out and change the focus. With two devices and one operator, perhaps camera A remains stationary and the other grabs close-ups. Another trick involves physically moving the camera during different segments of the shoot to increase variety.

Effective, convincing on-camera acting relies less on raw talent and more on preparation. To bridge the gap between naturals and novices, have inexperienced performers practice in front of the lens. Other filming pointers:

1. Be sure cameras are oriented correctly, whether landscape or portrait.
2. If a video camera must capture primary audio, get close to the sound source.
3. Frame each shot optimally so you don't discover unwanted clutter.
4. Follow *the rule of thirds*, placing your subject off center rather than right in the middle.
5. Keep cameras steady; avoid shakiness. Tripods are helpful.
6. Walk closer to the subject rather than zooming in.
7. While talking heads should generally look directly into the camera, filming from different places (above, below, the sides) adds interest.
8. Keep a given shot for at least 8 to 12 seconds before moving to something else. Viewers feel nauseous when the camera moves constantly.
9. At the end of a take, allow the camera to run a few additional seconds rather than shutting off immediately.
10. Keep notes while filming, indicating what worked or didn't for each take.

Editing the Content

Editing software ranges from free programs with limited capabilities to paid platforms offering sophisticated functionality. Video editing can be largely self-taught, thanks to a preponderance of free online tutorials.

Before editing begins, review all clips to determine what might be included. At this point, it isn't necessary to decide every second. Rather, eliminate losers and pinpoint potential winners. The more you clarify now, the quicker this process will go.

Piece together the primary audio track first. If you plan to add a soundtrack to support speaking, do that next, whether involving performances by artists in the video, specially composed music, or royalty-free clips downloaded from stock audio libraries. Sample multiple tracks until the mood is just right.

After audio timing is correct, edit the video: moving between takes, integrating B-roll, superimposing overlays. Video clips and still images such as photos can be mixed as desired. Start by getting the basic flow and fine-tune later. Be intentional about choices, researching other videos for inspiration. A final step involves aspects like:

1. **Transitions.** Control the look when moving from one clip to another, allowing for fades, wipes, and more. Without a transition, you have hard cuts, which may also be effective.
2. **Transformations.** Reposition, resize, crop, trim, or angle images. Apply the *Ken Burns effect* to pan or zoom in/out.
3. **Video effects.** Stylize the look by altering brightness, going black and white, getting "cartoon-y," or applying other specialized aftereffects.
4. **Video speed.** Apply slow motion or time lapse even as audio remains untouched.
5. **Color correction.** Fix saturation, brightness, contract, and white balance.
6. **Audio effects.** Beyond the mix, add reverb, equalization, panning, distortion, and special effects, as needed.
7. **Captions.** Add typed writing on top of the video.

Splitting the Screen

Composer Eric Whitacre started a revolution with his choral composition "Lux Aurumque." Rather than assembling a traditional choir, he *crowdsourced* the art. Fans recorded themselves singing while listening to a dummy track and uploaded the outcome. Mixing 243 videos from 185 singers in 12 countries into a cohesive video statement, the virtual ensemble was born.

Numerous projects emulate and expand this technique. One notable example is Jacob Collier's Grammy Award–winning "Moon River," where he harmonizes with literally hundreds of himself, showcased against various backdrops in different costumes and poses.

Trombonist Patrick Sullivan releases a steady stream of *split-screen* videos for low brass ensembles. His pop culture arrangements for up to 38 players include soundtracks from *Lord of the Rings*, *Star Trek*, and video games. After receiving individual recordings, Sullivan edits audio first, striving for a natural sound. Then he combines video clips with footage from the source film or game. Sullivan's multiscreen projects have been shared worldwide, demonstrating his brass instrument's *cool factor*. "Sometimes at a camp or clinic, kids come up and say how much they love my videos. I almost feel famous. It's weird!"

PROMOTING THE ART

Creating spectacular videos is just part of the process. Then there's the daunting task of getting noticed. While "going viral" means different things to different people (is it 1,000 views or 5,000,000?), set a goal for each release and try to beat it.

There are three paths to racking up views. The first is being famous already. Those with hoards of devoted followers may break the internet with any release, no matter how trivial. The second requires luck. Some influencer accidentally stumbles across your video and shares it widely. For the majority of us, however, the trick is—you guessed it—marketing! To gain traction, here are some tips:

1. Create unique, relevant content (not all videos have the potential to catch fire!).
2. Be consistent to your brand identity.
3. Ask your "tribe" to disseminate.
4. Share from a variety of platforms.
5. Partner with established influencers.
6. Incorporate relevant keywords in the description.
7. Ask people to subscribe to your channel during each video.
8. Post regularly.

Hum Me a Melody

"Could you please hum me a melody?" A stranger squirms and then blurts out five to eight *doo*s. Suddenly, a woman at the keyboard creates a fully orchestrated soundtrack inspired by the motive. This is but one type of video by Indonesian composer Eunike Tanzil that's racked over a million views. Others involve her composing on a flight, reimagining a ringtone, or adding harmonies to spoken words from trending personalities. She comes up with concepts by considering what (1) people like watching, (2) she likes creating, and (3) showcases her skills.

Tanzil's goal is to capture attention within the first five seconds. Her marketing strategy includes posting consistently (two to three times per week) and loading releases with hashtags. "Typically, you know if a video will blow up within 24 hours. I wish I could tell you the recipe. But it doesn't hurt when celebrities like H.E.R. repost my content." Such attention has led to film scoring opportunities, and even a major record deal, from folks who discovered her on Instagram. "Artists and brands are motivated to collaborate when you have lots of followers."

MUSIC VIDEO 2.0

Traditional online video creation is just the tip of the contrabassoon. New options continuously expand the realm of possibility, availing enthralling art never previously imaginable. Most equipment decreases in price and increases in quality each year. Better yet, fresh approaches offer the potential to reach new and wider audiences. Early adopters will be rewarded handsomely. How might you champion such breakthroughs?[1]

---

[1] In the pages that follow, I will not detail how each technology works. Intrigued readers should investigate additional resources. The goal here is to whet your appetite.

LIVE STREAMING

Concerts have been live streamed since the early 1990s. In 2006, the Metropolitan Opera began *simulcasting* performances to movie theaters, expanding their audience's size and geography. By 2008, YouTube began hosting live events. But it wasn't until COVID-19 that streaming went viral. (Apologies for the dad joke.)

The key advantage to streaming is that content can be viewed by anyone, anywhere. Doing so allows events to augment impact and audience, often significantly. But it can come at a cost. Online events are hardly comparable to live music. Viewers, less likely to focus completely, shift attention between the show and other activities. The very act of streaming can shrink in-person audiences, as locals opt to watch from home rather than braving traffic and parking. Then there is the question of money. Most streamed events are free.

Is streaming a good idea? As with so many things, that depends on your goals. Free online events help savvy musicians engage existing fans, expand reach, and promote other priorities. If direct monetization is a priority, several options exist:

- Ask for donations in a *digital tip jar*.
- Sell tickets through a pay-per-view service like *Qello Concerts*.
- Charge membership to your website, with events available to subscribers only.
- Seek corporate sponsorships.
- Host a streamed benefit concert.
- Sell ads, to be broadcast before/during the event or overlaid on top of the video.
- Use the occasion to promote other products and services.
- Invite VIPs who might hire you for subsequent work.

As is so often the case, *well known equals well paid*. How might streaming serve to grow your influence and fan commitment?

Living Room Concerts

Concert streaming has the potential to reach thousands of fans around the globe. But during the height of COVID-19, percussionist Peter Ferry explored another direction. "So many people suffered from extreme isolation. I desperately wanted to build a sense of tight-knit community."

When premiering a vibraphone commission from the comfort of his living room, Ferry had two ticketing priorities. First, audience size would be limited to 16, keeping things intimate. Second, if people paid at least *something*, their commitment to the streaming experience would increase. Attendees could choose any of four ticket prices: $5, $25, $50, or $100. Significantly, around 50% selected higher tiers. "These events provided me with respectable income during a period when other streams dried up."

At first, just 3 shows were scheduled, but high demand ultimately led to 20, which all sold out. At curtain time, Ferry introduced himself and met the audience. During the 15-minute performance, attendees turned off cameras. The evening concluded with 20 minutes of open discussion as spectators (cameras back on) conversed about the music and its subject matter. While Ferry plans to continue this model, that's not his main takeaway. "I learned to pay attention and innovate based on what feels most needed at that moment."

Live Projection

Videos aren't merely for home entertainment. Projection transforms live events, adding visual stimulation and enhancing the experience. When piecing together performance videos, work with a recording (no matter how rough) to ensure timings are accurate and visuals are appropriate.

- **Correlating content.** Scenes of nature, animals, news footage, digital art, anything else that enhances the music's meaning.
- **"Mickey Moused" content.** If imagery tightly aligns with compositional elements, staying in sync may require a click track.
- **Live shots.** A camera feed can project close-ups and additional views.
- **Silent films.** Add the soundtrack to a movie without one.
- **Processing.** Algorithms interpret how the music "looks."
- **Video cloning.** Perform in collaboration with other versions of yourself (e.g., a double quartet involves a live group plus a video recording)!
- **Unaccompanied content.** Standalone videos can bridge transitions and add variety.

Silent Film in Reverse

At a film festival, the new music sextet Eighth Blackbird was accompanied by video jockey (VJ) Patrick Nugent. VJs manipulate visual images in real time, much as DJs work with audio. "It's the reverse of musicians improvising to accompany a silent film," says Nugent.

This performance highlighted a flood that devastated the city a year prior. Studying the music beforehand, Nugent arrived with a huge video library. Combining a live feed with public domain archival footage and film clips about the flood, he mixed up to five layers at a time, manipulating color, saturation, speed, and other parameters. "Without being too obvious, I work to stimulate imaginations with funny, weird, or otherwise thought-provoking imagery."

Virtual/Augmented Reality

Virtual reality (VR) technology immerses users in an alternate universe. It is possible to look and move in any direction, thanks to videos filmed with omnidirectional 360-degree cameras that simultaneously capture everything around a sphere looking up, down, and around. Full surround sound changes depending on orientation, tying audio to video. VR can also engage the sense of touch when users holding joysticks or wearing smart gloves trigger virtual elements. Possibilities to impact music and education are endless.

Augmented reality (AR) adds elements to a real, physical environment. Pointing devices with a camera (smartphones, tablets, etc.) in a given direction reveals fresh visual stimuli: musicians, sheet music, program notes, animations, anything. Imagine the implications. Suddenly, it's possible to:

- Visit a musical venue and watch 3D performances by artists who aren't really there.
- Read supertitles while watching an opera without constantly shifting your focal point.
- Transform real-world objects like soup cans or ice cream containers into featured props within a music video!

Hyper Reality

Imagine standing in the middle of a symphony orchestra, controlling exactly what you see and hear, far away from any concert venue. London's Philharmonia Orchestra created just that opportunity with a thrilling, interactive VR experience featuring Sibelius's *Symphony No. 5*. Shared with 48,000 roaming shopping center customers—72% of whom had never before attended a classical music concert—an impressive 85% indicated an interest in attending future live events. Talk about cultivating audiences!

Current Rising is the world's first "hyper-reality" opera. Commissioned by London's Royal Opera House, this immersive 15-minute experience combines music, VR, and a multisensory set. While listening to a tone poem inspired by Shakespeare's *The Tempest*, audience quartets make their way through an installation wearing a VR headset and backpack computer. Exploring a series of spaces covered by newspaper headlines, participants witness magical digital imagery and the avatars of fellow group members. A doorway appears to cue when it's time to move on. "This isn't the future of opera, but it could be one of its futures," explains director Netia Jones.

VR and AR are also transforming music education. An app by ArtMaster teaches beginners to play piano. After selecting a virtual environment (outer space, mountains, opera house), users see their hands touching a real keyboard along with falling cylinders that indicate which keys to depress. Doing so gamifies learning while speeding up the process.

Projection Mapping

We are accustomed to viewing videos on ordinary, flat, blank screens. Why stop there? Projection mapping allows literally any stationary surface to become a "screen" for 2D or even 3D images: walls, tables, music stands, shoes, cars, statues, apples, you name it. Some examples involve skyscrapers and multi-million-dollar budgets. However, mapping technology is within reach for even independent artists. It requires specialized software but is cast with (one or more) ordinary projector(s).

> **Video Anywhere**
>
> The Sydney Opera House's façade, an architectural marvel, has served as a backdrop for multiple projection mapping spectacles. In *Lighting the Sails*, the building seemed to billow in the wind, stage larger-than-life dancers, and fold like collapsing origami. This project required 17 state-of-the-art projectors mounted 200 meters away.
>
> On a smaller scale, chamber ensemble CreArtBox regularly combines music with dancing, acting, acrobatics, and projection mapping. *Lighting the Dark* features a pianist surrounded by semitransparent screens installed at various angles. Audience members, positioned in three directions, experience unique visual relationships. Other CreArtBox programs use music stands, moveable walls, and pyramids of boxes as projection surfaces.
>
> Another remarkable example features the visioning of Korean artist Changhoon Nam. Set to Justin Huwitz's big band score from the movie *Whiplash*, about a talented percussionist at a prestigious music school, vibrant imagery is projected onto five drums of a trap set.

Holography

Much of the world first witnessed holographic projections through *Star Wars*. Holograms are optical illusions, people and objects that appear in three glorious dimensions. However, the image changes depending on your angle, making them more three dimensional than even 3D films. Better yet, they are visible to the bare eye. Think AR without the device. Consider the potential impact of holography on the music industry. Illuminating realistic, lifelike performers who aren't actually present—whether prerecorded (including artists who are no longer living) or playing live from a remote location—a single artist can theoretically perform simultaneously in dozens of venues around the globe!

They're There, But Not Really There

"Holography has been around for over 100 years," explains composer Eugene Birman. "But the technology has changed, offering exciting artistic potential." His opera *Aria* is installation art. As attendees make their way through a greenhouse, they encounter both a live children's choir and holograms of adult singers projected onto LED fans and an upside-down sprinkler system. *Slow Dance* maps avatars on top of an actual dancer, extending her anatomical capabilities to realize superhuman feats. In *The Longest Days*, a 100-member choir performed for 17 full minutes before literally evaporating. The audience gasped, suddenly realizing they'd been duped. What they just experienced wasn't "real." The show ended with a live choir singing alongside projected counterparts.

PART III
NICE WORK IF YOU CAN GET IT

"What do you do?" is often the first question asked by new acquaintances. Let's get specific. The music industry offers vast employment opportunities in diverse areas spanning education, performance, composition, technology, administration, artist support, retail, and beyond. Most savvy musicians balance assorted activities, often combining several categories.

Part III : Nice Work if You Can Get It considers:

- Which opportunities exist?
- What do they entail?
- How can you get the gig?

Chapter 16
The Art of Getting Hired

Landing a "gig" requires a sophisticated obstacle course. Each move is a hurdle in itself, one that must be adequately cleared before advancing to subsequent rounds. Assume that desirable opportunities motivate many applicants, often 50 to 300+. When embarking on a job hunt, don't be afraid to lean into your network. People you know can play an outsized role in sharing opportunities, personal reflections, and institutional history. They will serve as your references and support system.

Savvy musicians spend significant energy drafting cover letters, updating resumes, practicing for interviews/auditions. While many factors are outside your control, aim to *blow away the competition by every metric*. Beyond demonstrating expertise, showcase what truly makes you shine, putting to practice lessons we've already considered.

The art of getting hired is partially a creative pursuit, as you decide how to best frame your case. It also presents an opportunity to reflect on past achievements and professional gaps. While there are clever ways to mask shortcomings (always be honest or it WILL come back to haunt you!), use the process to reflect critically and determine next steps. Fundamentally, search committees are concerned with three core questions:

1. Is the candidate qualified?
2. Can they thrive here?
3. Will we enjoy working with them?

COVER LETTERS

Cover letters, typically a single page. are submitted when applying for jobs. Do not send the same document to every employer. While much content can remain constant, add a few customized statements demonstrating your sincere interest in THIS work.

An *opening paragraph* must articulate the position sought, your current role, and proof that you meet minimum qualifications (i.e., terminal degree for college teaching jobs). In addition, briefly describe what excites you about the role and why you are a compelling candidate. The *document's body* is used to make your case. Each paragraph addresses a different aspect of the requirements, citing past successes and distinctive approaches. Rather than restating a resume, offer insights on what makes you shine. Don't just say what you believe—substantiate! If you claim to be passionate about community building, provide a "for example." Strong *conclusions* summarize arguments, often adding a "but wait there's more." End strong.

Beautifully designed letterheads make a powerful first impression. In addition to displaying your name in large font, include an email and phone number. (Mailing address is not necessary.) Listing a website is an invitation for readers to take a look. Unify your application package with the same header topping your cover letter, resume/curriculum vitae (CV), and supplemental materials.

When people come to me with concerns that they aren't getting hired (or winning grants, for that matter), I ask to see the cover letter. Gaping shortcomings exist 85% of the time. Many musicians spend decades honing their craft but only hours scripting this vital document. If an opportunity is important, devote the time necessary. It may require weeks.

Like any promotional document, cover letters involve storytelling. After reading a letter, I often ask, "Suppose there are 100 candidates. What are the THREE most important reasons they should hire you?" Many people struggle initially but ultimately identify great features. "Fantastic! Did you mention these things?" To their surprise and horror, the answer is almost always "no." That's a problem. This brings up an important point: *Musicians tend to broadcast weaknesses while neglecting strengths.* For example, if somebody has limited teaching experience, they talk about it awkwardly in ways that underscore the shortcoming. Be sure to frame your case in the best possible light.

Other common cover letter mistakes include typos, weak opening/closing arguments, neglecting important parts of the job description, unsubstantiated claims, overusing "I," and writing weaknesses (wordiness, same vocab used repeatedly, lack of sentence variety). Understand that committee members do not start by identifying candidates to interview. Rather, they look for any excuse to purge. In fact, sometimes this initial review is conducted by AI, HR, a headhunter, or another outside entity. Be sure yours passes the bar so it will be given full consideration as the process unfolds.

Disqualified

Here are my all-time-favorite disqualifying cover letter mistakes. You can't make this stuff up!

1. If the committee chair is Dr. Shankovich, avoid beginning "Dear Dr. Frankovich."
2. Though strong design makes your letterhead stand out, think twice about fonts where letters resemble hearts or appear to be dripping blood.
3. While philosophy is crucial, keep some to yourself, such as, "I believe music educators should not have kids because it shows a lack of commitment to the profession."
4. Refrain from spending two paragraphs clarifying your time behind bars.

> 5. Here's one I made (ouch!!!). After my letter was finished, I subconsciously saved a few more times, just to be safe. In my haste, "control" and "S" were depressed in the opposite order, transforming "With *a* strong background in music theory pedagogy" into "With *ass* strong background in music theory pedagogy…"
> 6. Even if you are extremely famous, do not replace letters of recommendation with the phrase "For referrals, just talk to anyone in the business."
> 7. Do not conclude with "I believe my record of success makes me the perfect candidate for Eastern Iowa University"—at least not when applying to Yale.

Resumes

There must be a thousand resources about writing resumes, yet so many musicians get it wrong. This document is *not* simply a historic account of what you've done. It is a marketing tool used to gain employment, grants, and more. Present yours in the brightest light.

1. **Customize.** Documents sent to booking agents should highlight different points than those for teaching jobs. Include only relevant information.
2. **Opening.** Begin with a short paragraph emphasizing strengths, objectives, or philosophy.
3. **Essentials.** Typical headings: Work Experience; Skills; Performance Highlights; Awards and Grants; Recordings; Publications; Education; Teachers/Coaches; Conductors; Other Accomplishments. Include summer festivals, master classes, internships, volunteer work, and self-initiated projects, if relevant. List dates and locations. In particular, people want to know what you've done recently.
4. **Benefits.** Great resumes illuminate not only what you've done but also the value you bring. Clarify what sets you apart from the pack with action verbs and specifics.
5. **Accentuate.** Hold a resume three feet from your face and see what stands out. Emphasize strengths by strategically using **bold**, *italics*, ALL CAPS, and formatting.
6. **Strengths upfront.** Showcase major achievements early on. With the exception of academic positions, begin with professional accomplishments rather than education.
7. **De-emphasize weaknesses.** Combine headings to avoid bringing attention to lean activities. For example, if you have only one recording but perform frequently, merge these sections to create a general impression of success. Always tell the truth, however; never exaggerate. "Embellished facts" compromise reputation and integrity.
8. **Concise.** Choose words carefully. Resumes are typically a single page, though well-spaced two-page documents are better than cramming everything into one.

9. **Sparkle.** Approach resumes like artwork, mirroring your high-quality output.
10. **Consistency.** Keep formatting clear, logical, easy to navigate.
11. **Proofread.** Assume typos or inconsistencies will be noticed and count against you. Since *proofreaders' blindness* is real, have others double check your document.
12. **Combine.** Always submit resumes in conjunction with a cover letter.

Resume writing forces you to evaluate. Beyond illuminating successes, it makes shortcomings apparent (and everyone has these). Though documents can disguise weaknesses, confronting professional holes can be positive, identifying where energy should be focused moving forward.

Curricula Vitae

Far less information is available about curricula vitae (CVs). As a result, many people are unsure how to approach them. In fact, some mistakenly send resumes when CVs are required. CVs are the standard document in Europe. In the United States, resumes are more often requested apart from faculty searches, some grants, and specialized work.

CVs are longer, more in-depth accounts of your academic and professional history; someone fresh out of college might require 5 to 8 pages, while a seasoned professional could fill 15+. Both quantity and quality often count. Although it shouldn't turn into a novel, the luxury of space allows for details describing what and how you contributed to past employment. For example, when describing teaching, include the number of students, responsibilities, and unique contributions. Explain the significance and competitiveness of awards. Use concise bullets rather than run-on paragraphs. In addition to common resume categories, CVs may include repertoire or composition lists, professional memberships, community service, languages spoken, or even hobbies. Names and contact information for references—three to five colleagues, supervisors, professors, or collaborators who can speak to your skills and work ethic—often appear at the end.

Assume CVs will be skimmed rather than read. This makes it even more important that savvy formatting guides the eye. You never know which data will be noted.

Interviews

Candidates who advance beyond a screening round are invited to interview. Depending on the position, this can involve a single video call, an in-person visit, or a process combining multiple touchpoints. In addition to meeting with the committee, there may be conversations scheduled with HR, leadership, and other stakeholders.

Before the big day, research the organization thoroughly. Scour their website to understand practices, structure, and philosophy. Study names and backgrounds of people involved. Consider why you want this opportunity and which major points to convey. Mock interviews with friends/colleagues/mentors are invaluable.

Video-record these interactions and analyze your performance, paying attention to body language and nervous habits.

For virtual interviews, find a quiet, distraction-free zone. Turn off phones and refrain from chewing gum or checking email. Keep pen and paper handy to organize thoughts, jotting down important points as they arise. It is also helpful to have a resume nearby in case your mind goes blank. Do not interrupt, and keep answers short. Say just enough to intrigue, while creating positive rapport. The goal is typically to advance to the next, in-person round, so avoid the urge to divulge every last detail.

Dress the part for face-to-face sessions. Make eye contact, smile, and demonstrate enthusiasm. Maintain a professional aura while allowing your true personality to shine. Demonstrate that you are both qualified AND an outstanding colleague. Answer questions directly. Refrain from rambling, typically limiting each response to two to four minutes. Observers will follow up if interested. Speak honestly rather than guessing what interviewers want to hear, since there is no way to read minds.

Common interview questions, plus pointers:

1. *Tell us about yourself.* Be prepared for some variation of this. Don't simply provide a bio, regurgitate the cover letter (which they will have read), or reflect upon middle school. Instead, illuminate two to three essential points that emphasize your value. This is your opening argument. Start strong!
2. *Why are you interested in this position?* Rather than focusing solely on how you will be benefited (I need a job!), address organizational opportunities and how you are uniquely positioned to make a positive difference.
3. *How has previous work helped prepare you?* Articulate your approach and outcomes in ways that are relevant to this new position.
4. *What are your professional goals over the next 5 to 10 years?* Employers prefer ambitious colleagues but also want to gauge if you are likely to stay for a while.
5. *What is your artistic/business/teaching philosophy?* Many people give wishy-washy, nonspecific answers. Stand out by substantiating claims, providing examples of how your actions align with beliefs and deliver results.
6. *Can you describe a challenge with a colleague and how you resolved it?* This probes to see if you are self-reflective. Interviewers also want insights on what it will be like working with you.
7. *What are your strongest and weakest qualities?* Do not be shy sharing strengths. For weaknesses, the trick is highlighting meaningful growth potential (e.g., I'm just starting to wrap my mind around the potential of AI) that won't be unacceptable (I'm super lazy).
8. *What salary are you looking for?* This is a trap! Address broad considerations, but do not share a figure (!). Otherwise, you will never get a penny more.
9. *What questions do you have?* Always come prepared. Demonstrate sincere interest. Having no inquiries is a dealbreaker. So is asking about salary. The best examples address workplace culture, program design, institutional aspirations, etc.

Most committees are prohibited from discussing issues like marital status, children, sexual orientation, family structure, religion, or disabilities unrelated to the job. As an interviewee, you are welcome to bring up these topics, but it's best to stick to business.

In addition to interviewing, you may be invited to deliver a sample presentation or recital. For lectures, realize the topic is often less important than how it's portrayed. Content must be mastered, but you are likely the leading expert. Rather than packing everything in, focus on fewer points while emphasizing priorities, style, and philosophy. Do you integrate technology? Are you positive? Interactive? Likable? Funny? Similarly, recitals demonstrate more than musical excellence. The repertoire, words spoken, and rehearsals with collaborators are all noted. A final aspect of in-person interviews includes coffee breaks and meals. Even if these feel like times to relax, don't be fooled. Every interaction matters and plays a role in the final decision.

Interviews are two-way streets. Both employer and applicant must evaluate fit. Beware of red flags such as disorganization, workplace friction, disagreement around institutional priorities, or negative comments that indicate a toxic, dysfunctional environment. Sometimes applicants are so anxious to get any job that their better judgment is overridden.

A day or two following the interview, send a thank you note to the committee chair. If you are not offered the position, thank them again and solicit feedback. Frustratingly, some organizations never communicate results, forcing applicants to rely on grapevine gossip.

AUDITIONS

The act of auditioning starkly contrasts most everything in this book. Entrepreneurial inclinations won't help you here. The lengthy preparation phase has been compared to Olympic training, culminating in a highly competitive match permitting just one person to triumph. Particularly with blind auditions, where a screen between committee and applicant ensures complete anonymity, performance excellence—and little else—counts.

Consider, for example, a typical orchestra audition. Once a listing has been posted, up to 200 applicants submit resumes. Invitees are responsible for transportation, lodging, and food expenses. Hopefuls receive a repertoire list combining a solo piece (often a concerto) with a dozen or more standard excerpts, totaling up to 90 minutes. Either upon their arrival or at the audition itself, candidates learn which passages to play.

Onstage, the only human contact is with a proctor. The entire ordeal lasts six minutes. After an hour or two, the audition monitor announces a handful of players who advance to the next round (around 10%). Others are free to leave. A semifinal round usually follows, where committees listen longer and more discerningly to identify the few who advance further. Finals most closely approximate a concert performance. Removing the screen, candidates are announced by name and the music director is in attendance. One top performer is eventually selected, capping off a long and exhausting day for those on both sides of the screen.

Many variations exist. The process can be spread over several days, or finalists may be asked to join the ensemble for a trial period. Some groups mandate preview recordings. Individuals may be permitted to choose their solo piece(s). There can be a sight-reading component. The process also fluctuates when auditioning for festivals, chamber ensembles, teaching positions, regional groups, or other opportunities. In all cases, auditioning requires thorough preparation, focused concentration, nerves of steel, and top-notch performance.

Auditioning Tips

It is not uncommon to spend months training rigorously. The goal, many claim, is not to practice until music is right, but until you can't get it wrong.

- Devote two to three-plus months to the literature, working on a daily basis.
- Learn entire movements, not just excerpts, to understand context.
- Study scores, analyzing your part's role within the ensemble.
- Play along with multiple recordings that feature varied interpretations.
- Practice at a number of tempos (or even transpositions) to learn music inside out.
- Mock auditions simulating a high-stress environment are invaluable.
- Record and critique the results.
- At the audition, resist the self-destructive temptation of comparing your playing with others.

Opera and music theater work differently. Not only are singers seen, but also factors beyond performance influence the outcome. Productions often seek *triple threats*, those who sing, act, and dance. Multiple languages may be required. Physical attributes are paramount, since many roles are awarded to those who most look and sound the part. *Cattle calls* are commonplace in music theater, with many applicants auditioning simultaneously on the stage. Subsequent rounds may involve additional reps, staging scenes, or dance routines.

Great musicianship may not be enough to win competitive auditions. A single dropped note can mean instant disqualification. Even flawless renditions fall short, with many elements out of the applicant's control. For example, while adjudicators use specific rubrics, weighting is subjective. (What's the difference between a 7 and 8 in "tone"?) Judges look for different qualities. If they are unable to agree, nobody gets the job. In other words, auditions are a bit of a crap shoot. Most people serious about full-time ensemble work take many auditions before receiving an offer. Others never get that golden ticket.

Essentially all performers are required to participate in competitive auditions at some point. Discipline, consistency, and other important lessons can be gleaned from the process. The more pressure you heap upon yourself, the more likely you will crash. Try to enjoy the experience regardless of outcome. In the face of rejection, develop thick skin and stay positive. Make each audition a learning experience.

Audition Hacker

Percussionist Rob Knopper has taken 54 auditions. Forty ended in rejection. Despite intense preparation, his Achilles heel—uncontrollable nervous shaking—torpedoed any chance. After working through a sea of emotions, he experimented with preparation strategies, ultimately developing an effective practice regimen.

- Phase 0: **Excerpt research.** Listen to recordings, analyze the parts.
- Phase 1: **Learn the notes.** To instill muscle memory and confidence, he uses the self-coined technique ROAM: Repetitive, One note at a time, At tempo (never slower), Method. This involves *backchaining*, or starting from the end and working backward, adding one pitch at a time.
- Phase 2: **Self-recording.** Audio- or video-record run-throughs. Then scrutinize.
- Phase 3: **Mock auditions.** Realistic replicas of the audition environment include a waiting room, greeter to share the rep list, and makeshift screen.

This approach works! Among other successes, Knopper is now section percussionist with the Metropolitan Opera. He also shares strategies through an "auditionhacker" website and leads a yearlong program called "Rob's inner circle" that helps a cohort of 15 musicians polish auditioning skills and win jobs.

Negotiation

The title of a book by Chester Karrass is instructive: *In Business as in Life, You Don't Get What You Deserve, You Get What You Negotiate.* Remarkably, a whopping 49% of people fail this test before accepting their first position! After receiving an offer, realize that you likely have more capital at that moment than ever again. True, you don't want the prospect to evaporate. But the employer also doesn't want to blow it. They want you on their team!

When an offer is made, show enthusiasm and gratitude, but don't accept anything during an initial call. Instead, wait. Listen calmly and ask questions. Let them suggest the first number, and understand this is a starting place. In most cases, they anticipate a counteroffer. Investigate every facet of the proposal including salary, benefits, startup expenses, etc. You certainly won't want to haggle for something that is already part of the deal (e.g., a laptop).

On a follow-up call, negotiate from a position of power. Know your value and request what you want/need. In fact, it often makes sense to overshoot, as they will likely come back in the middle. Beyond salary, other elements may be negotiable: travel funds, summer schedule, office space, moving expenses, project support. Address only issues the negotiator can accommodate (as opposed to asking about health care, which is likely consistent across the company). Anticipate objections and come prepared with reasonable rationales. Though not easy to do, be willing to walk away if an employer can't meet your minimum requirements. Business is business. Don't take things personally.

Studies have found that women earn up to 30% less than their male counterparts for comparable work. Similar trends occur with people of color, members of the LGBTQIA community, and noncitizen applicants. While multiple factors are to blame for these unfortunate discrepancies, members of specified groups often feel apprehension about the negotiation process. Asking for too little or simply opting out can mean generating considerably less over the course of a career. As scary as it seems, know your worth and advocate for yourself. A carefully thought-out conversation can dramatically impact your future.

Self-Advocacy

Like so many musicians, jazz trumpeter Mark Morgan failed to negotiate his first big gig. *This must be the standard for cruise ships*, he reasoned naïvely. A different reality emerged. Some colleagues raked in $400 to $500 more per week, while a nonrequired booking agency claimed 20% of his fees. "I'd been bamboozled!"

Morgan ultimately got proactive. When a touring Broadway production reached out, desperate for a last-minute replacement, he was flattered and available. To make things work, however, he would need 40% more than what was offered. After the company explained they unfortunately had no flexibility, he thanked them and declined politely. Three months later, they called back with another offer matching his earlier appeal. Thrilled, he requested a few more perks like his own bus row and private hotel rooms. They obliged.

WHEN TO TAKE A GIG

Throughout their careers, savvy musicians are presented with numerous opportunities. Some are too good to pass up, others are riddled with problems, and still others are unclear. When deciding which to accept, *weigh the energy required against its benefits*, which may include:

1. **Pay.** Will the compensation make it worth your time?
2. **Connections.** Will it build relationships with potentially great contacts?
3. **Future.** Will it open the door to new opportunities?
4. **Satisfaction.** Will you feel fulfilled?
5. **Prestige.** Will it add to your reputation?
6. **Skill.** Will it help you develop a new ability?
7. **Gap.** Will it fill a hole in your work experience?
8. **Growth.** Will it help you evolve musically or intellectually?
9. **Debt.** Will it repay an obligation to someone who has helped you?
10. **Service.** Will it allow you to contribute meaningfully?

BENEFITS (#)	COMMENTS
8–10	Take it! This is a dream job.
5–7	The gig has much to offer. Pursue if at all possible.
3–4	Somewhat appealing. As long as you don't have too much on your plate, go for it.
2	If you really need work, accept. In the meantime, create more opportunities.
1	Only consider if desperate for work.
0	Run. Don't look back!!

Chapter 17
Teaching

Music education changes lives. Its teachers maintain an unrivaled role in the development of students, engaging on a daily/weekly basis for years on end. There is demand for this field almost everywhere, and you will be hard pressed to find more appreciative audiences. No wonder so many savvy musicians pursue teaching!

Above all, *what do you teach*? Readers may be tempted to answer "music," "my instrument," or "theory." Though logical, allow me to suggest an alternative. While artistic literacy is clearly valuable, it does not represent the entirety of what music instruction offers or contemporary learners need. This art form can cultivate self-esteem, collaboration, empathy, leadership, multiculturalism, attention to detail, technological fluency, communal engagement, creativity, and more. However, such priorities do not materialize automatically.

Curriculum matters. Do lessons celebrate the creative genius of composers past or creative genius of students present? Must learners work through open-ended problems (messy critical thinking) or implement "correct" solutions (efficient rule following)? Does performance center on competitive perfectionism or joyful community building? Of course, you can and probably should embrace a balance. But every decision comes at the expense of a thousand others. Be intentional. The most important thing you teach? *Students*.

TEACHING JOBS

Many musicians find teaching jobs attractive—whether primary, secondary, or collegiate—in part because of their unique framework for shaping learners over time. Additionally, full-time positions offer the perks of steady employment (consistent paychecks, benefits, etc.) and a professional community of colleagues.

K–12 Classroom

The vast majority of public and private K–12 schools hire at least one, and often several, full-time music teachers. With few exceptions, these educators must have certification and a related college degree. Part-time positions may also exist. According to a 2019 Arts Education Data Project study, 92% of US public school students have access to music education. Around 49% of them take advantage (with the highest percentage in elementary schools).

Common music classes include general music (elementary), choir, orchestra, band, jazz, and musical theater. Select programs, particularly at the high school level, offer music theory, history, technology, composition, songwriting, film scoring, guitar, rock band, percussion ensemble, chamber music, or Mariachi. Enlightened curricula led by savvy musicians may even offer music business and entrepreneurship.

Except for the occasional evening concert, most teaching occurs Monday through Friday during the school day. Nights, weekends, holidays, and summers are off, allowing time for family, personal projects, and additional work. The story is different for those leading marching bands or directing musicals, known for before/after-school rehearsals, weekend competitions, football game halftime shows, and summer training.

> ### Making Music Education a WIN
>
> When trombonist/guitarist Eric Songer was hired, his middle school teaching position involved multiple concert bands and small group lessons. "But I wanted to reach more people. Band, orchestra, and choir are great, but not for everyone." In a general music class he introduced, projects challenge students to create soundtracks for Pixar shorts and video games, stacking beats, guitar riffs, sound effects, and the human voice. "Our software allows you to write some pretty darn awesome things, even with limited training."
>
> His school requires students to attend three WIN (What I Need) sessions weekly. While this time can be devoted to academic tutoring, Songer's music options include workshops on DJing, songwriting, ukulele, and music production. He also supervises a fee-based after-school program (scholarships available!). Alternating ensembles, which meet once a week over the course of a term, include marching band, hip hop, guitar, bluegrass, garage band, jazz, Marichi, and more. "You don't want to be the teacher who does the same thing every year. We need to be open to change. Not just for change's sake, but to do what's best for our kids."

COLLEGE

I regularly hear musicians declare their unwavering interest in college teaching. With gentle prodding, it often becomes apparent they have little idea what that entails. While I can personally attest to the merits of this field, becoming a professor requires more than teaching theory or clarinet! Before placing all eggs in this basket, study actual job descriptions, observing requirements, preferences, and how many postings are available in your area. Also investigate the pay scale for your field. (Many aspirants are surprised to learn that college professors often earn less than public school teacher counterparts.)

> ### The Only Possibility?
>
> Some people pursue college teaching because they "cannot imagine anything else." It can be argued that someone incapable of survival outside academia should think twice before entering a field responsible for training future professionals. On the flip side, there is a need for savvy faculty committed to preparing the next generation for a quickly evolving world.

Music faculty positions exist in fields like applied instruction, ensembles, theory, history, education, and composition. Some universities also support music therapy or business. At small schools, instructors may be required to juggle multiple topics. Local orchestra members and freelancers, hired part time, often make up the majority of performance faculty.

Full-time college jobs are competitive—50 to 200+ applications are not uncommon. Most institutions consider only candidates with terminal degrees (typically a doctorate). Only the rare school dismisses educational pedigree, instead favoring international repute. Search committees increasingly gravitate toward musicians with a strong history of success in the field . . . plus something unique. Savvy musicians tend to stand out over those with traditional training only.

Around a third of college jobs are *tenure track*. After six to seven years at the rank of assistant professor, faculty apply for tenure through a rigorous review process. Once granted, promotion to associate professor guarantees employment (you can only be fired for doing something really stupid). However, a negative review in this process—not being granted tenure—means that employment is terminated. Some schools are infamous for never granting this distinction, while others boast a high success rate. It typically requires at least five more years before applying for promotion to full professor. Tenure-eligible employees balance three work requirements:

1. **Teaching** (approximately 40%). A full-time weekly load is typically 12 hours of classes or 18 hours for applied lessons. That may not seem like a lot, but it quickly adds up when combined with curriculum development, grading, office hours, and other responsibilities.
2. **Scholarship** (approximately 40%). Publications, performances, recordings, awards, and other field-specific activities. "Publish or perish" references scholarship.
3. **Service** (approximately 20%). Recruitment, committees, and other activities that serve music/university/local/professional communities.

Community colleges hire music faculty without the strict scholarship requirements, ideal for those interested primarily in teaching.

> **College Teaching with a Growth Mindset**
>
> After moving from Japan to the US for grad school, flutist Mihoko Watanabe got her first part-time college job when being discovered in a practice room by the director. Following a one-year sabbatical replacement, her first tenure-track position involved just 6 flute majors. (There were 18 when she departed after five years.) Teaching has included applied lessons, flute technique, chamber music, music history, world music, and ear training.
>
> After being approached by the search committee, Watanabe applied for her current post. Advancing past hundreds of applicants, she was one of three finalists. "Rather than guessing what they wanted, I shared my authentic philosophy. Great performance is important, but not enough. Strong musicians are driven to become better humans, always curious with a growth mindset." Hired as assistant professor with "credit," she was promoted to associate professor three years later and full professor after another five.
>
> "I'm always overloaded," reflects Watanabe with a smile. In addition to studio teaching, she founded and runs a music entrepreneurship certificate program. Her research specializes in solo flute music by Japanese composers. "And I love service!" Beyond recruitment, she serves on faculty senate, tenure and promotion, and search committees, and as program chair within several national organizations.

INDEPENDENT TEACHING

Independent music teachers guide life-changing journeys that often last for years. Career strategies could fill a book. (In fact, my publication *The Savvy Music Teacher* does just that, unveiling a blueprint for generating $50,000 to $100,000 annually while increasing impact.) For each opportunity that follows, two employment models are possible:

1. **Entrepreneur.** You take on the risk. If participation is robust, earnings can be significant.
2. **Employee.** Contracted by an existing organization with a lower but guaranteed salary.

Private Lessons

Fully customizable, one-on-one lessons meet students where they are. While it is common to teach your primary instrument, instruction is also possible on secondary instruments, various genres, musical skills (improvisation, sight reading, arranging), and extramusical perspectives (wellness, performance anxiety, career models). For some instructors, a handful of students is plenty. Others pack a

full-time, seven-day-per-week enterprise. With time and proactivity, it is possible to sculpt a studio that fits your goals.

The academic year (when most teaching occurs) includes 36 weeks, or 180 days. Because students invariably miss from time to time due to illness, travel, and other conflicts, the average person studies 32 to 34 weeks during this period. Summer break, around three months, offers an opportunity to embrace different musical priorities and scheduling approaches. A summer package might include six to eight flexible lessons, to be scheduled as convenient.

I recommend collecting tuition each term rather than charging by the lesson. Doing so minimizes cancellations, increases commitment, and secures income. It also makes things easier on families, allowing them to budget predictably. Tuition may also include activities such as recitals and workshop participation. Several online platforms geared toward independent teachers allow for automated invoicing, credit card payments, and income/expense tracking (a huge time saver during tax season!), in addition to helpful features like lesson reminders or even birthday well-wishing.

Shake Up Your Studio

Teachers typically offer 30-, 45-, or 60-minute weekly lessons. Though these frameworks make sense, they are not the only good options. For example, why not combine a half-hour in-person Monday lesson with 15-minute Wednesday and Friday online micro-sessions? Long meetings of 90+ minutes invite in-depth exploration. Not every week must be identical. To shake things up, an annual "intensive" with five consecutive daily lessons offers intrigue.

Teaching from home saves money in at least three ways: (1) eliminating the need to rent a separate space, (2) reducing gas expenses, and (3) creating a tax benefit for homeowners. It also avoids commute time and inconvenience when students cancel. Isolate a room or two solely for teaching if possible, separating work from personal life. Be clear about responsibilities placed upon household members such as cleanliness and quiet during lessons.

When a home studio isn't feasible, rooms can be rented in some office buildings and music stores by the month or hour. Another option involves traveling to students' homes. While this eliminates certain overhead, extensive driving is time-consuming and pricey. Is an hour round-trip ride for a 30-minute lesson reasonable? Add "travel fees," as appropriate.

Enlisting students is comparable to any other marketing. Word of mouth is most effective. Parents of students, in particular, make powerful allies. Sweeten the deal with discounts or other incentives in exchange for leads. Optimize your website. Get involved with local music programs (youth symphonies, school ensembles, church choirs, summer camps, etc.), volunteering to lead sectionals, offer master classes, or provide additional services.

ONLINE LESSONS

Synchronous lessons through video conferencing platforms are increasing in popularity, for good reason. Teachers can accept students from anywhere (including places with a higher going rate), expanding their footprint while populating difficult-to-fill slots with folks from different time zones. There is no need to cancel because of sickness or yucky weather. Commute time is eliminated. Despite some pedagogical disadvantages—the inability to physically adjust a student's posture, point to sheet music, or perform without lag—strengths include always playing in front of a "mirror" (the camera) and the ease of recording.

> ### Lesson Subscriptions
>
> Joseph D'Amico moved his entire piano studio online "before it was fashionable." Leveraging strengths of this technology while mitigating weaknesses, subscription-based *flex lessons* have transformed his pedagogical and business models. Students learn through three constructs:
>
> 1. **Tutorials.** An ever-growing curriculum of 800+ lessons (5 to 30 minutes apiece) is available on demand. Up to five videos per piece illuminate various approaches, tempos, and challenges. (Two free beginner courses, which have been viewed by thousands, "build trust, share my style, and serve as an incredible recruitment tool.")
> 2. **Submissions.** Subscribers can upload unlimited performance videos (typically 30 seconds to 3 minutes) to a private forum. D'Amico provides feedback through video responses, also viewable by the full community.
> 3. **Lessons.** One-on-one Zoom meetings purchased through an auto-scheduler, as desired.
>
> D'Amico's setup includes (1) a speaking microphone and piano stereo pair ("three mics makes a world of difference"); (2) a mixer; (3) a main camera; (4) an overhead camera capturing keyboard and hands; (5) an iPad for sharing/enlarging/writing on sheet music; and (6) OBS software, linked to (7) Zoom video conferencing and a (8) a *steam deck* loaded with buttons, which allows for instant view changes (e.g., main camera + keyboard + sheet music). "This approach works well because everything is simple and automated. I just teach and do my thing."

GROUP LESSONS

Private instruction is not the only effective option. Group lessons offer a slew of benefits. This format invites students to collaborate, learn from/teach one another, develop social skills, and overcome performance anxiety. It can cultivate friendly competition, which leads to quicker progress. When done well, communal learning is incredibly fun.

Financially, group lessons benefit all involved. Suppose your private lesson rate is $60/hour, while a 60-minute group lesson costs three participants $40 apiece. Each student saves one-third, yet teacher salary doubles ($40 × 3 students = $120/hour). Talk about a win-win!

It is not necessary to choose between private and group lessons. The Suzuki method often incorporates both on a weekly basis. Organizing even a few group experiences adds curricular variety. Though doing so introduces logistical challenges, the payoff can be enormous.

Amplifying Success

Early on, Daniel Patterson's studio involved a packed roster of 60 pianists taking mostly 30-minute private lessons. Requiring 42 work hours weekly (including travel), it generated $50,000 annually.

Fast forward five years. Patterson offered only one-hour group lessons (except for advanced players), with five headphoned students playing on keyboards in his dining room. "With lots of guided practice, an hour together was equivalent to three on their own!" Studio count jumped to 100; time requirement fell to 23 hours; annual income blew past six figures.

A decade later, Patterson took things to the next level. Two teachers plus two high school/college assistants in a 900-square-foot space now engage up to 480 students weekly over a 20-hour window. Twelve students at individual keyboards begin in the "assessment room" at, say, 4 p.m. Playing is evaluated solely by proprietary Piano Express software, gamifying the learning process. High scores allow learners to move on; those needing help ask the assistant. At 4:30, as a new dozen pianists arrive, the first group moves to one of two "discovery rooms" with six keyboards and an instructor for collaborative work on theory, rhythm drills, sight reading, and more. A study of this approach showed that beginning and intermediate students progress six times faster than with traditional lessons. That may explain why more than 500 studios of various instruments have converted to group lessons and licensed his platforms.

IN-PERSON CLASSES

Whether involving dozens of students or just a handful, classes allow for the exploration of fascinating topics. Some options can be administered at various skill levels (theory 1 through 4, beginning/intermediate/advanced guitar, etc.).

CATEGORY	TOPIC IDEAS
Musical performance	Chamber music, technique, literature, improvisation, conducting.
Musical skills/knowledge	Theory, ear training, music appreciation, music history, world music, sight reading, conducting, composition, songwriting, keyboard, Eurythmics.
Music technology	Recording, video, live sound, electronic performance, notation, sequencing, sampling.
Wellness	Alexander technique, body mapping, yoga for musicians, overcoming performance anxiety.
Professional skills	Career development, entrepreneurship, pedagogy, audition prep.
Early childhood	Programs like Music Together and Kindermusik, geared toward babies, toddlers, young children, and their parents.

Organizing your own class can be lucrative, particularly if it attracts healthy participation. Suppose you offer an hour-long course that meets 12 times over the course of a term. Tuition is $240, or $20 per session. If 15 students sign up, $300 is generated per hour ($20 × 15 students = $300). Even if a room must be rented for $25 to accommodate this community, this leaves $275/hour, a healthy wage!

Class recruitment requires savvy marketing. Introduce relevant offerings with intriguing titles, get the word out, and secure strategic partners. Then tap your network. Involve your own private students and ask for referrals.

Online Classes

Asynchronous eCourses allow students to progress on their own timeline and watch lessons multiple times, as desired. Unlike traditional classes, which consistently have the same duration (e.g., 50 minutes per week), the length of each video can vary. It often makes sense to release a library of short, bite-sized presentations.

Designing, filming, and producing a quality eCourse is time-consuming. But if there is demand for your product, it can produce handsome passive income for years. To emphasize the point, a $100 eCourse purchased by just 300 people generates an impressive $30,000! Surely you have something to offer that would motivate a few hundred people.

> ### Student to Teacher Ratio: A Million to One
>
> Guitarist and composer J. Anthony Allen has released over 130 online courses. Geared primarily toward hobbyists who don't read music, his best seller is Music Theory for Electronic Musicians. Others address topics like music production, sound design, and creative entrepreneurship. The average curriculum involves 60 short video lessons totaling four to five hours. It sells for around $9, purchased through his own website or dozens of others (which claim 50% to 90% of the profits, depending on "weird voodoo royalty math").
>
> Every day, Allen either records or edits five new lessons. He also answers questions submitted through a "fierce, email triage system, which can be quite intense when you have so many students!" To date, his products have reached north of 1 million unique users.

SUMMER CAMPS

Music camps offer rich artistic environments to children of all ages. They can address a specific instrument, any topic listed under the "Classes" section, or ensemble experiences like orchestra, choir, jazz, rock, music theater, or marching band (or specializations such as drum major). Both day and sleepaway camps allow attendees to cultivate skills, build friendships, and rejuvenate the soul. Campers and faculty alike often consider these events to be annual highlights.

Running your own camp requires a major time commitment. Even a single, week-long summer experience necessitates year-round effort to plan, hire faculty/staff, organize logistics, update the website, and recruit participants. If you are willing to put in the energy, however, high-demand offerings with a savvy business model can be lucrative.

> ### Cellobration
>
> The Cello Camp, founded by Danielle Merlis, is a one-week summer day camp for 5th through 12th graders. Hosted at a church in her hometown, it attracts 32 participants each August, 80% of whom are repeat customers. Many live locally, but hotel-renting campers are increasingly interested. A typical day, from 10 a.m. to 3 p.m., includes rehearsals, musical skill building, creative electives, and master classes. The week concludes with a public *Cellobration*, featuring an all-level ensemble. "When I was a kid, music camps were serious, competitive, and 100% classical. I aim to create a fun, supportive community that integrates many genres."
>
> Attendees pay $675 in tuition. Private lessons are available for an extra fee. Camp expenses include salaries for four faculty plus Merlis, venue rental, swag

> (T-shirts, water bottles, etc.), and supplies. Participants bring their own lunch. "It takes a lot of work, but this is the most rewarding week of my year."
>
> When students began requesting more—*How about a cello boarding school?*—Merlis invented Ensembles on Tour, a camp alumni ensemble that performs in zoos and senior centers throughout the school year. She also launched an a cappella camp for youth interested in singing and beatboxing, utilizing a similar business model.

Teaching for Hire

Teaching for an existing academy or music store lesson program offers several benefits. The best programs cultivate a collaborative, supportive community. They provide physical space, coordinate logistics, collect payments, and recruit students. In fact, there may already be a roster eagerly awaiting instruction, allowing instant access to a full studio. In exchange for these perks, expect a steep price tag. Hiring organizations claim 15% to 50% (!) of generated fees. This means you get paid less—often significantly—than students are willing to pay.

Consider flipping the model. What if you become the entrepreneur? Grow your own "school," contracting teachers on additional instruments, styles, and approaches. This way, you earn passive income from every session.

> ### Grow a School
>
> Guitarist Tim Benson grew his home studio from zero to 30 in year one. After he decided to rent a local music store room, another 20 signed up. "I made pretty good money. But teaching back to back, day after day, became exhausting. By Friday, I was burnt toast." Benson took a leap of faith, renting a 1,200-square-foot suite and contracting two additional guitar teachers. When the client list plateaued at 110, he began to believe this was as far as things could go. Fortunately, a mentor encouraged bigger thinking.
>
> Fast forward to today. Music Academy of Acadia, a 4,500-square-foot building with 12 rooms, employs 40 teachers on 20 instruments. (Tuition is split 50/50 with instructors.) Collectively, they teach 600 students, who take advantage of recitals, summer camps, a karate-like reward system, portrait days, even an in-house recording studio. With so much growth, Benson may soon open a second location. "I've learned to free my mind from self-limiting beliefs. There were times I never imagined I could get to 50, 100, or 200 students. Finally, I'm comfortable reinventing myself. I've already done that four times this year!"

OTHER OPPORTUNITIES

Additional teaching opportunities are central to the portfolio careers of many musicians.

KEYNOTES	**MASTER CLASSES**	**WORKSHOPS**
Featured plenary at conference or another event.	Coach performers in front of an audience.	Interactive, participatory sessions.
COACHING	**TUTORING**	**CONSULTING**
Provide musical, audition, career, or other guidance on a limited basis.	Assist students enrolled in a music-based class.	Advise a (music) business on strategy.
EDUCATIONAL MUSIC	**ADJUDICATION**	**EDUCATIONAL PRODUCTS**
Method books, easy arrangements, music for educational ensembles, etc.	Evaluate individuals/ ensembles at competitions or festivals.	Musical flashcards, curriculum guides, theory/history games, etc.

TEACHING ARTISTRY

A *musical teaching artist* is just what it sounds like: musicians who use their art form as a teaching tool. While there are rich opportunities through retirement homes, business gatherings, prisons, and other adult communities, the majority of this work is with children. Unlike traditional classroom teachers, who engage a fixed group of learners throughout the academic year, teaching artists typically serve one-hour to two-week residencies in a given community.

Teaching Talk Tips

- **Be user-friendly.** Omit technical jargon. This is not a conference presentation!
- **Build confidence.** Some attendees are shy about their lack of musical know-how. Build self-esteem with comments like "That's a great question." Always validate responses even if they're not 100% correct.
- **Read not.** Whether working from an outline or literal script, practice so that delivery seems organized but spontaneous. Verbatim recitations appear insincere and stilted.
- **Keep moving.** Kids, and adults to a certain degree, have short attention spans. Shift activities regularly.
- **Beware of know-it-alls.** There is often at least one participant who likes to show off. Find a polite, positive way to redirect, creating a safe space for all.

Designing Workshops

Teaching artists are known for delivering highly engaging, interactive workshops. The goal is sometimes purely musical but just as often links to topics like reading, math, science, and history. When done well, *arts integration* teaches important lessons about both music and the other subject. Sessions are typically 30 (K–3), 45 (grades 4–6), or 60 minutes (older students). Always consider the audience's attention span. As you design the experience, think about:

1. **Hook.** What BIG idea unifies the presentation? Programs can be built around a composition, musical element, genre, historical period, holiday/season, songwriting, leadership, multiculturalism, the environment, self-esteem, etc.
2. **Repertoire.** Which music will be presented? Use one piece to teach multiple lessons or integrate a variety.
3. **Entry points.** What musical elements will guide attendees to "enter" the music? Some options are rhythm, melody, motives, tempo, texture, density, proportions, etc.
4. **Exercises.** How will you get participants engaged? Build fun, interactive activities.

After a successful event, attendees often buzz with excitement for days or weeks. Not only are they inspired, but also musical literacy and appreciation has expanded.

Leadership Training through Music Composition

As a teaching artist, oboist Hassan Anderson has used music to teach K–2 students about global cultures, high schoolers to overcome adversity, and senior citizens to harmonize as a choir. One engagement involved business leadership training. After interviewing performers to learn about musical parameters, Anderson charged eight teams to compose a woodwind quintet piece, no easy task for nonmusicians! To amplify the challenge, every attendee had to somehow participate in the art making, whether conducting, singing, or playing percussion.

With little guidance, groups determined how to lead professional musicians in what felt like a highly ambiguous task. Through questioning, ideation, and iteration, they created graphic scores. Rehearsals and a final performance ensued. "Following a learning curve, participants began asking insightful questions, listening carefully, and building meaningful solutions. Afterward, they considered how to transfer lessons learned into business contexts. I was blown away by their transformation."

Lining Up Work

Some organizations have an established tradition of importing teaching artists, while others need convincing. Learn who has the authority to approve programs. In schools, this is often the principal or parent teacher association's director, though sometimes a music teacher handles bookings. For local organizations, it can be helpful to meet with the contact in person, presenting a compelling description of how your services fulfill their needs.

In some regions, booking agents specialize in educational programming, orchestrating events in exchange for a commission. Many city, county, and state arts councils, as well as private organizations like Young Audiences, pair schools with artists. Nonprofits like VSA Arts specialize in bringing the arts to those with disabilities.

Getting into Schools

Though guitarist/mandolinist/banjoist Dave Ruch works with kids of all ages, he finds third through fifth grade his "sweet spot." These students are engaged, curious, and not yet self-conscious. A typical day involves one to three 45-minute presentations in the morning, followed by afternoon programming at another school. Every session is immediately relevant, directly tied to social studies curricula. For example, his fourth-grade concerts address the Erie Canal, Native American culture, and colonial America. Most weeks, he spends three days in the field, with another two for marketing and invoicing.

To book each season, Ruch emails specific segments of his massive, hand-curated list of 10,000+ contacts within an eight-hour radius. Hiring managers can be principals, arts coordinators, or teachers. Though some organizations book a year in advance, two to three months' lead time is the norm. Teaching artistry pays "considerably better than other gigs." Ruch charges $600 to $2,500 per session, depending on distance traveled, school budget, and other factors. "I started with a three-piece band but quickly recognized that fees for the 'show' are more or less the same whether there are five musicians or one. Solo makes more sense for me." Just as important is the sense of fulfillment. "Every day, I get to be a special guest. You can see how inspired these children get, learning and growing in ways they never could from a lecture. What a dream job!"

Chapter 18
Performance

Singers, instrumentalists, and conductors are the public face of the music industry. We hear them in concert, watch them on video, obsess over their gossip in tabloid news. The range of paid performance opportunities is broad, particularly for versatile, accomplished, savvy musicians. Better yet, this work can be pursued just about anywhere.

So much goes into a performer's life beyond performing. Countless hours involve learning, rehearsing, and maintaining repertoire. Networking, marketing, logistics, event design, and financial planning are daily rituals. Attention must be spent maintaining physical fitness and avoiding injuries that threaten the ability to make music. Mental wellness is just as crucial to combat performance anxiety, stressful circumstances, and the inevitable sting of rejection.

Few people argue this career path is easy. Yet something about it is uniquely appealing. Motivated by the ability to build community and touch the soul, performers bring a humanity desperately needed in today's world.

OPPORTUNITIES TO PLAY

The best full-time performance positions involve inspired artmaking and collaboration. Consistent hours, dependable paychecks, health insurance, and retirement contributions offer stability. It probably comes as no surprise that such positions are rare and cutthroat. Contracted, per-service or per-project work comprises the majority of performance employment. Freelancers must hustle consistently but maintain autonomy when deciding which gigs, collaborators, hours, and work conditions to pursue.

Life at the Bottom

"I just wanted to make a living playing tuba," reflected Andres Trujillo. Easier said than done. Orchestra was the most obvious career choice, yet even ensembles boasting four to six horns, several clarinets, and dozens of string players had just one tubist (if that).

After grad school and a cross-country move, he received an offer to perform with a New Orleans–style brass band. Having played jazz in high school,

> he thought, "I could do that," and rented a sousaphone. Beyond enjoyable, it transformed his thinking about the realm of possibility. Trujillo has since performed with Klezmer, polka, marching, and Dixieland bands, in addition to brass quintets and orchestras. He even got hired by Disneyland. "The harder I work, the luckier I get!"

Large Ensembles

Large ensembles include various orchestras (symphony, chamber, pops, string, ballet, opera, film), bands (wind, concert, brass, jazz, marching, circus), and choirs (concert, chamber, women's, men's, symphonic, religious, radio/TV, gospel, etc.). Members—particularly those who are full time—are regularly asked to fulfill responsibilities beyond playing, such as educational programming, meeting with donors, or serving on committees.

LARGE ENSEMBLE BENEFITS
THE EXPERIENCE
Large ensembles program great repertoire (hopefully!). Some groups tour and record. Be celebrated for your art while making a difference in your community.
FINANCIAL SECURITY
Dependable (sometimes substantive) paychecks, full medical coverage, sick leave, and generous retirement pensions possible.
JOB SECURITY
Some positions are *tenured*, meaning that members can't be fired unless they do something horrible. Earning this status typically takes one to three years, involving multiple reviews focused on playing, professionalism, and compatibility.
CREDIBILITY
Landing a major job boosts reputation and opportunities. Music schools often hire applied faculty from local professional ensembles.
SCHEDULING
Many groups maintain reasonable schedules, perhaps eight services per week (around 20 hours) not including practice time. Some provide 8 to 10 weeks of paid vacation.

Full-time, salaried large ensemble employment is extremely competitive. To emphasize the point: There are around 60 American orchestras that work 40+

weeks per year. Just 18 maintain a 52-week schedule. Between them, circa 250 full-time openings appear annually. Instruments such as tuba and harp typically have just one, or zero, posts. Positions regularly attract 150 to 300+ applicants, and not all spots are awarded to newcomers. Many go to those with previous appointments in different ensembles.[1] These statistics are not meant to discourage but rather to present an honest picture. (Auditioning techniques are considered in Chapter 16.)

Groups also hire long-term musicians and subs on a per-service basis. Amateur and student ensembles may employ "ringers" to beef up their sound. Pay scale is dependent on the hiring ensemble's budget.

Orchestrating a Career

On her 13th audition, Cornelia Sommer landed a job as second bassoonist with the Detroit Symphony Orchestra (DSO). The DSO has a 43-week season, which includes one month paid vacation.* Additionally, players may (1) collect a supplement in exchange for an additional work "obligation" (teaching, chamber music, etc.), (2) accept add-ons on a case-by-case basis, or (3) opt out completely. To date, Sommer has chosen #2.

"I love the consistency of playing with the same people in the same hall, not to mention financial security." She even has time for independent teaching, recording, touring, and keeping up with 20,000 Instagram followers while exploring music inspired by fairy tales.

Members receive a small stipend for the remaining nine weeks. Though less than unemployment, it avoids the hassle of filing.

MILITARY "BANDS"

Few musicians dream of a military career from childhood. "Yet this is a good four-year job for just about anyone. It can be a GREAT 20+ year job for many," explains Michael Mench, commander of the US Air Force Band of Flight. The best candidates are solid, versatile players who read well and play multiple styles.

The term *band* here is not limited to wind or marching groups. In fact, most are umbrella organizations comprising several performing ensembles. For example, the US Army Field Band consists of a concert band, chorus, big band, and pop combo. The US Air Force Band oversees six groups, including string orchestra, chorus (cleverly titled "Singing Sergeants"), brass band, and big band. Large ensemble members are often assigned chamber groups as well: Dixieland, Baroque,

---

[1] This research was provided by Brandon VanWaeyenberghe, who conducted a comprehensive study on the supply-and-demand elements in the orchestra field for the past 25 years.

Celtic, rock, pop, country/western, brass/woodwind quintets, etc. Positions exist for instrumentalists (winds, strings, percussion, rhythm section), vocalists, conductors, composers/arrangers, and recording/sound engineers.

MILITARY MUSICIAN BENEFITS
MUSICAL OPPORTUNITIES
Many groups tour, record, and perform at high-profile diplomatic ceremonies. Members can be featured soloists or perform chamber music. Musicians have the time/opportunity to line up external work and income sources.
SERVE YOUR COUNTRY
Military musicians provide a patriotic service.
COMPENSATION
Pay is based on rank and time served. Members get a step raise every one to two years, in addition to annual inflation raises.
JOB SECURITY
Premier ensemble members can stay indefinitely. You can't be fired... unless you really screw up and are dishonorably discharged.
BENEFITS
The military may subsidize college debt, lessons, and/or instrument purchases. Comprehensive health care is available. Members live on base for free or receive nontaxable housing allowances, and collect food stipends. Retirement eligibility comes with 20 years of service. Retirees receive a pension equivalent to approximately 50% of their highest base pay.

Each branch of the US military—Army, Navy, Air Force, Marines, and Coast Guard—employs multiple full-time music ensembles.[2] In *premier bands*, players audition for a specific chair, usually before enlisting. Ensemble members have a guaranteed post, without the worry of being transferred. These musicians are immediately awarded the rank of E6. (Rankings range from E1 to E9; higher is better. Other enlistees must work 5 to 10+ years to reach that status.) Most of the 10 premier military bands are stationed in Washington, DC.

For *regional bands*, players typically audition after enlisting (... so, do you want to fly planes, work intelligence, or play clarinet?). Members can be reassigned freely. As with most enlisted soldiers, entering status is determined by education. Musicians with college credit often begin at E3. Regional groups are housed on bases across the country and abroad. Some are stationed in war-torn regions, though for shorter periods than nonmusician troops.

---

[2] Similar frameworks are found in many countries.

To join, you must be between the ages of 17 and 28 to 42 (depending on the branch), physically fit, a citizen or permanent resident, a high school graduate (or equivalent), and able to pass an Armed Services Vocational Aptitude Battery test. Basic training, which takes 6 to 13 weeks, is required for most military musicians. You must look the part—hair short, face shaved, boots shined— keep your house in order, and don't even think about drugs. Just about everyone has duties beyond performance, usually band related such as booking gigs, web design, making posters, and accounting. Unlike nonmilitary jobs, personnel have legally binding contracts that must be served in full (regularly four to five years of active duty).

Theatrical Productions

The majority of professional opera singers are freelancers. Engagements with different companies result in concentrated stays around the country/globe. Contracts involve a rehearsal period (weeks or months) followed by 2 to 12 shows. This career model allows performers to pursue various roles. It also leaves them unemployed between contracts. Though rarer, full-time positions within a single company exist. Resident artists play multiple minor/understudy roles over the course of a season. Chorus members are also cast in multiple productions.

Musical theater operates similarly, with one major difference. Some shows are extended for months, even years. Andrew Lloyd Weber's *The Phantom of the Opera* appeared on Broadway alone more than 13,000 times!

How large is the market? There are 150+ US-based opera companies, with a combined budget of $570 million. Worldwide, there are more than 1,100.[3] Some specialize in a particular genre (e.g., classics, contemporary works), while others span the gamut. For musical theater, New York City alone supports approximately 40 Broadway (500 to 2,000 seats), 50 Off-Broadway (100 to 500 seats), and dozens of Off-Off Broadway (usually less than 100 seats) venues. Other thriving scenes include London's West End and cities in Canada, Australia, Germany, France, and Japan. Touring casts take productions on the road.

He Is Not Giving Away His Shot

"The number of times my bank account went negative was wild," reflects singer/dancer/actor Vincent Hooper. "At one point, I was subletting an apartment, without enough money to leave Chicago—or to stay." He accepted literally any regional theatre role. Job surfing became a daily ritual.

Applying for an "unspecified role" in *Hamilton* required multiple video submissions and three flights to auditions in New York. A grueling year later, something incredible transpired: an offer to join the Puerto Rico cast! Over several seasons, he played multiple roles in that production. Tryouts for *The Lion King* on Broadway were different, and he was awarded the main character role

---

[3] According to a 2022 Opera America report.

> of Simba within a two-week window. "It was surreal, working toward something for a decade, and having everything change in the span of a three-minute call."
>
> Hooper's current life model involves performing eight shows per week, recording a solo album, workshopping a new show, going to the gym, and communicating with fans. "The grind doesn't stop when you get a big break, just changes. I'm less interested in applause or autographs, but rather performing genuinely with my own spin."

Conducting

Just about every large ensemble—whether professional, semiprofessional, community, or educational—is led by a principal conductor. (In addition, groups may hire assistant and/or guest conductors.) Typically the highest-paid musician, for good reason, these professionals are charged with a lot more than waving batons! Addressing a great many musical and extramusical issues, entrepreneurial problem-solving is every bit as important as artistic visioning. Responsibilities include understanding instrumentation, knowing scores inside and out, determining rehearsal strategy, and driving interpretation. They often double as artistic directors, institutional leaders, board liaisons, fundraising champions, public personas, and motivational speakers who keep morale high (or face revolting constituents).

Obtaining conducting work is akin to other performance jobs, though the degree of scrutiny may be higher. Audition and interview processes can be extensive. Advanced degrees are rarely required, though the training, experience, and connections help.

> ### Leading Ensembles, and an Industry
>
> Mexican American Enrico Lopez-Yañez balances a career as principal pops conductor of four major American orchestras and guest conductor with dozens of others. "What I love about this profession is incorporating many of my passions on a daily basis. While musical excellence is paramount, that is just the beginning of a conductor's work. Much of my energy centers around designing engaging experiences."
>
> Though his first major ensemble had an established tradition of theatrical shows, scripted moments featured guest actors and never the conductor. Aiming to expand that paradigm, Lopez-Yañez produced *Symphony in Space*. Playing the character Cadet Enrico, he and assistant A440 (a C3PO-style robot) interacted with green-screen footage of the music director posing as Head of Star Fleet. Together, they protected the universe from Evil Lieutenant Tritone.
>
> Building on the popularity of this type of program, Lopez-Yañez founded Symphonica Productions, which licenses family, education, and pops shows to dozens of orchestras. For an affordable fee, organizations receive a package

> including music, script, actors, props, video, and often soloists plus conductor. Performances such as *Three Mexican Tenors* (featuring his father!) and *La Vida Loca* (a 1990s/2000s pop show) explore his Latin roots.

SMALL GROUPS

Working with small groups—rock bands, classical ensembles, jazz combos—offers numerous perks. When all goes well, collaboration is inspiring. Members have artistic freedom and opportunities to shine. Long-term ensembles, like marriages, leave no place to hide. Engage with people you like.

There is a continuum of organizational models. On one end, a single leader controls all artistic/business decisions, with others hired as sidemen. In exchange for more responsibilities and power, the boss gets paid extra. The opposite extreme entails a democratic co-op. Each member serves as an equal partner. Responsibilities are delegated, preferably in writing. For major decisions, voting takes place and majority rules. The more people involved, the more bureaucratic this model. The majority of chamber groups operate on a project basis—more gigs mean more pay. How much depends on the type of work, presenter budgets, and your reputation. Opportunities include:

- **Concerts.** Each series maintains a unique mission. Some specialize in an experience type, while others embrace a cross-section.
- **Parties.** Standalone engagements like weddings, B'nai mitzvahs, retirements, and corporate events can pay handsomely.
- **Background music.** Bar, restaurant, and hotel gigs often pay modestly, but the deal may be sweetened with semiregular employment, tips, or free food and drinks.
- **Miscellaneous.** Cruise ships, amusement parks, circuses, retirement communities, and casinos often employ small groups. Featured acts command respectable paychecks. Longer-term compensation is less impressive, though consistent.

House Concert

House concerts are potentially lucrative, fabulously fun, and often overlooked. Organized virtually anywhere, here's how it works: Find someone to host a performance in their home. They invite friends and colleagues, who each contribute a certain amount. For example, 50 guests might pay $30 apiece, or $1,500 total. You show up, play for 30 to 60 minutes, and mingle. A great time is had by all. Numerous variations exist: potlucks, barn or backyard events, getting paid by the host, soliciting donations rather than charging a fee.

Soloists

The smallest group is an ensemble of one. Presenters love solo acts that speak to an audience because of their lower fees and simplified logistics (hotel bookings, people to manage, etc.). Chordal instruments like piano, guitar, and harp stand on their own. Another option combines single line instruments with electronics, whether that involves looping, prerecorded tracks, or interactive software. From the artists' perspective, working alone eliminates the need to coordinate schedules or compromise with collaborators. On the flip side, extensive touring can be lonely, and delegating tasks to fellow bandmates is impossible.

Sacred Music

Sacred music employment is available almost anywhere. Most cities and suburbs are packed with houses of worship. Even tiny rural communities support at least one organization. Positions include music director, conductor, pianist, organist, cantor (vocal soloist), and arranger. Performers sing in choirs and play in bands/orchestras. Even jobs like worship leader, program director, creative arts pastor, or camp counselor may encompass artistic components. Institutions regularly hire one to two full-time musicians, plus freelancers. While some jobs require a related degree, personable performers with sufficient skills may quickly be embraced.

> ### Holy Musician!
>
> Eric Mathis has held two full-time positions titled associate pastor for music and worship at places called First Baptist Church (different states). Music responsibilities have included conducting adult, children, and youth choirs; playing organ and piano; overseeing handbell ensembles; leading worship bands; and directing special programs. He also manages a music budget, contracting professional performers, section leaders, and coordinators.
>
> Another critical job element involves pastoral care. Mathis spends hours each week connecting with congregants as they mark significant milestones, be it a birthday, wedding, illness, or death. "My personal philosophy is that I'm only as good of a musician as I am a minister, and vice versa."
>
> Major changes to the religious landscape mandate entrepreneurial thinking. "Fifty years ago, people came to church in droves simply because we existed. Today, folks demand particularly relevant activities. We must consistently rethink and reframe."

GIG GETTING GUIDE

Someone looking to hire musicians stumbles upon your website. After inquiring, they immediately book the group. You perform, get paid handsomely, and everyone lives happily ever after. Is this scenario conceivable? Absolutely. Is it likely? Probably not. Embracing marketing techniques from earlier chapters, contemplate approaches that distinguish your product, generate buzz, and seal the deal.

12 Steps to Booking Concerts

Presenters must secure exciting acts that sell to the public. Please understand if they don't jump for joy at the mere mention of your proposal. The more desirable a series or venue, the more overwhelmed they are with solicitations. However, if your product, fan base, and persistence are compelling, doors will open.

1. **Develop marketable products.** Design high-quality, buzzworthy shows.
2. **Compile promotion.** Optimally position your electronic press kit and website.
3. **Research options.** Compile a list of venues/series and their specs. Generate ideas from colleague bios, internet searches, trade journals, and newsletters. Local/state arts councils and union offices also maintain presenter lists.
4. **Think through logistics.** When booking a tour, consider time between shows, travel distances, and lodging/transportation. Lock in major events first and then fill in the blanks with conveniently placed and timed options.
5. **Script sales pitch.** Proposals must quickly hook presenters, explaining (a) what you do, (b) why it's attractive, (c) when you're available, and (d) how much you cost.
6. **Reach out.** This is your chance to shine . . . you have one minute. If interest is demonstrated, deliver requested materials ASAP. Be persistent.
7. **Agree on a price.** Fees must cover transportation, lodging, meals, performers, taxes, and other expenses that arise. Inquire if the presenter will cover hotels, meals, or other extras.
8. **Sign contract.** Major presenters prepare their own contracts. You may be responsible for drafting one with smaller organizations. Consult an attorney to clarify questions.

Under Contract

When booking a gig, clarify all essentials in a typed contract, to be signed by both parties. Which music? Any requests? Start/end times? When should musicians arrive, set up, and sound-check? What's the address? Parking? Elevator? Stage size? What's the attire? May performers eat catered food or is a separate meal provided? With whom should you communicate? How much is the fee? Deposit?

A *technical rider* is a document outlining specific needs that must be provided by the presenter: stage dimensions, electricity, amplification (microphones, speakers, monitors), piano tuning, lighting, instruments,

> chairs, stands, risers, computer, projector, screen, crew, dressing rooms, and backstage snacks. A diagram should illustrate stage setup. Request only what is absolutely necessary.

9. **Follow through.** Send requested information (bios, photos, and program notes) in a timely manner. A week beforehand, confirm all is on track. Always be accommodating. Inquire how you can be helpful: radio interviews, fundraiser appearances, etc.
10. **Market.** Do all you can to help populate the audience. In some cases, artists are responsible for much or all promotion.
11. **Have a great show.** Arrive early, be good to the crew, deliver a knockout performance!
12. **Keep in touch.** Long-term relationship building is the name of the game. Send a thank you note. Keep the presenter posted with career developments.

Some Thoughts on Touring

Will you primarily serve local (short drives), regional (long drives), or national/international (flights) audiences? Widening the area can open fresh opportunities, expand your network, and bring personal fulfillment. It also introduces logistical and financial complications.

Musicians often dream about becoming international sensations. Successful touring allows you to explore the world, receive thunderous ovations, and be revered as a celebrity. As glamorous as this sounds, it's not for everyone. Extensive touring takes a toll. It is difficult to maintain healthy personal relationships when on the road for extended periods. Professional travel can be exhausting and lonely and require extreme stamina. The money is not always spectacular considering preparation required. Are you OK putting many miles on your car? Sleeping in hotels? Dealing with airport hassles? Leaving kids and pets with others?

When sculpting your profile, consider how much touring makes sense. What is the ideal number of days you'd like to spend out of town? Perhaps the most difficult model is semiregular travel, say, half the year. While not enough to survive exclusively, this schedule makes it difficult to secure opportunities at home.

On the Road Again

Bassoonist Monica Ellis, founding member of the Grammy Award–winning woodwind quintet Imani Winds, finds herself touring around 150 days per year. The group has been featured across 49 US states and in Europe, Asia, Australia, and the Americas. "Performing regularly with my musical family" is what she loves most.

Touring is fulfilling but not easy. "I often wonder why doing what I do has to happen somewhere else. It takes two days to make a two-hour concert possible." As a single mom, she is committed to creating quality memories with her son when at home, particularly because their quantity of time together is so limited. This lifestyle is only possible thanks to Ellis's devoted mother, sister, and friends, who provide loving support when tours are underway.

Imani is striving to build a more sustainable life/business model. Early on, literally any gig was accepted. Now, they are choosier. By charging higher rates, the same amount can be earned with fewer road days. A university residency and summer music festival make some work local, allowing members to stay in their own beds, off the road again.

Landing a Contract

Music contractors hire freelancers to fill out ensembles for concerts, recordings, film scores, private parties, religious services, and other projects. They work for either a predetermined fee paid by the employer or 10% to 20% commission. Many performers supplement income as contractors themselves. Get paid twice when booking and playing!

Contractors often contact several people. The first to respond gets the gig, so be prompt. Do they tend to hire "pals"? You bet! Do what's necessary to join the "A-list." When seeking employment, network with local contractors. Request an appointment, perhaps over coffee. Most are constantly on the lookout for talent. They may request a resume, demo, or audition. On the job, go the extra mile. Be prepared, dependable, and likable. One mistake can tarnish your reputation. Think twice before turning down offers or risk being overlooked next time.

Making the "A-List"

As a contractor, cellist Karen Garrity books over 100 engagements per year spanning every setting imaginable: chamber groups for weddings, huge orchestras for feature film recording sessions, and a variety of ensembles to back rock bands. After agreeing to a ska concert, she had to research what that was. "I make it my policy to always say 'yes.' Sometimes I think *crap, how can I pull this off?* Then I do my research and make it happen."

Garrity meets players in a variety of ways. As a busy freelancer, she is always on the lookout for promising talent. Referrals carry weight and cold calls are welcome. "If you're not willing to put yourself out there, it will take years to get discovered." Her database of 1,500 musicians allows artists to be sorted by instrument, contact information, and up to 12 ranked specialties. To get hired, players must be technically strong, amazing sight readers (particularly for recording sessions, where time is money), quick communicators, and drama free. "I want no surprises. They should arrive early, look good, smell good, and be a fun colleague."

Competing Priorities

Most music competitions are, well, incredibly competitive. Designed to identify the best performer/ensemble/conductor/recording/composition/artistic statement, those talented and lucky enough to win may be showered with cash, gigs, management, instruments, a record deal, and/or other rewards. Every performance-based contest has a unique structure. Most target a specific instrument, ensemble type, or genre. Some or all repertoire may be prescribed, and age restrictions are common. In most cases, artistic excellence is the primary criterion. That said, there is always a degree of subjectivity.

How important should competitions be to your career trajectory? In the past, success here represented one of few paths to a big break. Today, that is less often the case. Single wins (or even multiple accolades) are unlikely to trigger a career jackpot. And there are many other ways to establish yourself, as this book has surely illustrated. With just 24 hours in a day, does it make sense to devote the intense energy necessary for a chance at competitive victory? Or are you better served devoting these minutes to entrepreneurial pursuits and other professional development? This is a strategic question of time/project management.

World Champion, Entrepreneurial Wiring

Over a decade, Taiwanese American harpist Noël Wan entered two dozen competitions, placing in two-thirds and scoring a few impressive wins. Before competing in the 12th USA International Harp Competition, she trained as if preparing for the Olympics. Though literature for the first two rounds was set, her interpretations were unorthodox. The third *free-choice round* included original transcriptions. For the finals, she selected an obscure new music work to complement the compulsory "French, quite harpy" concerto. "Most people (including my younger self) stick to standard rep. I took a chance that stood out. Either judges would like it or they wouldn't."

This time, her risk paid off. Awarded the gold medal, Wan received two high-profile showcases, a "bucket of money," a $60,000 harp, and visibility through a prominent magazine article. The accolade strengthened her case when applying to college jobs and is valuable for recruitment. "Competition success has been great for boosting confidence and elevating my professional profile. But building a career still requires having a strategic, entrepreneurial mindset. Even when competing, it's important to stay true to my personal brand, built around this important mission: to explore the complexity of living and making music as a woman."

The Deal with Management

Many performers fantasize about obtaining management, believing this is the silver bullet to solve all professional challenges. Yet those with representation often blame their firm for holding them back. Which is it?

In an ideal world, artist managers are part coach, part advocate, part business executive. Unlike contractors, who work on a gig-to-gig basis, managers are concerned with long-term development of artists they represent. They address career strategies, book concerts, negotiate payment, set up contracts, market and promote, and arrange logistics for local, national, or international events. Who wouldn't want this?

In reality, things are complicated. It is difficult to obtain management. And it's really hard to get *great* management. More than a few artists make grumbling about their company a daily ritual: "They charge too much and don't get enough gigs." This suggests the next point: Management is expensive. Withholdings may be considerably more than individual musicians make. In some cases, compensation is required when no work is secured. Finally, even the world's best manager will not magically secure stardom. *Musicians are always responsible for their own success.* Without a proactive agenda, representation proves futile.

Every manager operates differently. Some handle scores of clients, while others take on just one or two. There are companies specializing in specific types of acts, while others represent an assortment. Less experienced managers with fewer contacts might devote more time to your cause than someone juggling an extensive roster. On the other hand, they may be unequipped to land much work. Regardless, it is essential that your manager has a substantial network, clear understanding of your vision, and exceptional people skills.

Getting Managed

Most often, managers sign artists after:

1. Seeing a remarkable performance and approaching the artist.
2. Someone from their roster makes a recommendation.
3. Another manager or industry professional makes a referral.
4. An artist's reputation grows and the manager becomes interested.
5. An artist wins a competition and management is part of the deal.
6. Cold calling and an outstanding press kit. This is the exception, rather than the rule.

Also possible is for artists to hire a personal contact with good administrative/people skills to serve as their "manager."

Most touring artists eventually employ management. Some opportunities are open only to those with representation, and managers can save tremendous time and energy. Contracts are usually one to three years, with the possibility of an extension. A 20% commission on gross (total) earnings is typical, including even engagements the artist initiates. Expenses such as physical promotion, postage, etc., are also billed. Less established managers require a *retainer*, or monthly fee, even if no gigs are secured. Because it takes time for efforts to work, this entails risk. Is money wasted, or patience needed? Look elsewhere if your company fails to deliver over time.

Many performers self-manage. This allows them to secure higher profits, greater control, and opportunities below the radar of firms. Of course, in many cases the debate is moot, since representation may be impossible to obtain.

Managing Success

By high school, Canadian violinist Timothy Chooi started winning international competitions. Each unlocked opportunities to solo with orchestras worldwide. When he was 21, a management firm extended an invitation to join their roster. Without truly understanding what that entailed, he accepted. Since then, Chooi has worked with four companies, each with a different focus.

"My current manager and I have a fantastic relationship." In exchange for a 20% commission, the manager books shows, negotiates fees, collects payment, does taxes, does marketing, provides career advice, and does "all the other yucky stuff." During the busy booking season, Chooi and his manager communicate at least twice per week. The rest of the year involves touching base after each show. Chooi serves as his own publicist and personally initiates many collaborations, concerts, and projects. "Even with representation, the artist is still their best manager. It is my responsibility to build and maintain relationships, optimize social media, and be an engaged collaborator."

A Musical Union

Musicians' unions exist to support and lobby for their members. They ensure affiliates are presented with favorable conditions, negotiate contracts, determine pay scales, establish/oversee royalty payments, provide information, and offer pension plans. Many professional orchestras, choirs, opera companies, and musicals hire only union musicians.

The largest example in North America is the American Federation of Musicians, but there are others for singers, recording artists, and theatrical productions. An initiation fee and annual dues are charged. Members are often forbidden from taking nonunion work and may face fines, suspensions, or even expulsion for doing so. Occasionally, it is possible to be granted an exemption or waiver. Joining more than one union is sometimes desirable, particularly for artists pursuing different types of employment (e.g., live performance vs. recording). Before committing, have a clear understanding of how the rules will impact your career decisions.

Chapter 19
Composition

Propelling a unique artistic "voice" is crucial for *composers*—the umbrella term used throughout this chapter to describe various musical creators including orchestrators, arrangers, songwriters, producers, etc. Hopefully these creative impulses translate naturally into career strategy, because for this group, entrepreneurial perspectives are not just an option. They are the only way. Savvy musicians must be proactive about self-promotion and expanding their network, constantly thinking ahead while juggling multiple projects.

Composer income generally includes a combination of commissions, arrangements, orchestrations, sheet music sales, performance royalties, mechanical royalties (Chapter 14), licensing (Chapter 14), grants/fundraising (Chapter 10), competitive awards (Chapter 18), copy work, and other activities (performing, conducting, teaching, etc.). Diverse possibilities intersect with every genre. Most composers develop a reputation within a given niche, but there are plenty of crossover artists.

> ### Composing a Profession
>
> Below are examples of ways in which composers earn income.
>
> - Steven Melin's composition credits include the video game *Beard Blade*, TV show *The Bachelor*, audio dramas, and podcasts.
> - Andrew R. Butler has composed several musicals, including a science fiction Off-Broadway production about a future underground music club in the mid-2200s.
> - Beyond nine full-length operas, including *Dead Man Walking* about a convicted killer on death row, Jack Heggie has composed numerous one-acts and hundreds of art songs.

- Concert music composer Jennifer Jolley, whose work addresses political themes like climate change and feminism, has received commissions by symphony orchestras, chamber groups, the US Navy Band, and other wind ensembles.
- The first Black female composer inducted into the Academy of Motion Picture Arts and Sciences, Kathryn Bostic has made a name scoring documentaries and feature films.
- Each year, hornist JD Shaw arranges two shows for drum and bugle corps (12' each), three to five for competitive marching bands (7'), and four to seven university marching half-time shows (5.5').
- Kevin Olson's 200 educational collections and arrangements for pianists, beginner through advanced, draw from classical, jazz, and popular styles.
- Composer and singer-songwriter Heather Sorenson has penned hundreds of church music works for choir, orchestra, and praise band.
- French composer John Baguette is most known for his iPhone ringtones.[1]

Commissions

Commissioned works guarantee the composer a premiere performance, engaged collaborator, and payment. They expand the canon, particularly valuable for instruments/ensembles with limited repertoire, while allowing performers to forge unique identities. Many of these works fulfill functions, such as supplying the score for a documentary. Finally, commissioning leaves a legacy, offering the gift of art to musicians and the world at large.

Stipulations such as timeline, commissioning fee, and premiere/performance rules should be clearly outlined in a contract. Factors contributing to the price tag include duration, ensemble size, composer reputation, and commissioning party budget. A separate charge may be requested for copying score and parts, though many composers do this themselves. Commissions are funded by:

- **Independent artists.** Soloists or ensembles who pay directly.
- **Consortiums.** Cosponsors who split the expense burden while proudly taking credit for its creation. The composer is rewarded with a healthy fee and multiple performances.
- **Grants.** Some commissioning programs accept applications from ensembles or composers.
- **Competitions.** Some awards may result in a commission.
- **Donors.** Even a single donor can commission new work. It is also possible to involve multiple patrons.
- **Companies.** Film scores, jingles, video game themes, and other functional music may be funded by for-profit companies that create the supported product.

---

[1] OK, so this composer is actually fictional. I do recommend the video about his ringtones, however. Hilarious.

Some commissions come with strings attached. Initiating ensembles may require a premiere performance, first recording, or even exclusive performance rights for a given period. *Works for hire* require composers to relinquish copyright ownership to the sponsor (though they retain the writer's share of performance royalties). The American Composers Forum publishes additional guidelines and considerations.

When artists or ensembles subsidize new music, who do they approach? Most often, this involves friends. Hopefully they love that composer's music. But only a fraction of commissions go to strangers. In fact, some composers report solicitations by personal colleagues who are unfamiliar with their musical creations!

> ### Power (and Art) in Numbers
>
> Australian Ukrainian composer Catherine Likhuta has organized eight consortiums. Co-commissioners are credited on the score and have exclusive performance rights the first year. "These are important to my business model—generating interest, performances, and royalties—and a great way to make new friends."
>
> Her first, a six-minute wind ensemble piece about children and the planet we are handing them, is often performed alongside displayed or projected artwork by local students. This was sponsored by 40 programs from around the globe, with a portion of Likhuta's fee being donated to support child victims of domestic violence. "Requesting an ensemble director to pay $10,000 for a new work is a heavy lift. Contributing just $250 to $500 is a no brainer."
>
> While attending dinner alongside 19 horn players at an international conference, someone declared: "It's high time for a Likhuta horn concerto!" Her response? If everyone there paid $750, this wish would come true. All attendees agreed. Word spread quickly, and the consortium roster crept up to 46!

PRODUCTION MUSIC

Just about every type of media—podcasts, TikToks, independent films, video games, audio books—incorporates music. Rather than commissioning new works, content creators can license recordings, offering composers who own their rights potentially significant income.[2]

A *sync license* permits third parties to utilize music in exchange for a specified fee. Agreements are typically narrow, outlining allowable usage (where it can be included, for how long, in which territories, under which conditions). Contracts should clarify whether an agreement is exclusive to a single project or if other sources may simultaneously license the clip(s). Composers can submit recordings to stock music libraries, allowing users to preview tracks and license what is needed. Profits are typically split evenly between the library and artist.

---

[2] It is illegal to embed someone else's intellectual property without permission.

Micro-Licensing

After moving back to Minneapolis, William Van De Crommert wondered how he could make a living. Though passionate about film music composition, the local scene was sparse at best. While waiting for a career to materialize, he discovered the world of *micro-licensing*. Here's how it works: Composers submit original recordings to platforms that house audio libraries. Paying subscribers, typically content creators without a budget for original music, preview options after inputting terms describing mood, style, or instrumentation. Downloading what is desired, they may legally embed music royalty-free (assuming media are not broadcasted). Composer payments are dispersed through profit-sharing models comparable to streaming services.

"I love the creative freedom of writing evocative music without a video reference. That said, there are rules and conventions. It is essential to get inside the head of an editor." For example, most tracks are 90 seconds to 4 minutes. They start with an intro (which can be omitted) and incorporate repetitive progressions easy to truncate. Button endings are more helpful than gradual fadeouts.

North of 1,000 Van De Crommert tracks—including variations with different orchestrations or durations—are available through several micro-licensing platforms. They are heard on tens of thousands of commercials, films, and social media clips.

Acquiring Performances

Conductors, soloists, ensembles, and educators constantly seek good music to perform. True, some only consider works by composers long dead. But many are enthusiastic about contemporary expressions. Just because a fantastic work exists, however, doesn't mean performances accrue magically. Visibility is key. Musicians consider a work only after they:

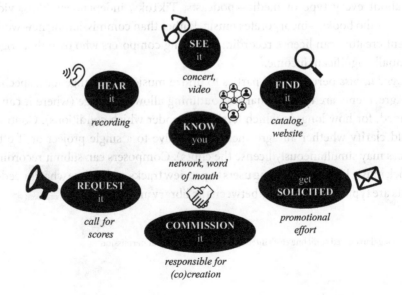

There are many steps a composer can take to expand visibility. Devote time each week to marketing. Submit works to competitions and calls for scores. (Think twice about opportunities that charge for consideration.) Never take networking opportunities for granted. Approach musicians directly, understanding that emerging artists—as opposed to famous ones—may be most likely to champion your music. Distributing unsolicited materials almost always wastes time and energy. Instead, share materials upon request.

Not all compositions have the potential for comparable demand, even if composer, quality, and marketing are equivalent. This is not a value judgment, just a fact of life.

ASPECT	EXPLANATION
Accessibility	Most artists seek works that resonate with audiences. Overly esoteric statements, no matter how well written, may have limited appeal.
Duration	Shorter pieces are often preferable.
Difficulty	Extreme complexity has limited appeal, since few players have the chops and pro ensembles shy away from extensive rehearsing. Alas ... time is money.
Score clarity	Sloppy notation or careless mistakes are turnoffs.
Orchestration	Traditional settings (piano, violin, string quartet) compete against endless alternatives. Nonstandard combinations may be beautiful, but securing performances can be a challenge. Instruments/common ensembles with limited rep (English horn, harp, sax quartet) optimize potential.
Transcriptions	To increase demand, rescore works for multiple instrumentations, voice types, and settings. Flexible educational arrangements increase usability.
Popular themes	There is considerable demand for arrangements of classics, pop hits, film soundtracks, video game music, etc. Works connecting to education, sacred ceremonies, pop culture, or contemporary issues generate broad appeal.
Uniqueness	Quirky, fun, out-of-the-box experiments quickly garnish notoriety.

She's Getting Played!

Why is it that Melissa Dunphy's compositions receive so much attention? In part, she lucked into it, taking an early interest in choral music. "Composers who write for groups hungry to champion new rep, like choirs and wind ensembles, have an easier life." She also received great advice from a mentor: *If you must choose, attend choral rather than composition conferences, where everyone wants what you offer.*

Another secret: "A shortcut to reaching nontypical audiences involves hooking them on the subject matter." When a scandal-ridden politician was blowing up the news, Dunphy wrote a 40-minute choral work about his Senate judiciary hearings. Before its Fringe Festival premiere, she created and promoted a related parody website. This generated buzz among journalists, which led to features in the *Huffington Post*, on Fox News, and on MSNBC. On primetime television, Rachel Maddow declared, "[This piece] is honestly probably the coolest thing you've ever seen on this show."

Other works tackle provocative themes like immigration (as an immigrant herself), local issues, and forgotten historical figures. Her deep interest in archeology has opened lucrative opportunities with museums.

Selling Notation

Composers generate capital when selling sheet music to individuals, ensembles, educational programs, and libraries. Even in our era dominated by digitization, many performers, teachers, and students prefer physical scores. To oblige, publishers must either print on demand (expensive) or prepurchase large quantities and maintain inventory. If you anticipate rare sales, personal printer copies may make the most sense. When demand is high, explore other options.

Electronic sheet music eliminates the expense and hassle of shipping. However, files can easily be copied and forwarded without your knowledge or permission. Digital rights management (DRM) protects copyright holders by limiting how files can be shared or printed. Unfortunately, this technology is expensive and out of reach for most composers and small publishers. The best policy is to clearly communicate conditions. Watermarks, sternly worded warnings, and password protection may help. Most performers respect these boundaries.

Much ensemble music, especially for orchestras, wind ensembles, and large chamber groups, is rented rather than sold. Groups pay to borrow scores and parts for a given period, to be returned after the performance. Rentals ensure that publishers and composers receive payment each time a work is programmed.

Traditional versus Self-Publishing

Historically, publishing houses were necessary to distribute music. Beyond their engraving function, these companies provided the only effective way to reach clients.

The situation is different today. Most composers use notation software to create attractive, professional-looking manuscripts. In fact, publishers often reproduce or slightly alter submitted computer scores. Music can be self-distributed through personal websites, and many online vendors work with anyone. Therefore, the dilemma of whether to sign with a publisher closely parallels considerations for record labels and artist management.

Bragging rights are earned when a publishing house champions your music. They provide services such as editing, packaging, duplication, collecting payment, overseeing copyright, obtaining permissions, licensing, and digital rights management. Some (rare) companies even cultivate career development. Publishers are particularly helpful when selling music in large quantities, since handling orders requires time and energy.

Accessing these benefits comes at a cost. Control is relinquished. Mechanical royalties (payments for record sales) must be split with the publisher (typically 50/50). Print and digital music sales have a more significant split (90/10 is the industry standard, in the publisher's favor), further decreasing the bottom line. Additionally, publishing deals are not always feasible, particularly for emerging composers.

> **Big Enough, Small Enough**
>
> After learning that many creators lacked a good system for marketing and distributing their print music, saxophonist Sean Murphy—who is not a composer—thought, "I could do that!" He founded Murphy Music Press (MMP) with the goal of disseminating works for his instrument. The venture exploded when he expanded to include wind ensemble arrangements. Ten years later, it represents 1,500 products by 350+ composers.
>
> Why would someone choose MMP representation over a big-box publisher? Murphy's company is established enough to reach substantial audiences yet small enough to provide individualized attention. Their lean model allows for speed; scores are quickly brought to market and ship within 24 hours. Talented composers who can't get the time of day from "the big guys" are welcomed with open arms. Financially, the company splits profits 50/50, a significantly better rate than most competitors. "I'm proud as hell of this business, which is run from my basement. It has been exhilarating watching sales go from hundreds to thousands to tens of thousands."

Self-publishing requires more work and upfront expense, but the revenue difference adds up. You set the price and are entitled to keep everything minus duplication, shipping, and marketing. More money can be earned even if charging less or selling fewer units. Better yet, you maintain ownership, directing performance royalties solely into your bank account. You are also a better advocate of your music than a publisher representing a profusion of products. To access these benefits, some veteran composers pay considerably to buy back rights to older music.

If self-publishing, keep excellent records and pursue all leads. Research prices for music of comparable duration and instrumentation. Ship orders promptly along with professional-looking invoices. Run this entrepreneurial venture with commitment and strategy.

> **DIY Publication**
>
> When demand for the wind ensemble compositions of John Mackey got very big, very fast, a major publisher made an offer. "But they only wanted to represent high-selling scores, not my entire catalog. That didn't feel right. Publishing just means making music available, and I could do that on my own." Beyond printing, binding, shipping, and collecting payments, he built a sophisticated website that automates watermarks while communicating performances to his performing rights organization.

> Mackey's top rationale for self-publishing is financial. Rather than relinquishing 50% of performance royalties, 50% of rentals, and a whopping 90% (!) of sheet music sales, he claims the entire amount. As the sole decision-maker for licensing, he controls which pieces may be rearranged, excerpted, or placed on YouTube, and what to charge (if anything). Conference booths promote just his music, rather than diluting attention across many represented creators.
>
> As Mackey's reputation and composition list grew, publishing responsibilities overwhelmed. He ultimately hired two part-time, salaried personal assistants (starting with his mother-in-law) to help with contracts, shipments, payment collection, and more. "I suddenly had an abundance of time, still earning much more than with traditional publishers."

Performance Royalties

Royalties are paid to composers and publishers by performing rights organizations (PROs) when works are played publicly (concert halls, churches, etc.) or recordings are broadcast (radio, television, film, etc.) and streamed. Most American composers belong to one of the three largest PROs:[3] ASCAP (American Society of Composers, Authors, and Publishers); (BMI) Broadcast Music, Inc.; or (SESAC) Society of European Stage Authors and Composers. Though they have slightly different policies and royalty formulas, all are ardent advocates for members. SoundExchange, which is free to join, pays royalties for music played on satellite radio, digital cable, and internet radio.

To get paid, each composition must be registered through the composer's PRO website. This is the publisher's responsibility (which means you when self-publishing). To ensure performances are noted, send programs or other documentation such as cue sheets for film and television to your PRO. The royalty amount depends on several variables and is typically divided equally between publisher and composer. Checks are mailed on a quarterly basis.

> ### Dividing the Pies
>
> Austin Wintory—composer of film, game, and concert music—made history by writing the first-ever Grammy-nominated video game score (*Journey*, for PlayStation 3). Breaking down his financial model provides a glimpse into complexities facing many music creators.[4]

---

[3] Each country has its own PRO. Examples include SOCAN (Society of Composers, Authors, and Music Publishers of Canada); MCSC (Music Copyright Society of China); and PRS (Performing Rights Society) in the United Kingdom.

[4] For a more detailed breakdown, view Wintory's video called "Income and Expenses for a Composer."

REVENUES

Gross income, "not to be conflated with take-home pay," includes a chunk of money that must then be paid to others.

- **Packages.** Composer receives the entire budget for a project but is responsible for all related expenses. (Amount remaining is the composer fee.)
- **Fees.** Direct payment for writing projects.
- **Royalties.** Passive income through sources like the ASCAP, Spotify, Bandcamp, and merch. "I would notice if this money were gone but don't depend on it to live."
- **Miscellaneous.** Sheet music rentals, speaker/conductor fees, etc.

EXPENSES

A variety of expense categories play a role in his financial model.

- **Subcontractors.** Money owed to subcontracted artists, recording studios, copyists, PR agency, etc.
- **Taxes.** Federal, state, city, business, franchise.
- **Commissions.** Payments to his agent.
- **Studio.** Rental and utilities for his workspace.
- **Wages.** A full-time and part-time assistant help with various tasks.
- **Professional expenses.** Work-related travel, meals, entertainment, studio supplies, professional dues, and more.
- **Living expenses.** Housing, personal travel, utilities, food, dog.

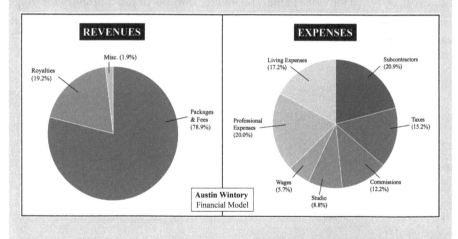

Austin Wintory Financial Model

Copyright Protection

Technically, a musical idea is protected the moment it is recorded or notated. If someone steals or plagiarizes your intellectual property, however, more proof is required in court. To safeguard works, file each score and sound recording with your country's copyright office. Doing so requires an application, fee, and audio or physical copy. It is possible to register multiple compositions with the same filing.

Logistical Considerations

Composers must be particularly disciplined when mapping their work schedule. Though some projects can be knocked out in a matter of hours, ambitious undertakings require weeks or months of grueling work. Because it takes time to line up commissions and funding, many creators secure projects years in advance to avoid the risk of future underemployment. Promotional efforts must be juggled even during composition-intense periods.

Startup and ongoing expenses are required. At the least, most composers need access to a powerful computer, music software, and MIDI keyboard. Those working with electronics are known to invest heavily in gear: sample libraries, effects processors, audio/video equipment.

Composers face a unique dilemma. The act of writing can be lonely. They are dependent upon performers, yet many operate in relative isolation. Unlike instrumentalists and singers, who interact regularly when rehearsing and gigging, composers must manufacture interpersonal encounters. Make this a regular ritual, visiting concerts by colleagues, attending the "after hang," and exploring other techniques from Chapter 8.

Theoretically, music creators can reside anywhere. In reality, a nonnegotiable requirement involves deep relationship building with potential collaborators. For this reason, cities known for given industries attract a disproportionate number of composers (places like Los Angeles, New York, or London for film; Seattle, Montreal, or Tokyo for video games; Nashville, Toronto, or Johannesburg for songwriting). Some creators adopt a secondary market as their home base, making it easier to emerge as a big fish even with less overall demand.

Chapter 20
Industry

While teachers, performers, and composers are on the front lines of the music ecosystem, a vast, sprawling industry exists to support them. Think of this final chapter as a barebones teaser of additional industry professions. If something captures your imagination, investigate further. As a savvy musician, consider which options might influence your career trajectory, either by pursuing a given track or by partnering with those who do. The trick is finding your place within this maze of potential, creating a financially feasible and personally rewarding profile.

ARTS ADMINISTRATION

Arts administrators work within cultural institutions, predominantly nonprofit, such as orchestras, opera companies, performance venues, education providers, and community arts hubs. Typical roles involve:

- **Leadership.** An executive director, who reports to the board, sets the vision, manages people, oversees operations, and ensures organizational success.
- **Programming.** Planning and executing events requires logistical oversight, creative problem solving, volunteer coordination, and the ability to get things done.
- **Marketing.** Promotional efforts focus on tactics like web development, social media, public relations, publicity, advertising, press releases, media coverage, and related efforts.
- **Education.** Develop programming for youth and other community segments.
- **Development.** Just about every music nonprofit is cash strapped. The ability to secure grants and galvanize patrons is paramount.
- **Finance.** Manage budgets, maintain spreadsheets, disperse/collect payments.
- **Human resources.** Responsible for hiring and training (and perhaps firing) employees, as well as enforcing legal regulations.

In large organizations, a separate team is responsible for each activity category. In smaller ones, a single employee may be required to address several single-handedly.

> ### U-turn on the Slopes
>
> Wyoming's Grand Teton Music Festival proudly embraces the world's only concert hall on a ski slope. In this gorgeous setting, some 20,000 guests enjoy solo, chamber, and orchestral concerts each summer over an eight-week period. Performances are broadcast on 100 public radio stations.
>
> When trumpeter Emma Kail accepted the position of executive director, however, there was "trouble in paradise." Musician stipends had stagnated for 15 years. Three long-time musicians had been disinvited, opening a painful rift between artists and administration. Many staff had resigned. "My first job was to unify people behind our shared love of music!"
>
> Over several years, Kail led an intensive strategic planning effort, redefining their mission, vision, and values. She prioritized a programming expansion (including their first ever staged opera!) and created a framework for renovating the hall and energizing past/new donors. One passionate supporter decided to underwrite a $10 million project to house musicians for the next 50 years. "As an arts administrator, I face hard problems every day. But the opportunity to be creative, dream big, and impact communities makes this work incredibly fulfilling."

Artist Support

Performing artists appear center stage, but getting them there requires a team. A number of behind-the-scenes professions center on securing opportunities, negotiating details, promoting bands and brands, coordinating logistics, and ensuring all goes well.

JOB	OVERVIEW
Artist management	Solicit opportunities, negotiate contracts, oversee logistics, and advise. Most managers accept five or fewer clients so they aren't spread too thin. Those representing established artists charge a 15% to 20% commission. Emerging professionals with less demand may be charged a retainer.
Contractor/ booking agent	Contract gigs and performers in exchange for 10% to 20% of gross revenue. Secure the venue, arrange logistics, collect/distribute payments, serve as the contact.
Tour manager	Arrange flights, hotels, ground transportation. Deal with problems that arise. Possibly travel with musicians.
Music publicist	Public relations expert who writes releases, creates press kits, and secures media features through podcasts, TV, radio, magazines, newspapers, and other sources. Paid by the month or project.

Social media manager	Develop strategy for increasing followers, build a calendar, create and release content, review analytics, coordinate with the artist.
Stage manager	Supervise sets, props, audio, and lighting during performances and rehearsals. Help realize the director's vision.
Sound/lighting technician	Salaried or contracted employees who set up and operate audio/lighting systems used during live events.

Audio Recording

The recording industry offers a variety of employment opportunities. Record labels are run by a CEO/president, responsible for its overall vision and success. Various divisions address key activities such as artist development, marketing, publicity, legal, and sales. At the heart of each label is an A&R (artists and repertoire) division, charged with talent scouting, signing artists, negotiating contracts, coordinating recordings, and keeping projects under budget.

Record producers have a hand in every aspect of the process, beginning with what to record and how. Part cheerleader, part coach, they listen from the booth during sessions, offer suggestions, and make notes on each take. Producers determine edit choices and collaborate with engineers to optimize a final product.

Whether working for a label or independent studio, audio engineers are responsible for recording, editing, mixing, and mastering recordings. Effective professionals possess technological fluency, strong musicianship, and patience.

Recording Studio Loser

While pursuing an MBA, guitarist Jeremy Mang recorded and produced music in his basement as a side hustle. Years later, he converted a 3,000-square-foot commercial location into Whisper Studios, which boasts a large control room, primary recording space, secondary studio/lounge, and several isolation chambers. Frugal about spending, he purchases a lot of gear that is broken, to be repaired and integrated or resold.

Mang's career combines studio recording, album production, mixing and mastering corporate videos, and live sound engineering. His YouTube channel Recording Studio Loser has helped generate incredible demand despite being in rural Indiana. "Lower overhead allows me to attract clients of all genres from across the country. They know they can get a high-quality product, and in the end, it's all about the hang."

Music Retail

Music retail is a multi-billion-dollar industry, peddling everything from instruments to accessories to software to sheet music to swag. While demand for brick-and-mortar stores has diminished with the dominance of e-commerce, most cities house traditional vendors with full- and part-time employees. Some retailers specialize, while others carry a breadth of products. Startups often launch as home businesses, relocating as necessary. Beyond physical products, dealers commonly sell related services: repairs, lessons, recording, etc.

> ### It's All About Da Harp
>
> Despite living on a Hawaiian island, harpist Sylvia Woods sells a huge variety of products related to her instrument. "When I started, there were few retailers committed to the harp. I was at the right place at the right time and did something about it. Monopolies are really good when you own them!"
>
> Woods performs locally and teaches online. Pedal harps can be purchased/rented by neighbors and island visitors through a small home "shop." Those ordered through her website are *drop-shipped* from manufacturers to the US mainland. Over the years, she has sold every conceivable harp-related item through her store and mail-order catalogs: accessories, jewelry, figurines, candles, rubber stamps, stationery, mugs, music boxes, stained glass, greeting cards, soap, salt and pepper shakers. Downloadable items include original sheet music (85 arrangements, compositions, and collections), works by 40 additional composers, MP3 recordings, and PDF quilt blocks.
>
> In today's world of options, why do consumers continue to shop with Woods? "Because they love me," she jokes, though this is clearly the case. Whether inspired by her content-rich e-newsletters or friendly nature, the personal relationships she cultivates generate loyalty.

Instrument Repair

Technicians are needed to repair, restore, and tune (keyboards) every type of instrument. They are hired by music stores, school districts, universities, and independent customers. Many people in this field begin by working magic on beat-up instruments purchased at pawn shops or stolen from junkyards. Skills are developed by (1) apprenticing with a master technician and (2) attending a trade school. For a glimpse into the profession, join a national/international organization focused on your area. These associations offer conferences, educational resources, career advice, and networking opportunities.

> **The Fixer**
>
> From a young age, saxophonist Tony Barrette could be found deconstructing bikes and building Legos. Fixing instruments was a natural extension. His woodwind shop, TB Winds, offers warranty repairs, vintage saxophone restoration, and reconditioning for K–12 schools, colleges, and walk-in clients (who travel up to 13 hours for his personalized attention!). It also sells high-end accessories and new/used instruments.

Software Development

Shape the future by developing music-related software or apps. It isn't necessary to become an engineer to make a mark. Entrepreneurial visionaries can hire their own team. Technology companies employ musicians to test functionality and offer feedback.

> **Musical App-titude**
>
> As Slovenian guitarist Mak Grgić itched to dip his toe into the startup world, he noticed a marketplace gap. While there are many online music education platforms and many music-oriented video games, none successfully combine the two worlds. Partnering with a coder, he began working on an app.
>
> *Notey's World* is a mobile music education game that takes place within an exploratory "sandbox environment" (think Roblox). Users playing any musical instrument control what happens: play a particular chord to jump; downward scale to duck; repeated note to punch the boss. Triggers work only when the requisite technique is performed adequately, encouraging practice and mastery. Currently, there are 150 levels.
>
> Building such a massive app is expensive. To pay for it, Grgić raised capital first from family and friends, and then in a preseed round with angel investors. Revenue is generated from both individual subscribers and schools that license the platform for their community of students. They even have the opportunity to integrate customized curricula.

Music Therapy

Music therapy uses evidence-based artistic interventions to treat health conditions as diverse as depression, anxiety, Down syndrome, autism, diabetes, self-esteem, insomnia, dementia, and stroke. Patients may be asked to sing, play, dance, compose, listen, improvise, or reflect upon what they hear. Sessions are typically one on one, but group settings can also be effective. Music therapists either run private practices or find full-/part-time work within psychiatric hospitals, nursing homes, community health centers, halfway houses, schools, and other organizations. A music therapy college degree and certification are required.

> ### Music Heals
>
> Passionate about helping others, trumpeter Meredith Pizzi initially assumed her career would be in education. That changed when a mentor suggested music therapy. As a clinician, she helps children, adolescents, and adults with complex medical and developmental disabilities. "This unique profession truly makes other people's lives better. It is magical when individuals who struggle with challenges or limitations make music together."
>
> Whether working individually or with small groups, Pizzi observes what drives people and designs activities accordingly. "I am not here to perform. My role is to facilitate, building a synergistic triangle between the client, therapist, and music." Sessions may involve piano, guitar, percussion, singing, or augmentative communication devices like an iPad or button triggering a sound. Sometimes the objective is to create communal art and experience shared joy with otherwise isolated participants. Music can be used to trigger emotional responses, bringing comfort to a hospice patient or supporting pain management following a surgery. Therapeutic benefits also positively impact caretakers, who have emotionally demanding responsibilities.
>
> There are approximately 10,000 board-certified music therapists in the United States today. "With baby boomers aging and a rise in mental health crises, there would be no shortage of work if we tripled the field."

MUSIC LIBRARIAN

Music librarians are hired by universities, public libraries, special libraries (like the Rock and Roll Hall of Fame), museums (like The Getty), and large performing ensembles. Responsibilities involve curating collections, making new purchases, organizing rentals, cataloging acquisitions, developing technological support, providing guidance on research techniques, and interfacing with patrons. Most employers require a master's degree in library science, coupled with deep knowledge of music history and repertoire (often through another degree).

> ### Best of Both Worlds
>
> While enrolled in a music undergraduate degree, Rebecca Littman realized she didn't want the constant hustle of a performer's life or *publish or perish* requirements of university professorships. Pursuing a Master's Degree of Librarianship led to several jobs within academia before she became managing librarian for music and recorded sound at the New York Public Library.

> "I couldn't imagine a career outside music, and was raised in academia. Becoming a music librarian allowed me to stay connected to teaching and learning without being on the professor track."
>
> Littman's responsibilities have evolved with each position. Beyond working reference desks, she has cataloged materials, built a search engine website for resources, designed library instruction guides, and curated music collections. Currently, she also manages a team. "Libraries are no longer quiet places just for books. Music librarians must be creative problem solvers, champions of technology, and well versed on industry issues."

Nonmusic Employment

Tales of starving artists forced to work dreaded "day jobs" are painfully common. Though they swear the gig is temporary until better times emerge, the opposite often transpires. Grueling, unfulfilling work induces physical and mental exhaustion. Employees are too drained to make significant progress toward meaningful ambitions. Avoid this trap. That said, there is no shame in working outside music. The best employment offers several of the following:

1. Fulfilling, purpose-driven work
2. Good pay
3. Flexible scheduling
4. Professional/personal growth
5. Sense of community
6. Valuable new connections

Do musicians make strong candidates for nonmusic employment? I've spoken with many hiring managers who brazenly declare they would immediately discount any such application. To be considered, the thinking goes, discipline-specific training is requisite. But the more we talk, thinking starts to shift.

The nature of musical training requires careful attention to detail, an ironclad work ethic, and the pursuit of excellence. We musicians understand the value of practice and regularly convey clear, committed communication with an audience. Chamber players are experienced collaborators and decisive leaders (let's hope!). Improvisers become creativity gurus. And as argued previously, musicians are financial wizards, squeezing more from every dollar than just about anyone (thanks to years of frugality-mandated bootstrapping).

We haven't even gotten to #SavvyMusicians, known for spotting opportunities where others see only roadblocks. This group has a track record of addressing important problems with innovative BIG ideas differentiated by WOWables. They come armed with empathetic listening, a comprehensive marketing approach, fundraising prowess, and a propensity for time/team/project management.

Finally, musicians are driven by passion. They pursue things they love and love things they pursue. *Isn't that who you want on the payroll?*

> **Play. Rest. Repeat.**
>
> Jeff Laibson already had a busy career as a jazz pianist and educator when he tried his hand at visual art. He was amazed how similar the processes felt. "I learned jazz by transcribing cats like Thelonious Monk and Bill Evans. Teaching myself to paint was virtually identical. I'd check out modern art books, emulate techniques, and improvise." At times, his income has split evenly between music and art. Paintings are sold online, at galleries, and through around 25 road shows annually. Never one to wait for the phone to ring, he hustled.
>
> Laibson's creations incorporate a personalized set of rules, tools, and color combinations. Though abstract, everything somehow relates to music. "The onset of a jazz solo is a blank canvas upon which players express idiomatically connected melodic invention. My art works the same way." Somewhere on each canvas, three words can be found: *Play. Rest. Repeat.* To see an example of Laibson's art, look no further than this book's cover.

CODA

As *The Savvy Musician 2.0* comes to a close, take a moment to reflect upon the remarkable journey taken. We've explored overlapping aspects like entrepreneurial perspectives, business models, finance, life management, and more. The most important priority is summed up in a single word: SUCCESS.

The path to extraordinary success is rarely easy. Yet, just about every puzzle can be solved with enough creativity and grit. That includes your career. In Chapter 1, I dared to suggest a success formula balancing three essential elements: INCOME, IMPACT, and INSPIRATION. Realizing this combination almost always requires INNOVATION.

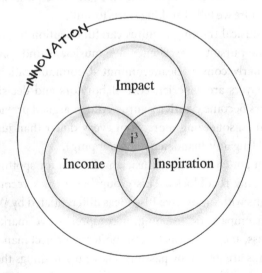

In today's complex, fractured world, our art form is unique in the ways it can positively impact wide-ranging problems, big and small. Music, and the acts of its creators, has the power to heal, inspire, entertain, challenge, communicate, educate, fulfill, tell stories, and build community. Savvy musicians offer value on a daily basis and leave lasting legacies that truly matter.

Isn't it time YOU got savvy?

Further Savvy Reading

Rather than overwhelming you with options, five top book recommendations are listed for a variety of topics. Edition numbers are omitted since books are regularly updated. Subtitles are included when necessary to clarify content.

MUSIC CAREER GUIDES

1. *THE SAVVY MUSICIAN: Building a Career, Earning a Living, and Making a Difference*, by David Cutler
2. *BEYOND TALENT: Creating a Successful Career in Music*, by Angela Myles Beeching
3. *THE ENTREPRENEURIAL MUSE: Inspiring Your Career in Classical Music*, by Jeff Nytch
4. *THE MUSICIAN'S JOURNEY: Crafting Your Career Vision and Plan*, by Jill Timmons
5. *THE MUSICIAN'S CAREER GUIDE: Turning Your Talent into Sustained Success*, by Ulysses Owens Jr.

ENTREPRENEURIAL PERSPECTIVES

1. *MINDSET: The New Psychology of Success*, by Carol Dweck
2. *SO YOU WANT TO BE AN ENTREPRENEUR: How to Decide If Starting a Business Is Really for You*, by Jon Gillespie-Brown
3. *PURPLE COW: Transform Your Business by Being Remarkable*, by Seth Godin
4. *CHANGE THE WORLD: How Ordinary People Can Achieve Extraordinary Results*, by Robert E. Quinn
5. *LIFE ENTREPRENEURS: Ordinary People Creating Extraordinary Lives*, by Christopher Gergen and Gregg Vanourek

PURPOSE AND LEGACY

1. *START WITH WHY: How Great Leaders Inspire Everyone to Take Action*, by Simon Sinek
2. *THE PURPOSE OF YOUR LIFE: Finding Your Place in the World Using Synchronicity, Intuition, and Uncommon Sense*, by Carol Adrienne and James Redfield
3. *MAKE THE IMPOSSIBLE POSSIBLE: One Man's Crusade to Inspire Others to Dream Bigger and Achieve the Extraordinary*, by Bill Strickland
4. *MUSICIANS WITH A MISSION: Keeping the Classical Tradition Alive*, by Andrew L. Pincus
5. *THE ARTIST AS CITIZEN*, by Joseph Polisi

INNOVATION AND CREATIVITY

1. *THE GAME OF INNOVATION: Conquer Challenges. Level Up Your Team. Play to Win.*, by David Cutler
2. *THE ART OF POSSIBILITY: Transforming Professional and Personal Life*, by Rosamund Stone Zander and Benjamin Zander
3. *THINKING FAST AND SLOW*, by Daniel Kahneman
4. *THE DESIGN THINKING PLAYBOOK: Mindful Digital Transformation of Teams, Products, Services, Business, and Ecosystems*, by Michael Lewrick, Patrick Link, and Larry Leifer
5. *CREATIVITY, INC.: Overcoming the Unseen Forces That Stand in the Way of True Inspiration*, by Ed Catmull and Amy Wallace

BUSINESS MODELS

1. *LEAN STARTUP: How Today's Entrepreneurs Use Continuous Innovation to Create Radically Successful Businesses*, by Eric Ries
2. *RUN IT LIKE A BUSINESS: Strategies for Arts Organizations to Increase Audiences, Remain Relevant, and Multiply Money*, by Aubrey Bergauer
3. *THE ART OF THE TURNAROUND: Creating & Maintaining Healthy Arts Organizations*, by Michael Kaiser
4. *THE E-MYTH REVISITED: Why Most Small Businesses Don't Work and What to Do About It*, by Michael Gerber
5. *THE VISUAL MBA: Two Years of Business School Packed into One Priceless Book of Pure Awesomeness*, by Jason Barron

NONPROFITS

1. *HOW TO FORM A NONPROFIT CORPORATION*, by Anthony Mancuso
2. *THE ONE PAGE BUSINESS PLAN FOR NONPROFIT ORGANIZATIONS*, by James T. Horan Jr.
3. *BRANDING FOR NONPROFITS*, by DK Holland
4. *JOAN GARRY'S GUIDE TO NONPROFIT LEADERSHIP*, by Joan Garry
5. *THE ART OF THE TURNAROUND: Creating and Maintaining Healthy Arts Organizations*, by Michael Kaiser

BUSINESS TOOLS

1. *BUSINESS MODEL GENERATION: A Handbook for Visionaries, Game Changers, and Challengers*, by Alexander Osterwalder and Yves Pigneur (for business model canvas)
2. *THE SWOT ANALYSIS*, by 50minutes.com

3. *SURVEYS THAT WORK*, by Caroline Jarrett and Steve Krug
4. *DEPLOY EMPATHY: A Practical Guide to Interviewing Customers*, by Michael Hansen
5. *THIS IS A PROTOTYPE: The Curious Craft of Exploring New Ideas*, by Scott Witthoft

MARKETING

1. *THE BRAND CALLED YOU: Make Your Business Stand Out in a Crowded Marketplace*, by Peter Montoya
2. *ARTS MARKETING INSIGHTS: The Dynamics of Building and Retaining Performing Arts Audiences*, by Joanne Scheff Bernstein
3. *GUERRILLA MARKETING: Easy and Inexpensive Strategies for Making Big Profits from Your Small Business*, by Jay Conrad Levinson
4. *MARKETING FOR CULTURAL ORGANISATIONS: New Strategies for Attracting Audiences to Classical Music, Dance, Museums, Theatre, and Opera*, by Bonita M. Kolb
5. *BUZZMARKETING: Get People to Talk About Your Stuff*, by Mark Hughes

CONTENT, DESIGN, AND STORYTELLING

1. *WORDS THAT SELL*, by Richard Bayan
2. *SEVERAL SHORT SENTENCES ABOUT WRITING*, by Verlyn Klinkenborg
3. *THE NON-DESIGNER'S DESIGN BOOK*, by Robin Williams
4. *UNLEASH THE POWER OF STORYTELLING: Win Hearts, Change Minds, Get Results*, by Rob Biesenbach
5. *MADE TO STICK: Why Some Ideas Survive and Others Die*, by Chip Heath and Dan Heath

ONLINE PRESENCE

1. *BEST WEBSITES: Simple Steps to Successful Websites*, by Nelson Bates
2. *THE NEW RULES OF MARKETING AND PR: How to Use Content Marketing, Podcasting, Social Media, AI, Live Video, and Newsjacking to Reach Buyers Directly*, by David Meerman Scott
3. *CYBER PR FOR MUSICIANS: Tools, Ticks, & Tactics for Building Your Social Media House*, by Ariel Hyatt
4. *CREATING A WEBSITE THAT SELLS YOUR BUSINESS: The Radical Blueprint to Turning Your Visitors into Buyers*, by J. R. See
5. *SOCIAL MEDIA PROMOTION FOR MUSICIANS*, by Bobby Owsinski

PEOPLE SKILLS

1. *HOW TO WIN FRIENDS & INFLUENCE PEOPLE,* by Dale Carnegie
2. *NEVER EAT ALONE: And Other Secrets to Success, One Relationship at a Time,* by Keith Ferrazzi
3. *MAKE YOUR CONTACTS COUNT: Networking Knowhow for Business and Career Success,* by Anne Baber and Lynne Waymon
4. *THE ART OF MINGLING: Easy, Fun, and Proven Techniques for Mastering Any Room,* by Jeanne Martinet
5. *COLD CALLING FOR COWARDS: How to Turn the Fear of Rejection into Opportunities, Sales, and Money,* by Jerry Hocutt

PERSONAL FINANCE

1. *THE AUTOMATIC MILLIONAIRE: A Powerful One-Step Plan to Live and Finish Rich,* by David Bach
2. *RICH DAD, POOR DAD: What the Rich Teach Their Kids About Money That the Poor and Middle Class Do Not,* by Robert Kiyosaki
3. *THE MILLIONAIRE NEXT DOOR,* by Thomas J. Stanley and William D. Danko
4. *THE MONEY BOOK FOR THE YOUNG, FABULOUS, & BROKE,* by Suze Orman
5. *YOUR MONEY OR YOUR LIFE: Transforming Your Relationship with Money and Achieving Financial Independence,* by Joe Dominguez and Vicki Robin

BUSINESS FINANCE

1. *THE ACCOUNTING GAME: Basic Accounting Fresh from the Lemonade Stand,* by Darrell Mullis and Judith Orloff
2. *VISUAL FINANCE: The One Page Visual Model to Understand Financial Statement and Make Better Decisions,* by Georgi Tsvetanov
3. *FINANCIAL INTELLIGENCE: A Manager's Guide to Knowing What the Numbers Really Mean,* by Karen Berman and Joe Knight
4. *ZERO TO SOLD: How to Start, Run, and Sell a Bootstrapped Business,* by Arvid Kahl
5. *MUSIC, MONEY, AND SUCCESS,* by Jeff and Todd Brabec

RAISING MONEY

1. *THE ASK: How to Ask Anyone for Any Amount for Any Purpose,* by Laura Fredricks
2. *BREAKTHROUGH FUNDRAISING LETTERS,* by Alan Sharpe
3. *GUIDE TO GETTING ARTS GRANTS,* by Ellen Liberatori

4. *YOURS FOR THE ASKING: An Indispensable Guide to Fundraising and Management*, by Reynold Levy
5. *THE ZEN OF FUNDRAISING: 89 Timeless Ideas to Strengthen and Develop Your Donor Relationships*, by Ken Burnett

TIME MANAGEMENT

1. *EAT THAT FROG!*, by Brian Tracy
2. *THE 7 HABITS OF HIGHLY EFFECTIVE PEOPLE*, by Stephen Covey
3. *THE 4-HOUR WORKWEEK*, by Timothy Ferriss
4. *GETTING THINGS DONE*, by David Allen
5. *HOW TO STOP PROCRASTINATING*, by S. J. Scott

RECORDING AND VIDEO

1. *RECORD LABEL MARKETING*, by Tom Hutchison, Amy Macy, and Paul Allen
2. *START AND RUN YOUR OWN RECORD LABEL*, by Daylle Deanna Schwartz
3. *THE GUIDEBOOK TO SELF-RELEASING YOUR MUSIC*, by Matthew Whiteside
4. *THE DIY GUIDE TO MAKING MUSIC VIDEOS*, by Jon Forsyth
5. *MARKETING RECORDED MUSIC*, by Tammy Donham, Amy Macy, and Clyde Rolston

GETTING HIRED

1. *RESUME MAGIC: Trade Secrets of a Professional Resume Writer*, by Susan Britton Whitcomb
2. *KNOCK 'EM DEAD COVER LETTERS*, by Martin Yate
3. *BEHIND THE SCREEN: A Winner's Guide to Preparing Your Next Audition*, by Ralph Skiano
4. *GET THAT JOB! The Quick and Complete Guide to Winning an Interview*, by Thea Kelley
5. *THE ART OF NEGOTIATION*, by Tim Castle

MUSIC TEACHING CAREERS

1. *THE SAVVY MUSIC TEACHER: Blueprint for Maximizing Income and Impact*, by David Cutler
2. *THE DYNAMIC STUDIO: How to Keep Students, Dazzle Parents, and Build the Music Studio Everyone Wants to Get Into*, by Philip Johnston
3. *TEACHING MUSIC IN HIGHER EDUCATION*, by Colleen Conway
4. *THE MUSIC TEACHING ARTIST'S BIBLE*, by Eric Booth

5. *A TEACHING ARTIST'S COMPANION: How to Define and Develop Your Practice*, by Daniel Levy

MUSIC PERFORMANCE CAREERS

1. *GETTING GIGS! The Musician's and Singer's Survival Guide to Booking Better Paying Jobs with or without an Agent*, by Mark W. Curran
2. *HOW TO BE YOUR OWN BOOKING AGENT: The Musician's & Performing Artist's Guide to Successful Touring*, by Jeri Goldstein
3. *ROMANCING THE ROOM: How to Engage Your Audience, Court Your Crowd, and Speak Successfully in Public*, by James M. Wagstaffe and Bruce Bean
4. *SIX-FIGURE MUSICIAN: How to Sell More Music, Get More People to Your Shows, and Make More Money in the Music Business*, by David Hooper
5. *THE INNER GAME OF MUSIC*, by Barry Green and Timothy Gallwey

MUSIC COMPOSITION CAREERS

1. *THE PLAIN & SIMPLE GUIDE TO MUSIC PUBLISHING*, by Randal Wixen
2. *A COMPOSER'S GUIDE TO GAME MUSIC*, by Winnifred Phillips
3. *FAMILY FIRST COMPOSER*, by Stehen Melin
4. *SIX STEPS TO SONGWRITING SUCCESS*, by Jason Blume
5. *WORKING AS A FILM COMPOSER*, by Bill Brown

MUSIC INDUSTRY CAREERS

1. *ALL YOU NEED TO KNOW ABOUT THE MUSIC BUSINESS*, by Donald Passman
2. *THIS BUSINESS OF MUSIC*, by William Krasilovsky, Sidney Shemel, John Gross, and Jonathan Feinstein
3. *START YOUR MUSIC BUSINESS*, by Audrey K. Chisholm
4. *HOW TO MAKE IT IN THE NEW MUSIC BUSINESS*, by Ari Herstand
5. *ARTIST MANAGEMENT FOR THE MUSIC BUSINESS*, by Paul Allen

OTHER CAREERS

1. *HOW MUSIC HELPS IN MUSIC THERAPY AND EVERYDAY LIFE*, by Gary Ansdell
2. *CAREERS IN MUSIC LIBRARIES*, edited by Misti Shaw and Susannah Cleveland
3. *THE RECORDING ENGINEER'S HANDBOOK*, by Bobby Owisinski
4. *ARTIST MANAGEMENT FOR THE MUSIC BUSINESS*, by Paul Ellen
5. *WHAT COLOR IS YOUR PARACHUTE? Your Guide to a Lifetime of Meaningful Work and Career Success*, by Richard Bolles

Featured Artist Index

For the benefit of digital users, indexed terms that span two pages (e.g., 52–53) may, on occasion, appear on only one of those pages.

Abigana, Hilary, 31–32
Ahmann, Jesse, 204
Allen, J. Anthony, 247
Anderson, Hassan, 250
Anderson and Roe, 214
Anthony, Ryan, 178
Antonio, Karisa, 50–51, 64
AquaSonic, 184
Arkells, 75
ArtMaster, 223

Baguette, John, 268
Balliett, Brad, 39–40
Barrett, Michael, 48
Barrette, Tony, 281
Bashi, Kishi, 77–78
Benson, Tim, 248
Birman, Eugene, 225
Bodkin, Sam, 57–58
Bostic, Katheryn, 268
Boston Festival Orchestra, 154
Bowden, Mary Elizabeth, 171
Bowland, Jimmy, 202–3
Brown, Nick, 154
Bryukhno, Sergey, 207
Burnside, Denise, 138
Butler, Andrew R., 267

Callahan, Audrey, 20–21
Cancer Blows, 178
Carling, Guinhild, 23
Castle of Our Skins, 30
Cauchemar, Vladimir, 216
Caverns, the, 184
Cello Camp, The, 247–48
Chan, Nathan, 110
Chase, Claire, 214
Chicago Philharmonic, 77–78
Childish Gambino, 214
Chooi, Timothy, 266
Clarkson, Joey, 208
Collier, Jacob, 219
Concert Truck, The, 14–15
Concerts for Compassion, 33
Concerts in the Barn, 184
CreArtBox, 224
Cutler, David, 91, 195

D'Amico, Joseph, 244
Danyew, Ashley, 125
DaPonte String Quartet, 138–39

De Vettori, Tiamo, 53
Deaf Broadway, 71–72
Death of Classical, 34
Decoda, 39–40
Detroit Symphony Orchestra, 50–51, 64, 255
Doris Duke Foundation, 159–60
Drunken Tenor, The, 32
Dunphy, Melissa, 271–72
DuPree III, Tom, 210

Eighth Blackbird, 222
Einaudi, Ludovico, 184
Ellis, Monica, 262–63
Emeneth, Katherine, 103
Emerald City Music, 193
Ensemble π, 187

Farley, Matt, 204
Felder, Hershey, 185
Ferguson, Emi, 91–92
Ferrin, Brecklyn, 139–40
Ferry, Peter, 221–22
Fischer, Andrea, 10
Forbes L'Estrange, Joanna,
Fourth Wall Ensemble, 31–32
Francis-Hoad, Cheryl, 21–22
Fripp, Matt, 111

Garrity, Karen, 263–64
Goldstein, Andrew, 193
Gomez, Esteli, 31
Gordon, Ashleigh, 30
Grand Teton Music Festival, 278
Grande, Mike, 76
Gransden, Joe, 152–53
Green, Jazelle, 216
Grgić, Mak, 281
Groupmuse, 57–58

Hanes, Seth, 117
Harkins, Elisa, 156
Heath, Jason, 165
Heggie, Jack, 267
Helix Collective, 19
Holloway, John, 150
Hooper, Vincent, 257–58
Howell, Tonya, 153
Hunter, Rebecca, 195
Huwitz, Justin, 224
Hyken, Sam, 194

294 FEATURED ARTIST INDEX

Intonation Music, 153
Invoke, 28–29

Jazzfuel, 111
Johnson, Dereck, 107
Johnson, Emlyn, 183
Jolley, Jennifer, 268
Jones, Joshua, 108–9
Jones, Netia, 223
Jukes, Greg, 31–32

Kail, Emma, 278
Kaufman Music Center, 74
Ketter, Daniel, 183
Knighton, Maurine, 159–60
Knopper, Rob, 236
Korman, Idith, 187

Laibson, Jeff, 284
Lakeland Cultural Arts Center, 156
Likhuta, Catherine, 269
Littman, Rebecca, 282–83
Liva, Ferdinand, 138–39
Living Earth Show, The, 184
Lopez-Yañez, Enrico, 258–59

Mackey, John, 273–74
Mang, Jeremy, 279
Marcoux, Krystina, 186–87
Martin, Janice, 186
Mathis, Eric, 260
Matteson, Zach, 28–29
McAllister, Tim, 176
McPherson, Robert, 32
Melin, Steven, 267
Merlis, Danielle, 247–48
Meyerson, Andy, 184
Milliken, Cathy, 188
Moab Music Festival, 48
Morgan, Mark, 237
Multi-Story Orchestra, 183
Murphy Music Press, 273
Murphy, Sean, 273
Musaics of the Bay, 158
Music For All Seasons, 156

Nam, Changhoon, 224
New York Public Library, 282–83
Notey's World, 281
Nu Deco Orchestra, 194
Nugent, Patrick, 222

Oclassica, 207
OK Go, 214
Olson, Kevin, 268
Orchestrating Diversity, 175
Ousley, Andrew, 34

Pacific Opera Project, 87–88
Parsons, Neil, 31–32
Patterson, Daniel, 245
Penningroth, Lydia, 77–78
Periapsis Music and Dance, 156

Philharmonia Orchestra, 223
Pizzi, Meredith, 282
Play On Philly, 151
Popham, Phil, 19
PRISM, 176

Real, Hal, 45
Rizzo, Rhonda, 120–21
Rock Out Loud, 76
Rockstar Bingo, 59–60
Rodriguez-Wolfe, Marlén, 173
Roomful of Teeth, 31
Royal Opera House, 223
Ruch, Dave, 251

Salon Salut, 214
Sandbox Percussion, 214
Sarich, Mark, 175
Seattle Chamber Music Society, 150
Seraph Brass, 171
Shaw, Caroline, 214
Shaw, JD, 268
Shaw, Josh, 87–88
Sheeran, Kate, 74
Shyu, Jen, 156
Simmons, Jade, 127
SMASH, 138
Sō Percussion, 214
Sommer, Cornelia, 255
Songer, Eric, 240
Sorenson, Heather, 268
Sullivan, Patrick, 219
Sydney Opera House, 224

Tanzil, Eunike, 220
Thompson, Stanford, 151
Tomkins, Leslie, 48
Trujillo, Andres, 253–54

Ukulele Kids Club, 173

Van De Crommert, William, 270
Van Der Brecken, Daria, 73
VanderHart, Chandra, 182
Vardanega, Audrey, 158
Voisey, Rob, 183

Wallbridge, Sean, 59–60
Wan, Noël, 264
Watanabe, Mihoko, 242
Wein, Gail, 95
Whitacre, Eric, 219
White Stripes, The 214
White, David, 118
Wilson, Frances, 96
Wintory, Austin, 274–75
Woods, Sylvia, 280
World Cafe Live, 45

Zazou, Zic, 214
Zeucher, Garrett, 71–72
Zhang, Susan, 14–15
Zhu, Jocelyn, 33

Subject Index

For the benefit of digital users, indexed terms that span two pages (e.g., 52–53) may, on occasion, appear on only one of those pages.

360 deals, 206
401(k), 142
403(b), 142
7 Habits of Highly Effective People, The, 162
97% Rule, 40, 70

A&R, 279
active income. *See* income
adjudication, 158–60, 249
advertising, 65–66, 74
After the Golden Age, 196
American Federation of Musicians (AFM), 137, 266
annual giving, 146, 150–51
annual percentage rate (APR), 139
A-roll footage, 215
arranging, 267
artificial intelligence (AI), 3, 39
artistic biography. *See* bio
artistic excellence, 11–15
artist management, 91, 265–66, 278
arts administration, 12, 150, 172–73, 277–78
arts marketing "A" list, 68–69, 77–78
ASCAP, 274
   After, 76–77
   Allies, 73–74
   Angle, 72–73
   Arsenal, 74–76
   Art, 70, 73, 75
   Audience, 70–72
   canvas, 68–69, 77–78
asking for something, 118–19
assumptions, 60–61, 62–63
attorney, 44
audiences, 13
audio recordings. *See* recording
auditions, 10, 12, 13, 40, 165, 202, 234–36, 255, 256, 257–58
   blind, 11
augmented reality (AR), 39, 223
authentic performance practice A(APP), 194
award income. *See* income

background music, 259
bands, 240, 254–55, 260
basket career, 18
benefits, 75
best in the world, 22–23

BIG idea, 46, 48, 150
bio, 9, 81, 88–89, 91, 100, 161
blogs, 39, 100, 161
BMI, 274
board of directors, 73
   personal, 173
booking agents, 91, 95
brainstorming, 80
brand identity, 25, 75, 85
B-roll footage, 215
budgeting, 80
business
   business model canvas, 54–56, 57–60
   concept, 49
   etiquette, 126
   plan, 43, 54, 81
BUZZ, 72–73, 75, 81, 210
BUZZ hook, 72, 94, 95
Buzzmarketing, 72

call to action, 76
camps, 247–48
capital campaign, 147
captions, 215
career model, 49
   basket, 18
   hat, 18
   portfolio, 17
certificates of deposit (CD), 141
Chamber Music America, 137
channels, 55
Chappell, Rebecca, 203
choirs, 240, 254–55
choreography, 185–86
classes, 245–47
   online, 246–47
   in person, 245–46
classical music
   rethinking the cannon, 193
   vs. popular, 189
coaching, 249
cold calling, 120–21
collaboration, 31
commissions, 176, 267, 268–69
communication, 171
   professional, 119–20
competitions, 9–10, 11, 264, 267, 268, 271

competitive array, 53–54
competitor
  direct, 53
  indirect, 53
composition, 4–5, 38
  lifestyle, 276
  opportunities, 267–76
compound interest, 141
compulsory mechanical license, 211
concept collision, 41–42, 53
concept development, 35
concert music composition, 268
concerts, 259
  booking gigs, 261–62
conducting, 187, 245, 250, 258–59, 270
consortiums, 268, 269
consulting, 249
contractor, 91, 263–64, 265, 278
contracts, 132, 261
contributed income. *See* income
copyright, 210–11, 272, 275–76
corporation, 135
cost of goods sold (COGS), 133–34, 208
cost of living, 138
cost structure, 56
costuming, 184, 185, 188, 189, 217
cover letters, 229–31
Covey, Stephen, 162
COVID-19, 3
creative performance practice (CPP), 195
creativity, 10, 40
crowdfunding, 146, 151–53, 205
  Kickstarter, 151
  Patreon, 152
  rewards, 152
curricula vitae (CV), 156–57, 232
customer, 61, 70
  relationships, 55
  segments, 55, 70

data, 50
day jobs, 16, 18, 163
deadlines, 167, 170
debt, 139–40, 142
deductions, 135–36
demand, 25–28, 60
demographics, 60, 61, 70
digital service providers (DSPs), 209
digital tip jar, 221
diversity, 40
donor fundraising, 148–50, 268
donors, 73
dreaming, 35
dream jobs, 16

eCourse, 111, 246
education, 38
educational products, 249, 268
elation points, 49–50

electronic press kit (EPK), 9, 91–92, 101, 118–19, 261
elevator pitch, 87
email, 81, 110, 119, 121, 149, 171, 233
  signature, 120
  solicitation, 149
emergency funds, 137
empathy points, 49–50
employee, 17
endowment, 147
entrepreneurial
  framework, 35–36, 49
  idea, 38–39
  journey, 36
  mindset, 4, 9–10, 19
  ventures, 40
entrepreneurship, 3, 4, 9–11, 13
  definition, 10
equity investment, 147
everything bagel approach, 30
excellence, 11–15
executive director, 44, 74, 138, 150, 153, 178, 277
expectations, 114
expenses, 126, 132–40
  cost of goods sold (COGS), 133–34, 208
  fixed, 134
  overhead, 134
  recording, 205
  variable, 134

facts, 50
family and friends, 116
fans, 116
fantasy points, 49–50
features, 75
feature tweaking, 41, 53
feedback, 60–63, 173
film scoring, 268, 274
financial
  literacy, 3
  management, 35
  strategy, 4
focus groups, 50–51
fonts, 82, 119–20
form 1023, 44
for-profit businesses, 44–45, 135
Founder's Syndrome, 170
freelancers, 17, 118, 124, 253
freemium, 201
fundraising
  crowdfunding, 146
  events, 147
  goals, 146
  in-kind donations, 147, 154
  large gifts, 147, 149
  major gifts, 147
  mistakes, 148
  reasons for giving, 148–49
  special events, 147, 153
  sponsorships, 147, 154, 205

funnel, 111
futurecasting, 165
fuzzy goals, 168

gesamtkunstwerk, 196
gigs
    booking, 261–62
    when to take, 237–38
GivingTuesday, 146
Gladwell, Malcolm, 22
goals
    fundraising, 146
    fuzzy, 168
    short/medium/long-term, 164–65
    SMART, 168
Godin, Seth, 26, 110
grants, 44, 81, 147, 154–60, 205, 267, 268
    adjudicating, 158–60
    budget, 157
    opportunities, 155
    submissions, 156–57
gratification, 10
gratitude, 115
green screen, 216
gross profit, 133
group lessons, 244–45
guerilla marketing, 3, 66–67

Hamilton, Kennith, 196
handshakes, 117
Harry Fox Agency, 209, 211
hat career, 18
health care, 137–38
Henry Ford, 49
holography, 224–25
hook, 95
house concerts, 259
Hughes, Mark, 72
human-centered design, 49–51

i^3, 15, 284
image, 86
impact, 15, 60, 284
important urgent matrix, 162–63
income, 15, 123–32, 284
    active, 123–24
    amplifying, 130–32
    award, 124
    contributed, 124
    high-ticket item, 126
    loaned, 124
    passive, 124, 131–32
    price points, 126
    projecting, 127
    reaching your goal, 128
    recording, 202
    recording artists, 208–9
    streams, 125

income tax, 44, 135–36
    1040EZ, 135
    1099-MISC, 135
    deductions, 135–36
    W2, 135
in-kind donations, 147, 154, 157
innovation, 3, 13–14, 15, 169, 284
    GAME, 3
insights, 50, 62
inspiration, 15, 284
intellectual property (IP), 210–11
Internal Revenue Service (IRS), 44
internet, 99
interviews, 50–51, 229, 232–34
investing, 142

jingles, 268
jobs
    day job, 16, 18
    dream job, 16
    transition job, 16
Jobs, Steve, 49
Jordan, Michael, 169

key activities, 55
keying, 216
keynotes, 249
key partnerships, 56
key resources, 56
Kickstarter, 151

large ensembles, 254–55
leadership, 2
lead magnet, 111
legacy, 4, 11, 161, 175–78
legacy giving, 147
lessons
    group, 244–45
    online, 244
    in person, 242–43
librarian. *See* music librarian
lighting. *See* video
limited liability company (LLC), 135
listening, 114
list price, 133
live performance, 4, 181–88
    attire, 184
    audience participation, 187
    choreography, 185–86
    duration, 182
    interdisciplinarity, 187
    music as theater, 181–82
    set design, 186
    setlist, 182
    speaking, 184–85
    surprises, 188
    venue, 183
live projection, 222
live streaming, 221–22

298　SUBJECT INDEX

loaned income. *See* income
logos, 86–87
long-term goals, 164
luck, 20

mailing list, 110–11
management. *See* artist management
marketability, 12–13
marketing, 35, 65–84, 99, 207–8
    arts marketing "A" list, 68–78
    compositions, 270–72
    definition, 67–68
    goal, 79–80
    guerilla, 66–67
    myths, 65–68
    recordings, 207–8, 210
    strategy, 99
    video, 219–20
    website, 105
master classes, 249
mechanical royalties, 209, 267
media, 92–97
medium-term goals, 164
meetings, 171
Mench, Michael, 255
mental health, 18
micro-licensing, 270
military music, 255–57
minimum viable product (MVP), 59–60, 104
mission, 176
mission statement, 32–33
multi-talent, 31
music academy, 248
musical theater, 257–58, 267
music education. *See* teaching
Musician's Journey, The, 147
music industry, 4–5
music librarian, 282
Music Teachers National Association (MTNA), 137
music therapy, 281–82
mutual funds, 141

name recognition, 65
names, 86
Napster, 201
negative vision statement, 33–34
negotiation, 236–37
networking, 115–17
newsletters, 101, 110–11
newsworthy, 94–95
niche, 29–30, 71, 79
nonmusic employment, 283–84
nonprofit, 44–45, 148–49, 154, 155, 173
nontraditional audience, 32, 70

online lessons, 244
opera, 257
opportunities, 36
opportunity creation, 3

optimism, 117
orchestras, 40, 41–42, 122, 126, 192–93, 198, 234, 240, 254–55, 260
    jobs, 12
orchestration, 267
Outliers, 22
overhead. *See* expenses
overlay, 215
owner. *See* venture owner

pain points, 49–50
pandemic, 3
passive income. *See* income
pass-through, 207
people skills, 3, 113–22, 169
perfectionism, 13
performance, 4–5, 38, *See* live performance
performance opportunities, 253–66
    large ensembles, 254–55
    military, 255–57
    musical theater, 257–58
    opera, 257, 267
    sacred music, 260
    small groups, 259
    soloists, 260
    touring, 262–63
performance royalties, 267, 274
performing rights organization (PRO), 274
Permission Marketing, 110
persevere, 166
persistence, 121
personal board of directors, 173
personality, 32
philanthropy, 145–50, 155
    definition, 145
photos, 89–91, 101
pivot, 166
podcasts, 39, 101
portfolio career, 17, 124
posters, 74
post-its, 56–60, 167–68
powerhouse positioning, 27–28
powerhouse proposals, 45–48, 87–88
    BIG idea, 46, 48
    a little something extra, 47–48
    WOWables, 47, 48
practice, 181
premiere, 268
    recording, 211
presentation, 82–84
    cover letters, 230
presenters, 95
press release, 81, 95–97
pricing, 53, 60, 67, 126–27
print media, 93–94
prism concerts, 186
private lessons, 243
problem-solving, 3, 4, 35
problem statement, 36–38

producer, 279
product development, 4
production music, 269–70
productivity, 161
professional communication, 119–20
professional frameworks, 16–18
project management, 4, 164–69, 264
    mapping, 167–68
projection mapping, 224
protocols, 109, 171
prototype, 58–60
public domain, 211
publicity, 93, 278
publishing, 211
    traditional versus self, 272–74
purple, 27, 40
Purple Cow, 26–27

rainy day fund, 142
rat race, 18
real estate, 138, 141
record labels, 198, 205, 206–8
record producer. *See* producer
recording, 4, 39, 67, 102–3, 197–211
    choice, 200–1
    costs, 199, 205
    downloading, 197
    engineer, 28, 41–42, 205, 255–56, 279
    financial objectives, 199–200
    product psychology, 201
    rationales, 202
    for video, 217
reflecting, 165
rejection, 21
relationships, 115–16
relevance, 13
repair, 280
rep list, 91
resources, 62
restricted giving, 145
resumes, 9, 156–57, 229, 231–32
retail, 42, 210, 280
retainer, 266
retirement, 140–41, 142
revenue, 43
    projecting, 127
    streams, 56
reviews, 101
risk, 19
Roth IRAs, 142
rule of thirds, 218

sacred music, 260
savings
    liquid, 142
    career, 142
    retirement, 140–41, 142
savvy, 1–2
    definition, 1

scheduling, 164
schmoozing, 117–18
scope, 43, 99, 109
self-management, 266
self-publishing, 272–74
SEP-IRAs, 142
services, 39
SESAC, 274
sheet music sales, 267, 272
short-term goals, 164
simulcasting, 221
Sinek, Simon, 32
slogans, 86
small groups, 259
SMART goals, 168
social media, 3, 66, 70, 74, 91, 99, 108–10, 118, 149
    messaging, 108–9
    platforms, 108
    protocols, 109
    solicitation, 149
software development, 281
sole proprietorship, 135, 136
solutions, 38–39
speaking, 184–85
spending habits, 137
sponsorships, 154, 205
spreadsheets, 80
Start with Why, 32
statistics, 50
staying current, 121–22
stocks, 141
storytelling, 46, 85, 87, 127, 150, 182, 230
strategic partners, 73–74
strategic planning, 35
streaming, 3, 197
stretch goal, 146
subtitles, 215
success, 1, 2, 4, 9–10, 18, 80
    formula, 15
SUCCES(s) approach, 86
survey, 60–64
    design, 61–63
SWOT diagram, 51–52
sync license, 269

target users, 50
tax-deductible donations, 44
teaching, 4–5, 11
    college, 240–42
    independent, 242–49
    K-12 classroom, 239–40
teaching artistry, 249–51
    designing workshops, 250
    getting work, 251
team management, 169
    ailments & remedies, 169–72
    makeup, 172–73
technology, 3, 39
tech rider, 91, 261–62

tenure-track, 241
therapist. *See* music therapist
time management, 161–64
    matrix, 162–63
    to do lists, 162
timeline, 81
Timmons, Jill, 147
title, 95
touring, 262–63
Traditional IRAs, 142
transition jobs, 16
TurboTax, 136

unions, 266
unrestricted giving, 145
US Air Force Band, 255–56
US Army Field Band, 255–56

value amplification, 42–43
value proposition, 55
venture owner, 17
venues, 38, 183
video, 4, 39, 91, 102–3, 213–25
    cameras, 217–18
    cloning, 216, 222
    color correction, 219
    concept, 213
    crowdfunding, 152
    editing, 218–19
    filming, 217–18
    keying, 216
    lighting, 217
    live projection, 222
    masking, 216
    set, 216
    transitions, 219
video game music, 267, 274
VIP list, 147
virtual reality (VR), 39, 223
vision, 2
vision statement, 33
    negative, 33–34
visioning, 62
VJing, 222
voiceover, 215

web presence, 76
web representation, 91, 99
websites, 9, 43, 81, 99–107, 110
    content, 101
    domain, 99
    home page, 101, 102
    reasons they fail, 105–7
    sitemap, 100
work ethic, 35
work for hire, 269
work-life balance, 174
workshops, 249
WOWables, 47, 48, 49, 60, 61, 70, 87, 88, 150
writing, 81, 88, 102, 104
    content, 83
    cover letters, 229–31
    giving letter, 150
    grants, 156–58
    presentation, 83

yield, 141

Author Bio

An award-winning, multigenre composer, pianist, and Yamaha Master Educator, **Dr. David Cutler** balances a varied career as a speaker, author, consultant, musician, and educator. A self-proclaimed "weekend traveler," his artistic statements seamlessly weave classical, jazz, popular, folk, and world music. Stretching what it means to be a performer, he regularly includes extreme eclecticism, choreography, humor, interdisciplinary collaboration, and more in his events.

One of the world's leading voices on arts entrepreneurship training, Cutler has authored acclaimed books *The Savvy Musician* and *The Savvy Music Teacher*, which provide tools for amplifying income, impact, and innovation and have shaped a generation of artists. His recent full-color, illustrated book *The GAME of Innovation* guides readers to conquer complex challenges, align teams behind shared visions, and invent the extraordinary.

Cutler is known for leading immersive "innovation GAMEs." These powerful, team-based experiences empower arts, education, and business communities to solve creative challenges while becoming better collaborators.

Cutler serves as Distinguished Professor of Music Entrepreneurship and Innovation at the University of South Carolina, where he also leads a living-learning community called IDEA (Impact, Design, Entrepreneurship, Arts). He is an active member of the Liberty Fellowship and Aspen Global Leadership Network, associations aimed at building a more just society.

More information:
- **www.savvymusician.com**
- **www.thepuzzlercompany.com**

The manufacturer's authorised representative in the EU for product safety is Oxford
University Press España S.A. of El Parque Empresarial San Fernando de Henares,
Avenida de Castilla, 2 – 28830 Madrid (www.oup.es/en or product.safety@oup.com).
OUP España S.A. also acts as importer into Spain of products made by the manufacturer.

Printed in the USA/Agawam, MA
July 11, 2025

890307.003